The NEA and AFT:

Teacher Unions in Power and Politics

California 1993 Voucher Initiative

p. 75-76

by

Myron Lieberman
Charlene K. Haar
Leo Troy

PRO > ACTIVE PUBLICATIONS

The NEA and AFT: Teacher Unions in Power and Politics

Published by:

Pro>Active Publications
10 Hale St.
Rockport, Massachusetts 01966

Printed in the United States of America

10   9   8   7   6   5   4   3   2   1

Main entry under title:

The NEA and AFT: Teacher Unions in Power and Politics

ISBN No. 1-885432-00-3

CONTENTS

CHAPTER ONE

INTRODUCTION:
THE RATIONALE AND POINT OF VIEW

This book is an effort to describe the structure, operations, and influence of teacher unions, especially the National Education Association (NEA) and the American Federation of Teachers (AFT). The context should make it clear whether the organization titles include their state and local affiliates. The authors believe that an NEA/AFT merger will take place in the 1990s, but whether or not this happens, the emergence of strong teacher unions is an important development in education, in the labor movement, in the economy, and in American politics. Because their role is so pervasive but also so widely overlooked, a brief comment on the subject may serve as an introduction to this book.

Ostensibly, school boards formulate educational policy, whereas terms and conditions of teacher employment are negotiated with teacher unions. In the real world, however, employment terms and conditions inevitably impact educational policy; indeed, in many situations, a term or condition of teacher employment is simply an educational policy viewed from an employment perspective. For instance, suppose a school board decides to assign its most experienced teachers to schools in which pupil achievement is especially low. The board may characterize this as an educational policy; to the teacher union, however, the board would be changing transfer and/or assignment policies, matters normally considered terms and conditions of employment. As such, the school board is required to bargain with the teacher union over the change, which frequently does not materialize as a result of teacher union opposition to it. Thus the unions play a critical role with respect to educational policy, and they do so even when such policies can be distinguished from terms and conditions of teacher employment. Most school district expenditures are for teacher compensation, and collective bargaining contracts set forth the policies under which teachers are employed and compensated. With over 70 percent of the nation's 2.9 million public school teachers employed pursuant to collective bargaining agreements, teacher unions clearly play important roles in making and implementing educational policies.

The educational importance of teacher unions is especially evident in controversies over educational vouchers, privatization, and efforts to introduce market-oriented reforms in public education. Indisputably, the teacher unions

1

are the major obstacles to such efforts. Despite their pivotal role in such controversies, there is little public awareness of the dynamics and modus operandi of teacher unions; their critics especially reveal a remarkable lack of sophistication about how and why they function as they do.

The unionization of teachers also marks a basic change in the character of the American labor movement. For instance, in 1953, public employees constituted only six percent of union membership. By 1994, approximately 40 percent of union members were public employees, and we anticipate that the public sector unions will soon enroll a majority of union members in the United States. Actually, public sector unions will be predominant in the AFL-CIO if and when the NEA, the nation's largest public sector union, becomes affiliated with the Federation. As will be explained shortly, however, it is a fundamental mistake to think of public sector bargaining and public sector unions as merely an extension of private sector concepts to the public sector.

Politically, teacher unions are major players at all levels of government. One of every ten delegates to the 1992 Democratic National Convention was a member of the NEA or the AFT, and no serious observer doubts their important role in state and local politics. Inasmuch as elected officials shape policy on noneducational as well as educational issues, the political influence of teacher unions extends far beyond the field of education. Although teacher unions are usually the most influential interest group on educational issues, their impact on noneducational issues may be even more important from a public policy perspective.

To illustrate, the teacher unions play a pivotal role in the politics of health care. First, they were a key element of the coalition that carried Bill Clinton to victory in the 1992 Democratic primaries and in the general election. Not surprisingly, the Clinton administration's emphasis on health care is also a major union interest. Unfortunately, the media treatment of health care often fails to reveal the union stake in the issue; a casual observer might think that the union's interests are concern for the poor or the uninsured or some other humanitarian concern. In the real world, however, the union interest is a practical one, based on union interests as perceived by the unions. As they consider health care, they see the following union benefits in government's absorption of a larger share of its costs and of forcing all employees to share the costs:

1. To the extent that government spends more and employers spend less on health care, more funds would be available for wages and other economic benefits. If the federal government absorbed some of the costs of health care that are currently paid by school districts, the teacher unions could negotiate for the savings to be distributed to teachers' salaries.

2. Privatization would be less attractive because contractors could not offer fewer benefits to their employees. All employers would have to share whatever costs of health care devolve on employers per se. Employers would be required to pay for health care for employees of independent contractors working for a single employer.
3. Unions could bargain for the employer to pay for any costs of health care not included in the federally subsidized plan (*AFL-CIO News*, 1993).

Citizens not familiar with collective bargaining often fail to appreciate the importance of health care issues to unions and employers. At the present time, health care is a frequent obstacle to agreement in both the private and public sectors. Disagreements over who should pay for the rising costs of health care sometimes lead to impasse or even strikes. The point here is not whether the Clinton administration's health care policies are good or bad public policy; it is that teacher unions play a critical role in how the health care issues are resolved. By the same token, the teacher unions play a major role on other domestic policies as well.

Because of their educational and political roles, teacher unions inescapably play a major role in our nation's economy. The sheer size of our educational system means that every major educational interest group is also an economic actor of some importance. More importantly, many educational issues are also economic issues, or should be so regarded. For example, the maximum age of compulsory education affects the extent of public and private expenditures, the level of taxation, lifetime earnings, social security funding and benefits, and labor markets, to cite just a few of its economic aspects. The field of education involves scores of such issues; their economic ramifications are often more important than their educational ones. In short, the teacher unions are major actors in the nation's economy, and like all such actors, should be subject to critical analysis.

Needless to say, the influence of teacher unions, as distinguished from the rationale for their positions, can be a controversial issue in its own right. Quite often, it is impossible to characterize the unions' influence with any degree of confidence. Nonetheless, uncertainty over their role in specific situations does not invalidate the rationale for this book; the latter is based on what is known, not what is uncertain.

THE POINT OF VIEW

The authors' point of view toward teacher unions should be laid on the table at the outset. We believe that the absence of competitive markets in

3

K-12 education is a major weakness of our educational system. The teacher unions are opposed to competitive markets in education; they could hardly do otherwise and remain viable unions. Consequently, we are at times critical of union positions; the positions and our criticism of them are not always articulated in this book. In some instances, our criticisms are not limited to union efforts to stifle competitive markets in education.

Despite our objections to the anticompetitive policies espoused by teacher unions, we recognize that organizations that represent public employees have a legitimate role to play. Public employees need an organization to protect themselves against unjust government action. In totalitarian societies, governments control the organizations that represent public employees. Consequently, the latter are unable to resist unjust government action, whether directed against themselves or others. In a democratic society, the problem is that the power to oppose government action for legitimate reasons is or becomes the power to promote the interests of public employees for indefensible objectives. Our view is that teacher unions illustrate both the positive and negative aspects of public employee organizations. The discussion of one aspect is not a denial of the existence of the other.

Has our point of view resulted in a biased treatment of teacher unions? We define "bias" as the omission of data and arguments that might reasonably be expected to influence the conclusions of a reasonable person on the issues at stake. While recognizing the possibility of bias, we have tried to consider the data and arguments that support conclusions different from our own. Of course, bias may be reflected in what issues are selected to analyze as well as the way issues are discussed; we have tried to avoid both kinds of bias. Of course, readers must decide for themselves whether we have succeeded in doing so.

Throughout this book, we use the term "NEA/AFT" (1) to refer to the organization that results or would result from a merger of the NEA and AFT, or (2) as a term applicable to both unions. Thus "the NEA/AFT" position on contracting out is the position taken by both unions. In some contexts, both meanings are appropriate because the positions the unions have adopted separately will be the positions adopted by the merged organization. Where only one meaning is intended, the context should clarify any ambiguity in the meaning.

Readers who are familiar with previous books about teacher unions will be aware that we have not relied heavily on them. One reason is that their data are no longer accurate or fail to take account of recent developments that are critical to a realistic assessment of the issues. In addition, we believe that several of these earlier books are characterized by a naive point of view that impedes an objective analysis; this is true for favorable as well as unfavorable books about the teacher unions (Berube, 1988; Blumenfeld

1985; Donley, 1976; Johnson, 1984; Kerchner, 1988; Lieberman, 1956; McDonnell, 1988; Reed, 1980; Selden, 1985; and West, 1980). In addition to the fact that such matters as membership, revenues, and organizational structure have changed considerably, changes in the political and demographic context impact several organizational issues in unprecedented ways. Our analysis is more akin to a sketch than a comprehensive analysis; indeed, one of our objectives is to call attention to various dimensions of the teacher unions that deserve intensive research and analysis.

NEA/AFT MERGER

In view of the influence of the teacher unions, the possibility of their merger is not to be taken lightly. It would be overly optimistic to treat merger as a fait accompli; at the same time, an analysis that assumed that the NEA and AFT will continue as separate organizations might be out of date when published. Our solution to this dilemma is to describe the status of merger in early 1994 as best we can, and leave it to the reader to assess the likelihood that it will materialize. We will offer our assessments of both the issues in the merger talks and the prospects for merger, but reiterate the importance of teacher unions, merger or no merger.

For present purposes, the critical event relating to merger is the NEA's invitation to the AFT to engage in merger talks. This invitation was included in New Business Items 1993-A and 1993-B, adopted by the NEA's Representative Assembly (RA) on July 2, 1993. In our view, the adoption of these items, especially since it was by a substantial margin, renders it likely that an NEA/AFT merger will take place in the next three to five years.

The size and resources of a merged organization would be awesome, yet retain the potential for substantial growth. Table 1.1 provides some idea of the membership and revenues that would result from an NEA/AFT merger.

Table 1.1

Merged Membership and Budget
National Organization Only
NEA/AFT

1993-94 Membership		Budget
NEA	2,100,000	$173,206,000
AFT	820,000	60,000,000
Total	2,920,000	$233,206,000

5

The figures in Table 1.1 overestimate the membership and underestimate the revenues of the merged organization; since the revenues will be discussed in more detail in Chapter 3, we will comment here only on the membership figures.

From its *Strategic Plan and Budget, Fiscal Year 1993-94*, the total NEA 1993-94 membership figures includes the following:

Active—Professional Education Positions	1,605,000
Active—Educational Support Positions	202,000
Active—Life	105,000
Agency Fee	23,000
Retired	98,500
Associate and Reserve	4,100
Student	50,000

For some purposes, these categories differ from the regular full-time teachers who constitute the overwhelming majority of NEA members. In addition, it should be noted that the NEA does not categorize its membership publicly into "professional" or "teacher" on the one hand, and educational support personnel on the other, although the distinction is made in the NEA budget.

The AFT membership figures must be interpreted even more cautiously. As shown in Table 1.1, the AFT claimed a membership of 820,000 in 1993. The Federation also stated that its members are in one of five divisions. Although the AFT did not provide an official breakdown, its informal breakdown to one of the authors was as follows:

Public and Private School Teachers	600,000
Paraprofessionals and School-Related Personnel (PSRP)	110,000
Federation of Nurses and Health Professionals (FNHP)	50,000
Federation of Higher Education Faculty	*60,000
Federation of Public Employees (FPE)	—

*Author estimate

Nevertheless, just prior to the October 1993 AFL-CIO Executive Council meeting in San Francisco, the AFL-CIO released a report that showed the AFT with 574,000 paid up members, a gain of only 1000 over 1992. Meanwhile the AFT was claiming that its membership was 796,000, a gain of 50,000 over 1990-92.

Undoubtedly, some of the discrepancy is due to the fact that the AFL-CIO

6

counts only fully paid up members who are included in the count for determining union representation at the AFL-CIO convention; in contrast, the AFT is counting all members, whether or not they are included in the membership count for convention purposes. Furthermore, the AFT does not pay the full per capita tax on certain categories of membership, such as associate members. This is another reason why the AFT membership figures released for public relations purposes are much greater than the AFT membership figures cited by the AFL-CIO. It is possible, however, that the AFT's larger membership figures may be a more accurate guide to its political influence, since the Federation is often successful in persuading retirees to be campaign activists for union candidates and causes. It should also be noted that a small number of teachers are members of both the NEA and AFT, hence the memberships and revenues of both groups would have to be adjusted downward to reflect this fact if and when an NEA/AFT merger materializes. Nonetheless, even on the most conservative estimates of membership and revenues, the NEA and AFT would constitute a towering presence in education, the labor movement, politics, and the economy.

DIFFERENCES BETWEEN THE NEA AND AFT: DO THEY MATTER?

At various times, we refer to "teacher unions." This usage implies that there are no significant differences between the NEA and AFT on the issues under discussion. Elsewhere, the analysis points out how the NEA and AFT differ in some way. To avoid any misunderstanding, let us explain our perspective on the similarities and differences between the two national unions.

Clearly, the NEA and AFT differ in membership, resources, governance structure, and leadership personnel, to cite some of the more obvious differences. In addition, the demographics of the two unions differ considerably; the AFT's strength is more concentrated in large urban centers; the NEA is much stronger in suburban and rural areas. These demographic differences sometimes result in policy differences that are erroneously viewed as different concepts of unions or union objectives. Also, the AFT is affiliated with the AFL-CIO; the NEA is not, although its policies on non-educational issues are invariably supportive of or consistent with AFL-CIO policies.

Some differences between the NEA and AFT are important, but they are not necessarily the ones that receive the most attention in the media or among academicians. Generally speaking, the NEA is perceived as the more conservative in terms of teacher militancy but the more liberal in terms of

7

social policy generally. In our view, this perception is unwarranted, or at least requires significant modification.

At the district level, the local affiliate of either union bargains for the objectives of its membership. To illustrate, suppose the teaching staff is composed predominantly of senior teachers dissatisfied because the salary schedule does not offer high maximum salaries for teachers with many years of experience. These senior teachers will seek higher maximum salaries, regardless of whether they are represented by an NEA or an AFT affiliate. Younger teachers are more likely to emphasize reducing the number of steps required to reach the maximum salary. If and when they reach the maximum, their bargaining objectives will change, but at any given time, the bargaining objectives of a local union are a compromise between such conflicting interests. Similarly, if most teachers are concerned about extra-duty pay or school safety, the local union that represents them will emphasize these objectives. These objectives are not affected by whether the union is an NEA or AFT affiliate. Inasmuch as the demographics will be the same, willingness to engage in hard bargaining or strike action is likely to be the same or very similar, regardless of national affiliation. In short, the local union's national affiliation rarely plays a significant role at the bargaining table.

Of course, the NEA and AFT assert that their affiliates are more effective than their rivals. The NEA claims that its support services are superior to the AFT's; the AFT asserts that its affiliation with the AFL-CIO enables AFT locals to gain labor support for teacher objectives. Neither reason is very persuasive. Teacher salaries and benefits are public information; in any given district, an AFT negotiator is as likely as an NEA negotiator to know how much teachers in comparable districts are being paid. As for AFL-CIO affiliation, many AFT locals are in districts where there is no AFL-CIO organization; even where there is, its active support cannot be taken for granted. In short, from a bargaining standpoint, it makes little or no difference in theory or practice whether teachers are represented by an NEA or AFT affiliate.

In the era when the NEA and AFT were competing for bargaining rights, their rhetoric greatly exaggerated the differences between the unions from a bargaining perspective. Today, however, displacement of an NEA affiliate by an AFT local (or vice versa) is relatively rare, and neither national union is making a systematic effort to replace the other at the local level. This truce would not continue to exist if either union were superior to the other in achieving benefits in the bargaining process.

Although not critical from a bargaining standpoint, NEA/AFT differences are important from other standpoints. We shall discuss these differences, but one caveat should be emphasized at the outset; the differences

8

are not necessarily a guide to which union is "better" from either a teacher or public interest point of view. These are complicated issues that must often be resolved on the basis of the circumstances facing the decisionmaker. Furthermore, the NEA and AFT, like other unions, constantly undergo changes that might affect one's assessment of them.

CHAPTER TWO

TEACHER UNION
ORGANIZATIONAL STRUCTURES

This chapter is devoted to the governance structure of the NEA and AFT. The following chapters will discuss their financial structure and political activities.

THE NATIONAL EDUCATION ASSOCIATION (NEA)

It appears that almost 70 percent of all U.S. public school classroom teachers were members of either the NEA or the AFT in 1994; in fact, the NEA had become the largest union in the world well before 1994. As Table 2.1 (from the *1993-94 Handbook*) indicates, NEA enrolled over 2,100,000 members, including almost 2,000,000 classroom teachers and college faculty; the remaining members were support personnel: clerical staff, bus drivers, school health officials, food service employees, maintenance staff, students and retirees.

The NEA was founded in 1857, when the presidents of ten state educational associations issued a call to the teachers of the country to form a national organization. This call was answered by 43 persons who met in Philadelphia on August 16, 1857 and organized the "National Teachers Association." The original constitution of the National Teachers Association excluded women from membership, an exclusion which was eliminated in 1866. The next major change took place in 1870, when the National Association of School Superintendents and the American Normal School Association merged with the National Teachers Association to form the National Education Association. The Association was offered a charter by act of Congress in 1906; the charter was accepted in 1907, at which time the name of the organization was changed to "National Education Association of the United States." No other professional organization or labor union has been chartered by Congress; in addition to the NEA, Congress has chartered only the American Legion, AMVETS, American War Mothers, the American National Red Cross, the Boy Scouts of America and the Disabled American Veterans.

Membership in what is now the NEA grew very slowly until the years following World War I. Prior to 1918, membership had consisted largely of

10

Table 2.1
NEA Membership, July 30, 1993

State	K-12 Act & Life	Higher Ed Act & life	Retired Members	Student Members	Other[a] Members	Total[b] Col. 2-6	Incr. or Decr. in NFA Members over August 31, 1992 Number	Percent
1	2	3	4	5	6	7	8	9
Alabama	55,051	4,033	6,217	1,229	182	66,712	1,184	1.81
Alaska	8,555	50	474	39	318	9,436	840	9.77
Arizona	26,534	256	1,085	555	229	28,659	373	1.32
Arkansas	15,029	87	2,083	1,084	163	18,446	-240	-1.28
California	202,385	13,737	6,124	2,115	718	225,079	-678	-0.30
Colorado	28,691	544	1,069	417	180	30,901	322	1.05
Connecticut	29,003	120	1,564	232	215	31,134	-81	-0.26
Delaware	8,282	45	502	156	84	9,069	447	5.18
District of Columbia	305	408	93	10	145	961	8	0.84
Florida	52,497	3,482	1,338	1,168	170	58,655	-1,930	-3.19
Georgia	27,628	325	1,343	1,728	60	31,084	439	1.43
Hawaii	10,981	3,323	1,402	324	89	16,119	641	4.14
Idaho	10,026	4	328	79	116	10,553	82	0.78
Illinois	78,797	2,216	2,292	426	724	84,455	2,493	3.04
Indiana	44,157	203	762	1,197	284	46,603	816	1.78
Iowa	35,027	1,439	669	838	241	38,214	-78	-0.20
Kansas	23,591	1,163	859	1,607	255	27,475	721	2.69
Kentucky	34,319	940	664	2,213	114	38,250	760	2.03
Louisiana	19,407	173	472	765	240	21,057	-827	-3.78
Maine	17,007	2,243	4,870	50	212	24,382	-372	-1.50
Maryland	42,722	161	1,689	246	118	44,936	384	0.85
Massachusetts	58,569	9,514	3,368	137	505	72,093	1,855	2.64
Michigan	104,653	5,837	14,209	635	10,929	136,263	2,161	1.61
Minnesota	39,565	2,912	1,077	3,556	1,080	48,190	956	2.02
Mississippi	8,249	168	552	427	34	9,430	-395	-4.02
Missouri	22,452	358	1,071	892	179	24,952	993	4.14
Montana	9,585	130	341	310	171	10,537	168	1.62
Nebraska	20,531	895	1,188	1,054	1,112	24,780	210	0.85
Nevada	14,828	50	278	3	38	15,197	760	5.26
New Hampshire	10,660	130	338	24	98	11,250	87	0.78
New Jersey	123,102	3,385	16,003	531	1,478	144,499	3,481	2.47
New Mexico	6,717	118	510	167	90	7,602	-120	-1.55
New York	31,324	3,187	2,238	22	948	37,719	2,213	6.23
North Carolina	42,616	279	5,427	1,704	265	50,291	832	1.68
North Dakota	7,318	125	245	540	132	8,360	-85	-1.01
Ohio	99,341	1,552	2,998	1,594	274	105,759	1,438	1.38
Oklahoma	30,488	498	857	2,088	118	34,049	-821	-2.35
Oregon	33,911	1,474	968	248	125	36,726	1,165	3.28
Pennsylvania	109,204	4,687	4,134	6,377	2,053	126,455	1,582	1.27
Puerto Rico	14,831	48	5,375	0	168	20,422	-346	-1.67
Rhode Island	6,123	1,764	580	5	224	8,696	118	1.38
South Carolina	13,874	124	2,840	695	161	17,694	-82	-0.46
South Dakota	6,924	224	215	781	71	8,215	256	3.22
Tennessee	43,061	499	796	3,327	162	47,845	2,250	4.93
Texas	55,317	1,284	1,101	2,675	130	60,507	-1,787	-2.87
Utah	17,336	94	562	45	40	18,077	93	0.52
Vermont	7,668	50	419	33	41	8,211	120	1.48
Virginia	48,793	299	1,761	1,840	255	52,948	1,526	2.97
Washington	60,400	1,260	2,120	760	560	65,100	2,957	4.76
West Virginia	14,610	221	794	428	82	16,135	-251	-1.53
Wisconsin	61,175	1,789	3,116	1,227	310	67,617	3,058	4.74
Wyoming	6,039	135	250	55	112	6,591	-16	-0.24
Overseas	7,255	3	85	4	304	7,651	-511	-6.26
Other	181	26	64	0	31	302	4	1.34
TOTAL	1,906,694	78,071	111,779	48,662	27,137	2,172,343	29,173	1.36

[a] Substitute, Reserve, Staff, and Associate members, NEA life members who also hold annual or lifetime membership in NEA-R; and preretired subscribers to NEA-R

[b] The totals in Column 7 represent NEA members in all classes existing for the 1992–93 membership year—Active, Retired, Life, Student, Substitute, Reserve, Staff, and Associate. Only Active and Life members count toward a state's eligibility for additional directors.

men in administrative positions; however, after 1918 membership underwent an enormous expansion. Partly as a result of this expansion, the
organizational structure of the NEA was changed in 1920 to provide for
more representation from the state and local associations affiliated with the
NEA. By 1955 NEA had enrolled approximately 52 percent of all professional educators eligible for membership.

As a professional association dominated by school administrators, the
NEA was naturally opposed to collective bargaining by teacher unions;
however, as AFT membership increased from 60,000 in 1961 to 300,000
in 1970, mainly as a result of AFT support for collective bargaining,
the NEA reluctantly embraced it in order to survive as the nation's
leading teacher organization. In 1961, the NEA established the Urban
Project to oppose teacher unionization, but the outcome was to accelerate
it dramatically. The NEA began by declaring that it supported "professional negotiations" instead of "collective bargaining"; the difference turned
out to be that collective bargaining was termed "professional negotiations"
if implemented by an NEA affiliate but "collective bargaining" if by an
AFT affiliate. In any event, the budget for the Urban Project was $28,037
in 1961-62; in 1964-65, however, the Urban Project spent $884,665 to com-
pete with AFT locals for bargaining rights. Concomitantly, NEA positions
on teacher strikes and written collective agreements by whatever label were
rapidly becoming union oriented; in effect, the challenge from the AFT in
the 1960s and 1970s transformed the NEA into a union. Eventually, the
differences that supposedly distinguished the NEA from "unions" disappeared, and a new department devoted to negotiations was established in
1968. Staff oriented to union activities replaced educational specialists as
instructional and curriculum issues were deemphasized in favor of collective bargaining matters. As it shed its "professional" image, NEA leadership
sanctioned the use of strikes, and in the late 1970s, the U.S. Department of
Labor and Internal Revenue Service officially recognized the NEA as a
union. Despite its new and unfamiliar role, the NEA doubled its membership during the 1970s, and by the early 1980s, it was second only to the
Teamsters as the nation's largest union (Lieberman and Moskow, 1966).

During the NEA's evolution from "professional association" to labor
union, Terry Herndon, the NEA's executive director from 1973 to 1983,
was the most visible and articulate representative of "the new NEA."
Herndon, who served under five different NEA presidents, was committed
to teacher bargaining, and to the unionization of the NEA. He was also an
aggressive advocate of the liberal political agenda of his day. As its
executive secretary, Herndon led the NEA against what he charged was a
right-wing conspiracy of "chronic tax resisters, congenital reactionaries,
dangerous witch hunters, energized superpatriots, wayward dogma ped-

dlers and vitriolic race haters" bent on destroying public education. In 1981 the NEA published a teacher's guide to counter "attacks on public education" by "the radical Right" (Toch, 1991). This organizational posture has carried over to the 1990s; for example, in 1993, the NEA established the Center for the Preservation of Public Education. Funded for two years by the Representative Assembly, the Center provides staff support, materials and assistance to NEA affiliates actively opposed to the privatization of educational services. In addition to its opposition to voucher plans and parental choice initiatives, the Center received $50,000 to combat what NEA termed right wing stealth candidates who seek election to local school boards. In this effort, the NEA works closely with People for the American Way, a liberal policy organization that was formerly housed in the NEA building.

Representative Assembly (RA)

The NEA's organizational structure is shown in Table 2.2. Created in 1920, the Representative Assembly (RA) is the NEA's governing (legislative and policymaking) body. The RA approves the program budget, all resolutions, the legislative program, reports of committees and of officers, and amendments to the Association's constitution and bylaws before they are effective. The smaller administrative units of the Representative Assembly, such as the 164 member Board of Directors, nine member Review Board, and nine member Executive Committee, control the execution of major policies during the year. The Association's president, vice-president, and secretary-treasurer are also elected by the Representative Assembly.

For each 1,000 active NEA members, each affiliated state association is entitled to one delegate to the Representative Assembly. Local associations are allowed one delegate for each 150 NEA members or major fraction thereof. In 1993 there were over 9,000 voting delegates to the Representative Assembly.

As a result of the size of the Representative Assembly, individual delegates often find it very difficult to participate effectively in the business before the Assembly. A large RA does serve some useful purposes, such as involving more members in NEA business, nominally at least, and more members can be accorded the prestige of being delegates. Nevertheless, it seems likely that a merger of the NEA and AFT would lead to and require constitutional changes that would increase the ratio of members to delegates; otherwise, the governing body of the merged organization would be too large to function effectively.

Standing Committees of the RA

Five standing committees of the Representative Assembly facilitate the operations of the annual meeting by such activities as reviewing proposed

13

resolutions (294 resolutions were voted on and adopted at the 1993 RA), and preparing the annual budget. When the RA is not in session, the committees are accountable to the president, board of directors and executive committee.

Strategic Objective Standing Committees
Implemented September 1, 1993, five standing committees devise the NEA Strategic Plan used for program development and budget allocations. As a result of internal restructuring, NEA "Centers" now provide the organizational structure for achieving the union's goals. NEA goals developed as the basis for its 1994-95 budget include:

Strategic Objective 1. NEA shall expand and protect quality public education as a basic right (preK-G) and secure its adequate and equitable funding.

Strategic Objective 2. NEA shall achieve the restructuring of public schools and enhance the preparation, practice, and professional standards of education employees to improve student learning.

Strategic Objective 3. NEA shall achieve a pluralistic education work force and advance the economic interests, protect the job security, and improve the terms and conditions of employment for all education employees.

Strategic Objective 4. NEA shall promote equity for all and the elimination of discrimination and other barriers to learning generated by social, economic, and political conditions.

Strategic Objective 5. NEA shall strengthen its capacity to attract, represent, and serve members in all membership categories.

No standing committee exists to support the final strategic objective to maintain the organizational systems essential to fulfill the mission of NEA, although this goal receives a budget allocation of nearly $46 million.

Advisory Standing Committees
Five NEA Advisory Standing Committees develop and propose policies and programs on matters of concern to the constituencies that each represents: women's issues, minority and ethnic concerns, general membership needs, student members and retired members.

Special Committees
Special committees may be established by the RA, the board or the executive committee in order to accomplish specific tasks within limited periods of time. As of September 1, 1993, five special committees had been author-

14

Table 2.2

NEA Structure *

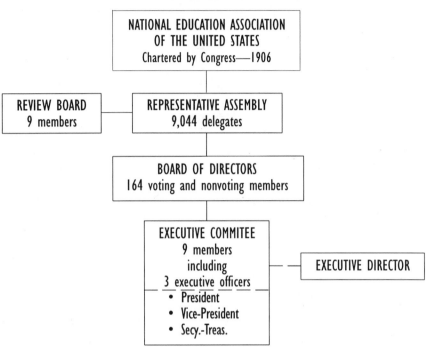

| NATIONAL EDUCATION ASSOCIATION OF THE UNITED STATES Chartered by Congress—1906 |

| REVIEW BOARD 9 members | REPRESENTATIVE ASSEMBLY 9,044 delegates |

BOARD OF DIRECTORS
164 voting and nonvoting members

EXECUTIVE COMMITEE
9 members
including
3 executive officers
• President
• Vice-President
• Secy.-Treas.

EXECUTIVE DIRECTOR

STANDING COMMITTEES OF THE REPRESENTATIVE ASSEMBLY	STRATEGIC OBJECTIVE STANDING COMMITTEES	ADVISORY STANDING COMMITTEES	SPECIAL COMMITTEES
• Constitution, Bylaws, and Rules • Program and Budget • Resolutions • Credentials • Elections	• Employee Advocacy • Human/Civil Rights • Legislation • Membership Services/ Affiliate Relationships • Professional Standards and Practice	• Women's Issues • Minority Affairs • Membership • Student Members • NEA-Retired Advisory Council **	• Health Care(1990-94) • Relationships with Other Organizations(1991-94) • Discipline, Order, and Safety(1993-94) • Candidate Questionnaires

  * As of July 1, 1993.
 ** The NEA-Retired Advisory Council is an elective rather than appointive body.

Note: This chart does not include ad hoc internal committees of the Board of Directors and Executive Committee.

ized, including the Committee on Health Care, and the Committee on Relationships with Other Organizations. The latter committee was charged with reviewing NEA's policies regarding a single national organization and merger with the AFT and/or AFL-CIO (*NEA Handbook*, 1993-94).

STATE EDUCATION ASSOCIATIONS

The first state educational association was organized in Alabama in 1840. By 1921 every state and territory except Alaska had such an association; today NEA's two million members are organized in 52 state affiliates and approximately 13,000 local organizations.

State teacher unions play a critically important role in the NEA's organizational structure. The fact that the state unions affiliated with the NEA usually function under a title that refers to an "association" reflects the historical development of public education in the United States. Education is not mentioned in the U.S. Constitution, hence it is constitutionally a power reserved to the states or to the people. In the early 1800s, education was regarded as primarily a local matter if it were a governmental concern at all, or an individual family matter. In any case, it was taken for granted that public education was to be regulated by the states, within the very broad parameters of the U.S. Constitution.

As a result, the early educational organizations were state associations organized to achieve state funding in various ways. Teachers and administrators alike were members. As a matter of fact, it was common practice for administrators to insist that candidates for teaching positions agree to join their local and state associations as well as the NEA as a condition of employment. Needless to say the associations at all levels were not very aggressive advocates of teacher welfare. Nevertheless, until the advent of teacher collective bargaining in the 1960s, the predominant way to achieve teacher benefits was through state legislation.

Eventually, this emphasis was inadequate, or at least insufficient, for three reasons:

1. Inasmuch as the associations allowed unrestricted administrator membership, administrators tended to dominate the legislative objective of the state associations. This was not a problem when the welfare objectives of teachers coincided, or at least did not conflict with those of administrators. For example, both groups had a common stake in improving benefits under the state teacher retirement system. On the other hand, their objectives sometimes were conflicting; for example, administrators were often op-

posed to teacher tenure and applied their influence in the associations to block or weaken teacher tenure legislation. Thus, unrestricted administrator membership and administrator domination of the state education associations often worked to the detriment of teachers.

2. Reliance on the legislative process often meant that no teachers could achieve a certain benefit unless and until all teachers received it. Teachers who could achieve various benefits if they had a strong local organization were disadvantaged by sole or even primary reliance on legislative processes.

3. To be effective at the state level, state organizations need local affiliates who can provide meaningful assistance to candidates for state office. The state education associations could not meet this requirement because their local affiliates were hardly more than social organizations.

For these reasons, the emphasis on state legislation as the vehicle for promoting teacher welfare ultimately was superseded by collective bargaining, that is, a procedure under which terms and conditions of teacher employment were negotiated by teacher unions and local school boards. Paradoxically, although teacher bargaining resulted from the ineffectiveness of the legislative approach to terms and conditions of employment, it strengthened enormously the political influence of the state teacher associations. It led to increases in their membership and to well-financed local affiliates which were much more effective politically in implementing the state legislative agendas.

The advent of teacher bargaining actually led to several basic changes in state association organizational structure and operations. Chapter 3 discusses the changes in union financial operations and Chapter 4 those in the political dimensions. Here, we shall limit the discussion to state association governance structures.

One of the most important changes was the adoption of unified membership throughout the NEA's organizational structure. Prior to teacher bargaining, teachers were usually allowed to join the local, state, or national organization without necessarily having to join at the other levels. A common pattern was for teachers to join the state association but not the NEA; at the same time, local dues were usually so low that membership at the local level was largely pro forma. In the 1970s, however, the state associations moved to require unified membership, and in 1975, the requirement was incorporated in the NEA's constitution. It is interesting to note that from 1972 to 1976, NEA membership increased from approximately 1,167,000 to 1,887,000, an increase of almost 62 percent. Some of the increase and a membership decline in 1977 were due to the addition and subsequent withdrawal of the New York State United Teachers, but the impact of unified membership was the predominant factor in the increase in NEA membership during these years.

Generally speaking, the state education associations have elected officers who are not eligible for reelection and staff headed by a full-time executive secretary. The prohibitions against reelection may be due to prohibitions in the state association constitution or to a tradition of changing the elected officials annually or biannually. Typically, local affiliates elect delegates to the state convention, and the delegates elect the policymaking officers, such as president, vice-president, and secretary-treasurer. The members of an executive committee are also elected, usually for staggered terms of office.

The executive secretary model of governance differs from the conventional union model. In the latter, the full-time officers are free to run for reelection as often as they wish; for example, Albert Shanker has been president of the AFT since 1974. Similarly, Tom Hobart has been president of the New York State United Teachers since 1968. Obviously, these governance issues will have to be resolved if an NEA/AFT merger is to take place, but it seems apparent that the NEA is moving toward the union model of governance. At the state level, some of the tendencies in this direction are as follows:

1. Terms of office in the state associations are being increased, usually from one to two years.
2. Restrictions on being reelected are declining. Increasingly, elected state officers may run for reelection for a limited number of terms.
3. In an earlier era, the state associations merely reimbursed the elected state officers for the days lost from teaching while on state association business. Today, the practice is to pay the elected officers a full-time salary which exceeds the salary of the executive secretary.

Overall, the tendency is to treat the executive secretary as the top ranking staff officer but not as one of the leading policymaking officers of the associations. Of course, regardless of any organizational chart, executive secretaries (or "executive directors") often do play important policymaking roles, by force of personality or tradition or simply because it is often impossible to separate formulating policy from implementing it.

Realistically, it is not to be expected that teachers who become officers of a state association will necessarily return to the classroom after their service as a state officer. The taste of high salaries, liberal expense accounts and fringe benefits, media attention, and the absence of supervision can hardly fail to affect the elected state officers. Of course, it is politically impermissible to acknowledge these advantages in so many words; in union politics, one must forego the joys of working with children for the thankless tasks of union office.

With the change from association to union functions, the state association structure changed dramatically. Prior to the change, the associations had devoted a great deal of their resources to instructional and curriculum matters. Like the NEA, the state associations supported departments along instructional lines, such as reading or mathematics or science. With the advent of teacher bargaining, however, the administrator organizations, such as the American Association of School Administrators, withdrew or were in effect expelled from the associations; at the same time, the curriculum and instruction organizations, such as the National Science Teachers Association, that had also been sub-units of the NEA and the state associations also became free standing organizations outside the NEA/state association umbrella.

LOCAL EDUCATION ASSOCIATIONS

Prior to the emergence of collective bargaining, local associations affiliated with the NEA were weak organizations. Quite frequently, they served mainly as social organizations, introducing new teachers and honoring retiring ones. Insofar as teacher terms and conditions of employment could be distinguished from educational policy, local associations played a marginal role in the former and a negligible role in the latter. Inasmuch as local associations usually included school administrators, it was seldom feasible for them to be aggressive advocates of teacher welfare. Such advocacy typically conflicted with administrative prerogatives. For example, the teachers might have preferred extra duty to be assigned by rotation or by seniority, but the administrators would often prefer to retain administrative discretion in such matters. Teachers were not likely to urge local associations to advocate limits on administrative discretion in the presence of the very administrators whose actions allegedly justified the limits.

Collective bargaining altered the NEA membership structure dramatically. Because teacher bargaining is regulated by state law, the following comments do not necessarily apply to every state; in fact about 16 states have yet to enact teacher bargaining legislation. Nevertheless, the overall thrust of the collective bargaining legislation that has been enacted is clear enough. Collective bargaining draws a sharp distinction between individuals who exercise supervisory/managerial responsibilities and the employees under their supervision and direction. The union represents the latter. Participation in union affairs by supervisory and managerial employees is dis-

19

couraged where it is not prohibited by law. Such restrictions are deemed essential to prevent employer domination of the organizations that represent employees. Thus, collective bargaining eliminated unrestricted administrator membership, one of the major causes of weak local associations.

At the same time, collective bargaining greatly expanded the role of local associations. School districts were required to negotiate terms and conditions of employment with the exclusive representative of the teachers, that is, the union by whatever name it adopts. The exclusive representatives were usually the local associations affiliated with the NEA, which embraced their union role despite their anti-union heritage.

Negotiations require experienced full-time representatives at the local level. In addition to negotiating the collective agreement, the union is responsible for ensuring that the school district does not violate the agreements. If teachers allege that the school district is violating the agreement, the union initiates a grievance and carries it through the grievance procedure, possibly to arbitration. And because teacher terms and conditions of employment overlap with or affect educational policy, local associations are important players in district affairs. The senior teachers who want higher maximum salaries, perhaps instead of reducing the number of steps on the salary schedule, had to become active in the local association to achieve this objective, just as do the teachers who want the reduction of steps to be a higher priority than raising maximum salaries. Teachers who want family insurance coverage to replace teacher-only coverage must become active in the local association to ensure that the local association bargains for family coverage, just as those who prefer that funds be allocated to the salary schedule must be active to achieve their objective. Thus, whenever teachers feel strongly about an employment issue, the local association becomes the organizational vehicle through which they can achieve their objectives. More precisely, teachers try to persuade their local association bargaining team to emphasize their particular objectives in negotiations.

As local associations became de facto unions, teachers had to invest more resources in them. Local association dues increased dramatically with the advent of collective bargaining. Inevitably, the changes affected their influence in the NEA's organizational structure. First, local associations became an independent power base within the state and national organizations; instead of being overwhelmingly dominated by the state associations, local associations emerged as a major caucus in the state and national organizations. Nationwide the local associations established the National Council of Urban Education Associations (NCUEA), which received official recognition and support from the NEA itself. Obviously, the allocation of resources between the different levels of union organization are influenced by the existence of a strong network of local associations with needs and priorities that differ from time to time from the priorities of other caucuses within the NEA.

Although the factors contributing to the increasing importance of local associations are clear enough, the way that their importance is reflected in the NEA's organizational structure is not always evident from the formal structure of the NEA. One might assume that the dues for each level of organization (local, state, and national) would cover the organizational costs at each level, but that is not how the NEA functions.

The NEA also spends millions annually on approximately 1,500 field representatives who link the NEA to its 13,000 local affiliates. These "UniServ directors" provide bargaining and political services in every state, the District of Columbia, Puerto Rico, and in four overseas areas. Supported in part by a special fee ($19 in 1993-94) assessed of every NEA member, UniServ staff tie locals to the NEA's national political network. UniServ directors, UniServ representatives, UniServ field representatives, UniServ consultants, by whatever title, typically serve as the chief negotiator for one or more local affiliates of the NEA. Where local associations do not have enough members to support a full-time representative, the UniServ programs enable them jointly to receive full-time representation.

Providing assistance to local affiliates in collective bargaining is UniServ's most significant service. As will be explained in Chapter 3, UniServ staff accords the highest priority to contract language that maximizes the union's income stream, as well as to articles that restrict the rights of competing unions. For example, the UniServ directors try to persuade school boards to deny the use of district mail facilities and bulletin boards to competing organizations.

For 1993-94 the budget allocated for UniServ implementation of collective bargaining programs was $48,631,161. The budget also targeted 16 state affiliates which did not have collective bargaining statutes in 1993. Plans included a pre-Representative Assembly conference, designed to secure bargaining rights for all education employees in those states. Coordination, evaluation, and expansion of NEA programs on collective bargaining for all education employees was also included in the funding.

De facto bargaining is a separate line item ($486,683) within the State Relations budget for 1993-94. In collaboration with state affiliates and other NEA program units, this budget item provides support and assistance to the bargaining efforts of state affiliates in states that have not enacted bargaining statutes. In practice, UniServ directors also often exercise the leadership in campaigns for or against school board members, state legislators, and other candidates for public office. By any criterion, they are a crucial component of the NEA's vast political as well as bargaining operations.

The UniServ program illustrates the difficulty of trying to assess the NEA's organizational priorities from a perusal of its organizational structure or gross budget figures. The UniServ funds are transferred from the NEA to the state associations; the latter are technically the employers of UniServ staff. Why not fund UniServ by having the state associations increase their dues by $19 and having NEA dues reduced by this amount? We do not know the answer to this question, but it is probably easier for the NEA to fund its field representatives through one appropriation at the national level than through 52 different state and association appropriations.

The preceding discussion is hardly more than an introduction to the NEA; indeed, it is an introduction mainly to the transformation of the NEA from a professional association with unrestricted administrator membership to a public sector union that excludes administrative personnel. It should be noted that the transformation affected all the state and local associations, not merely those in states which had enacted legislation that required school boards to bargain with teacher unions. As the union orientation began to dominate the NEA's national perspective, its constitution and policies became increasingly antagonistic to administrative personnel and to policies such personnel normally support. By 1994 the NEA was emphasizing the enactment of collective bargaining for teachers in the states that had not yet enacted it.

Our emphasis on the transformation is based on one overriding consideration; to wit, that the emergence of the NEA as a union is the key to understanding virtually every other dimension of its policies and programs. In some cases, the effects of its union orientation are not always apparent to persons not familiar with the dynamics of unionism, but the following chapters will help to confirm the importance of union status. First, however, let us review briefly the structure of the other national teacher organization, which adopted and proclaimed its union status since its inception in 1916.

AMERICAN FEDERATION OF TEACHERS (AFT)

Although teacher unions emerged before 1900, the first to affiliate with the AFL was one in San Antonio, Texas, in 1902. In the same year the Chicago Teachers Federation, which had been organized in 1897, affiliated with the Chicago Federation of Labor. Two patterns of affiliation thus appeared at the outset. One pattern was affiliation with a national labor organization, the other affiliation with a local labor body.

From 1902 to 1916, the teacher union movement had little success in enlisting the nation's teachers. In 1916, however, a number of teacher union leaders agreed upon the desirability of a national teacher union. At that time, there were three teacher unions in Chicago fighting with the Chicago Board of Education for their very existence. The Board had amended its rules in 1915 to

22

prohibit "membership by teachers in labor unions or in organizations of teachers affiliated with a trade union." The Chicago Teachers Federation secured an injunction which restrained the Board from enforcing this prohibition. However, at this time teachers in Chicago were hired on a year to year basis, and the Board refused to rehire many teachers who belonged to the unions. This action of the Board finally induced the Chicago teachers to take the lead in forming a national union of classroom teachers. An invitation to form such a union was sent to all teacher organizations affiliated with labor or those interested in such affiliation. Only four locals sent delegates to the first meeting in Chicago on April 15, 1916, but teacher organizations in Chicago, Gary, New York, Oklahoma City, Scranton, and Washington received charters from the new organization. An application for affiliation with the American Federation of Labor was granted on May 9, 1916.

In its first two years, the AFT had to struggle desperately to survive as a functioning organization. The Chicago Teachers Federation withdrew from the AFT in 1917 as the price for the reinstatement of the Chicago teachers who had been dismissed or not rehired as a result of union membership. Many other locals disbanded under heavy pressure from school boards. However, from 1918 to 1919, the number of AFT locals increased from 24, with a membership of less than 2,000, to over 160, with a membership of close to 11,000. For a short time, membership in the AFT exceeded the membership of the NEA, as teachers were increasingly dissatisfied with the Association's failure to raise teacher salaries in the inflationary period at the close of World War I.

After World War I, however, school boards and school administrators, encouraged by the anti-labor political climate in the early 1920s, launched a major effort to minimize teacher participation in teacher unions. As a result, by 1927, less than one-fifth of the AFT locals which had been issued charters were still operating. After 1927, membership increased steadily until 1939, suffered a short setback until 1941, and then slowly turned upward with only minor reverses until the 1960s.

Prior to the 1960s, the AFT had not been able to organize a higher proportion of the nation's teachers; its increases in membership merely kept pace with increases in the total number of teachers in the United States. The Federation's inability to enroll a higher proportion of all teachers ended with dramatic gains in the 1960s. These gains resulted from the AFT's overwhelming victory over the NEA in the 1961 representation election in New York City. This victory convinced AFT leaders that if given an uncoerced opportunity to choose, most teachers would prefer union to association representation. Consequently, AFT locals began calling for representation elections to choose a bargaining agent, even in districts where the AFT

23

enrolled far fewer members than the NEA. Because of administrator influence in the NEA at that time, the Association did not embrace collective
bargaining until a series of election losses to AFT affiliates in large cities
created an unavoidable dilemma for the NEA at every level. The dilemma
was to embrace collective bargaining and unionization or face staggering
losses to the AFT. Inasmuch as teachers far outnumbered administrators,
the outcome was more or less inevitable as the NEA and AFT competed in
representation elections in the 1960s and 1970s. In the mid-1960s, however,
the NEA and its affiliates realized that teacher bargaining could be used to
increase their membership, and they proceeded to take advantage of their
opportunities to do so as the association replaced its professional image
with a union one. Indeed, in struggling to overcome its earlier opposition
to collective bargaining, the NEA adopted extreme positions that were intended to demonstrate that it was a bona fide militant union. For instance,
the NEA asserted that all school board policies should be negotiable. As
experts on collective bargaining would unanimously agree, this position
was indefensible, but even AFT leaders embraced it publicly to avoid being
upstaged by the NEA. Unfortunately, many teachers who are not sophisticated about collective bargaining were convinced that they should have the
right to bargain on educational policies, or for that matter, on any school
district policies of concern to teachers. The possibility that negotiating public
policies with one interest group might be contrary to the principles of representative government was simply ignored.

Once the NEA embraced teacher bargaining, the NEA and AFT entered
into a rough stalemate. Both showed increases in membership, but gains
were made mainly by organizing the unorganized, not by persuading teachers
to switch from one organization to the other. By and large, the AFT is
dominant in large urban centers and the NEA in smaller cities, suburbs,
and rural areas. Both unions have achieved some success in organizing higher
education; their success in doing so has led to the virtual demise of the
American Association of University Professors (AAUP), which had formerly been the dominant organization of faculty in higher education.

In 1993 the AFT claimed a membership of 820,000 in 49 states (no affiliate in Nevada), the District of Columbia, Panama, Guam, Puerto Rico, the
Virgin Islands, and ten overseas countries, and 2,281 local affiliates. It was
also affiliated with the American Federation of Labor–Congress of Industrial Organizations (AFL-CIO), the national labor body formed by the
merger of the AFL and the CIO in 1955.

Biennial Convention

As shown in Table 2.3, the governing body of the AFT is the Biennial
Convention, which is analogous to the Representative Assembly in the

24

Table 2.3

American Federation of Teachers, AFL-CIO

TABLE OF ORGANIZATION

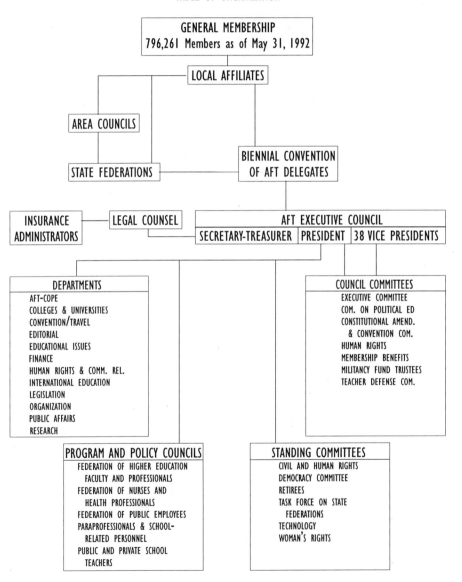

NEA. Locals are permitted delegates on the following basis: one delegate from each affiliated local having a membership of 25 or less; for each 100 members or major fraction thereof, one additional delegate may be elected, provided the full per-capita tax has been paid to AFT. Locals with fewer than 100 members each, but in the aggregate fewer than 300 members from a contiguous geographic area, may form area councils of locals for the exclusive purpose of electing a delegate to the convention. Voting for delegates and alternates is by secret ballot. Each state federation may elect one delegate to the convention, regardless of its at-large membership. In 1992 there were 2,862 delegates at the AFT convention, representing 461 locals, 25 state federations, and 2 councils.

The Executive Council consisting of the president, secretary-treasurer and 38 vice presidents is responsible for the direction of the AFT between conventions. In effect, its functions include those of the NEA's Board of Directors, Executive Committee, and Review Board. The Executive Council carries out the instructions of the Convention, takes action with respect to legislation, interprets and enforces the constitution, makes rules and bylaws which must be submitted to the next convention for approval or rejection, creates and appoints members in the committees, has the responsibility for settling intra-organizational disputes and/or violations, fills vacancies in its own membership, and in general handles the Federation's affairs in the interim between conventions.

AFT members are categorized into five divisions:

1. Public and private school teachers.
2. Paraprofessionals and school-related personnel.
3. Higher education faculty and professionals.
4. Nurses, allied health professionals and other health care employees.
5. State and local public employees and other workers organized in conformity with the provisions of the AFT constitution.

New language adopted by the 1992 convention provided that "all divisions must be represented among the 38 vice presidents" (*AFT Constitution*, 1992).

Committees
Standing Committees, Council Committees, and Program and Policy Councils report to the AFT convention delegates with findings and recommendations for convention action. Like the reports and scores of resolutions voted on at the NEA Representative Assembly, the reports and resolutions presented to the AFT Convention address such diverse issues as Haitian refugees, the balanced budget amendment, childhood lead poisoning, school finance issues, and endorsement of a presidential ticket.

CONCLUSION

Both the similarities and dissimilarities between the AFT and the NEA are not always apparent from their organizational structures; similarities are often obscured by terminological differences, dissimilarities by similar terminology. Several important organizational differences will be explored in the following chapters, but one that does not show up in their organizational structures should be recognized at the outset.

Because of the NEA's much larger membership, the policymaking process in the NEA is hostage to several interest groups that have veto but no "do power." The upshot is that NEA policy tends to be the result of compromises between various interest groups within the Association; as frequently happens in such situations, policymaking becomes a process of formulating the policies that offend the least influential constituencies.

Because of its recent history, the political dynamics in the AFT are very different. Prior to 1964, the AFT was divided politically into two caucuses of roughly equal strength; the Progressive Caucus and the Classroom Teacher Caucus. This situation is relatively rare in union affairs; usually, the incumbent officers are able to utilize the advantages of incumbency to eliminate or weaken significant opposition to their continuation in office. At any rate, the United Federation of Teachers (UFT) in New York City was in the Progressive Caucus in the early 1960s. As a result of its victory over NEA affiliates in a 1961 representation election, the UFT was able to organize a majority of New York City's teachers. Within a few years, the UFT enrolled from a third to a half of all AFT members. Consequently, election to national office within the AFT became practically contingent upon UFT support; since 1964, no candidate for national office opposed by the UFT has been elected to national office in the AFT. This situation has continued despite the fact that the UFT enrolls considerably less than one-third of total AFT membership.

It must be emphasized that these differences in the political dynamics do not necessarily justify any conclusions about the specific policies actually adopted by the two unions. Whether NEA or AFT policies are "better" in some sense can be assessed only by examining the policies themselves. The point here is that the AFT is more unified politically than the NEA. AFT leadership can commit the Federation in ways that would be politically dangerous or unpredictable in the NEA. If AFT membership were as large and as diverse as NEA's, the political dynamics within the AFT would undoubtedly be more similar to the NEA's.

27

CHAPTER THREE

THE REVENUES AND EXPENDITURES OF TEACHER UNIONS

The preceding chapter discussed the structural features of teacher unions. Although we have not discussed the full range of union programs and services, the teacher unions need substantial revenue streams to sustain their operations. This chapter, therefore, is intended to provide an overview of union revenues.

The NEA fiscal year begins September 1 and ends August 31 of each year; the AFT fiscal year is from July 1 through June 30. As labor organizations, each is organized under Section 501(c)(5) of the Internal Revenue Code and files IRS Form 990 annually. This designation exempts the unions from paying income tax, from paying certain state taxes (and the property tax in the case of the NEA), and from paying excise taxes. The Federal Election Campaign Act governs the national teacher union political action committees (PACs); federal committee reports are filed with the Federal Election Commission (FEC). State PAC organization and reporting requirements vary. In addition, both the NEA and the AFT file an annual labor organization report form (Form LM-2) which is filed with the U.S. Department of Labor. Table 3.1 shows NEA cash receipts and disbursements for the year ending August 31, 1992, as shown on the LM-2.

All data in Table 3.1 are for the national office only. Revenues and disbursements of state and local affiliates will be discussed later in this chapter.

Although the data in Tables 3.1 and 3.2 raise several unanswered questions, the following discussion may be adequate to explain how union operations are supported financially. We begin by reviewing budgeted receipts and disbursements of the general fund, one of several financial operations of the NEA. General Fund income is generated from three sources: 1) membership dues, 2) agency fees, and 3) external recoveries.

NEA GENERAL FUND INCOME

Membership Dues
NEA member dues account for over 90 percent of its general fund income. The dues payments are transmitted monthly from the state or local affiliate

Table 3.1

National Education Association
Period covered 9/30/91-8/31/92
Schedule B   Form LM-2

Receipts

Dues	$155,287,381.
On Behalf of Affiliates for Transmittal to Them	746,222.
Sale of Supplies	5,077.
Interest	1,081,579.
Dividends	1,630.
Loans Obtained	1,646,290.
Repayment of Loans Made	2,031,093.
From Other Sources	77,441,645.
TOTAL RECEIPTS	$238,240,917.

Disbursements

To Affiliates of Funds Collected on Their Behalf	$ 680,505.
To Officers	2,740,265.
To Employees	28,432,206.
Office and Administrative Expenses	8,846,870.
Educational and Publicity Expenses	7,661,790.
Professional Fees	9,390,124.
Benefits	12,276,727.
Loans Made	18,413.
Contributions, Gifts and Grants	47,846,097.
Purchase of Investments and Fixed Assets	9,551,998.
Direct Taxes	2,310,263.
Withholding Taxes	9,565,151.
Repayment of Loans Obtained	45,240,880.
For Other Purposes	52,634,642.
TOTAL DISBURSEMENTS	$237,195,931.

29

Table 3.2

National Education Association
Period covered 9/30/91-8/31/92
Statement A   Form LM-2

Assets

Cash on hand	$ 4,010.
Cash in banks	16,075,126.
Accounts Receivable	28,622,754.
Loans Receivable	2,925,529.
Other Investments	10,470.
Fixed Assets	73,634,852.
Other Assets	3,870,435.
TOTAL ASSETS	$125,143,176.

Liabilities

Accounts Payable	$16,163,110.
Mortgages Payable	51,404,013.
Other Liabilities	18,140,849.
TOTAL LIABILITIES	$85,707,972.

to the national headquarters. NEA dues are based on a formula set forth in NEA Bylaw 2-7. Accordingly, Table 3.3 indicates anticipated membership and membership dues for 1993-94:

Obviously, maintaining its 2.1 million dues paying membership is crucial to NEA's finances. Until 1975, it was possible for teachers to be members of the local, state, or national association without necessarily paying dues at the other two levels. Typically, NEA membership was much lower than membership in the state associations and local associations were often primarily social organizations with minimal dues.

The advent of collective bargaining changed the financial dynamics in several ways. With collective bargaining, there was imperative need for trained negotiators to represent local associations in bargaining and grievances. Local associations not large enough to pay for full-time representatives combined to support full-time union staff, usually a UniServ director. UniServ directors are union representatives who are funded partly from

Table 3.3

National Education Association
1993-94 Membership and Dues
(Based on full-time equivalents)

Membership Category	Individual Member Dues	1993-94 Membership	1993-94 Dues
Active—Professional Education Positions	$99.00	1,605,000	$158,895,000.
Active—Educational Support Positions	49.50	202,000	9,999,000.
Active—Life		105,000	–0–
Agency Fee		23,000	2,208,000.
Retired—Annual	5.00	65,000	600,000.
Retired—Life	10.00	33,500	400,000.
Associate	5.00	1,100	5,500.
Reserve and Staff	49.50	3,000	148,500.
Student	10.00	50,000	500,000.
Other			450,000.
TOTALS		2,087,600	$173,206,000.

NEA dues, but are not employed by the NEA. Instead, UniServ directors are legally employees of the state associations or local affiliates of the NEA. Most of the funds transmitted by the NEA to its state affiliates ($45 million in 1992-93) is for the UniServ program. UniServ salaries and working conditions are negotiated by the unions representing UniServ directors and the state associations. Table 3.4 shows the number of UniServ employees in the various regions. When fringe benefits are factored in, UniServ directors are paid $60,000 to $100,000.

In addition, the NEA operates six regional offices that employ field representatives who are NEA employees. These field representatives are represented by Association of Field Staff Employees (AFSE), which negotiates on their behalf with the NEA. These are also well-paid positions. As so often happens when unions are employers, the NEA pays its field representatives very generously. The field representatives argue that it would be hypocritical for them to urge school boards to provide certain benefits if the NEA itself did not provide them. Thus the NEA, like many other unions, provides extremely generous benefits to its employees—so generous that the NEA does not publicize the salaries and dollar value of all employee benefits to NEA members.

Table 3.4

UniServ Funding Summary
Contract Year 1993-94

Region	Unit Employees	NEA Funds
Pacific	278	$ 6,264,925.
Midwestern	361	7,869,144.
Southeastern	201	4,521,464.
Mid-Atlantic	239	5,450,200.
Northeast	119	6,280,567.
Western	165	3,828,880.
TOTALS	1,509	$34,215,181.

Inasmuch as membership dues pay for most of NEA's budgeted programs, and most state and local programs as well, a union focus on dues is readily understandable. In order to illustrate the sophistication as well as the relentless nature of the union approach to dues, let us examine a standard clause on the subject from a California school district:

ARTICLE XII
ORGANIZATIONAL SECURITY AND PAYROLL DEDUCTIONS

1. Any employee who is a member of the Association who signs and delivers to the District an assignment authorizing deduction of unified membership dues, initiation fees and general assessments of the Association, or service fee (representation fee), shall have such authorization continue in effect from year to year unless revoked in writing between June 1 and September 1 of a given year. Any such revocation should be effective for the next school year. Pursuant to such authorization, the District shall deduct such dues, fees or assessments (or service fee) from the regular salary check, in ten (10) equal installments each year, for the duration of this Agreement.
2. The District will provide bargaining unit employees new to the District with a copy of the Collective Bargaining Agreement and the employee will sign a form, a copy of which will be forwarded to the Association within ten (10) days of the employee reporting to work.

3. Any employee who is a member of the Unit, who is not a member of the Association in good standing, or who does not make application for membership within thirty (30) days from the first day of active employment or July 1, 1981, whichever is later (except as provided hereafter in the Optional Procedure), shall pay a service fee to the Association: an amount equivalent to the United Membership dues, initiation fee and general assessments uniformly required to be paid by members of the Association.
4. In the event an employee fails to comply with this Article, at the request of the Association, the Superintendent or his designee shall notify the employee within (10) days that he/she is not complying with his/her contractual obligation to the Association and the District. A copy of such notice shall be sent to the Association.
5. The District shall deduct service fees from the salary or wage order of the employee who is not a member of the Association, or has not complied with the Optional Procedure.

   Any employee may pay service fees directly to the Association in lieu of having such service fees deducted from the salary or wage order.

   In the event that a unit member shall not pay such fee directly to the Association or authorize payment through payroll deduction as provided in paragraph 1, the Association shall so inform the District and the District shall immediately begin automatic payroll deduction in the same manner as set forth in paragraph 1 of this Article.

   Any payment to a charity must be made on an annual basis.
6. The parties further agree the obligation of this Article shall be grounded in the individual contract issues after July 1, 1981, for employees, which shall state—"this contract is subject to a collective bargaining agreement heretofore or hereafter negotiated by the District and the exclusive bargaining representative of employees employed by the District. The terms of such collective bargaining agreement are incorporated herein, and by accepting this contract, you agree to be bound by all such terms, including Article XII, Organizational Security and Payroll Deductions provisions thereof."
7. The District agrees promptly to remit such monies to the Association accompanied by an alphabetical list of employees for whom such deductions have been made.
8. The Association agrees to furnish any information needed by the District to fulfill the provisions of this Article.
9. Upon appropriate written authorization from the employee, the

District shall deduct from the salary of any employee and make appropriate remittance for annuities, credit union, and savings bonds. Deductions for any other plans or programs shall be jointly approved by the Association and the District.

10. Dues Checkoff—Authorization in effect on date of the signing of this Agreement shall remain in effect but shall be subject to the conditions set forth in this Article.

11. The Modesto Teachers Association agrees to indemnify and hold the District harmless from any and all claims arising from a bargaining unit member represented by the Modesto Teachers Association concerning the implementation of Article XII provided such implementation is done by the District in good faith and in a non-negligent manner. In such case, the Modesto Teachers Association shall have the exclusive right to defend such suits and to determine which matters shall be compromised, resisted, tried, or appealed.

12. The District agrees to deduct dues or service fees pursuant to the schedule submitted by MTA for employees who execute a form currently in use or any mutually agreed upon form. The MTA is to submit the schedule each year by September 5. The schedule may be amended once each school year with thirty (30) days notice.

OPTIONAL PROCEDURE

13. *Exclusive optional procedure effective upon final ratification of the 1990-92 Collective Bargaining Agreement applicable to employees hired to commence service to the District thereafter and to employees employed before that date who were members of the Association or who were paying a service fee to the Association.*

Any employee of this unit who has bona fide religious beliefs which prohibit him/her from joining or financially supporting employee organizations shall not be required to join or financially support Modesto Teachers Association CTA/NEA. However, that employee shall utilize the following Optional Procedure:

a. submit a notarized statement to the Association with a copy to the employer by the end of the first month (September) of each school year. The statement shall state that the person does not desire to join or contribute to the Modesto Teachers Association because of religious beliefs that prevent him/her from joining or contributing.

b. Make payment equal to unified membership dues to a non-religious, non-labor organization exempted under Section 501 (c)(3) of Title 26 of the Internal Revenue Code. The list of designated charitable organizations is: Heart Fund, Cancer Fund, Cystic Fibrosis Foundation or others approved by the Association.

c. Proof of such payment (i.e., payment to one of the charities on the list of designated charities) shall be submitted to the Association with a copy to the District by the end of the first month of each school year (September).

Upon final ratification of the 1990-92 Collective Bargaining Agreement, this procedure is applicable only to employees who have elected to not join in financial support of Modesto Teachers Association CTA/NEA based on personal beliefs and who annually continue to exercise that option.*

A close examination of Article XII of the Modesto contract shows that it is much more convenient to pay the dues than it is not to pay them. Paragraph 1 continues the authorization in effect from year to year. The revocation must be in writing and submitted between June 1 and September 1, a period of time in which most teachers are not in school. Actually, the window in which a teacher can resign is not very helpful even to those who might wish to use it. One of the union's main functions, if not the major one, is to negotiate a contract. In many situations the contracts are not completed until after the beginning of the school year. When and where this is the case, the teachers have lost their most effective way to object to the union's performance—they can no longer withdraw their financial support for the union.

The 1993-94 unified dues in this district were $640; local dues $165, state (CTA) dues $376, and national (NEA) $99. Ostensibly, the contract allows teachers to revoke the dues deduction; note, however, that it does not allow them to avoid paying an amount equivalent to regular dues assessments and initiation fees. This is clearly stated in paragraphs 3 and 5 which will be discussed shortly. If the teacher does not pay, the union merely notifies the district, and the district is contractually obligated to deduct the amount from the teacher's pay.

---

*All School district contracts in California are public records. The Modesto contract is cited here because it also illustrates the importance of a long-range perspective on teacher bargaining. When one of the authors (ML) was employed by the Modesto board of education in the 1970s, the MTA contract did not include a service fee requirement. After several years of hard bargaining by the MTA, and a strike, the service fee was included. The service fee provisions illustrate the fact that the concessions school boards often make to achieve an immediate agreement often strengthen the union's ability to extract even more concessions from the board later on.

The Optional Procedure also illustrates the minimal concern for teacher rights on issues pertaining to dues. A relatively small group of teachers has or may have religious objections to paying dues or service fees to the union. Such bona fide objections do not release the teachers from an obligation to pay; they serve only to release the teacher from an obligation to pay the union. So the teacher has to pay, but to whom? The designated list of charities is extremely narrow, but cannot be expanded without union approval (section 13b). Finally, to safeguard against the possibility that teachers might drop their religious objections but continue to avoid payment, (section 13c) requires that the optional procedure be repeated every year, or the teacher pays the union. Parenthetically, it should be noted that one reason the unions are so adamant about restricting the religious objections is that the union receives no income from the religious objector. Unlike the teachers who object on religious grounds, objectors on other grounds must still pay the service fee to the union.

The union's emphasis on dues and service fees is further illustrated by Paragraph 7, which ensures that there will be no float accruing to the district, and that the union will be able to identify non-payers immediately. Paragraph 9 ensures that there will be no payroll deduction for any plans or programs opposed by the union. New employees will not be able to assert lack of awareness of Article XII as a basis for challenging the dues deduction.

NEA Service (Agency) Fees

Another important source of union revenues is compulsory payment of fees by nonmembers of the union. Such fees are widely referred to as "service fees" or "agency shop" or "fair share fees"; the former terminology will be used here. Paragraph 3, 4, and 5 of the Modesto contract illustrate the contractual provisions governing service fees. Inasmuch as these paragraphs are fairly typical, we shall cite them to clarify the issues.

The basic public policy issue can be stated as follows: Should public policy require, tolerate, or prohibit service fees? State legislators might adopt any of these divergent answers. Where the states allow but do not mandate service fees, the public policy question is also a bargaining issue at the table. In effect, the state legislatures have referred the public policy issue to local school boards, which must then decide what to do about it.

Although it is impossible to ascertain the precise amount of union revenues that results from service fees, they are an important source of union revenues. In the 21 right-to-work states, service fees are not allowed. In the states where such fees are allowed, the union must negotiate the inclusion of a service fee in the contract, and the amount varies from district to district and state to state. As a matter of fact, even the unions might have difficulty assessing the amount of union revenue resulting from service fee clauses in contracts. The reason is that some union income from membership dues actually results from service fee clauses in the contract. Teachers who pay service fees are not union members and do not participate in union affairs; for instance, they cannot vote on whether to accept proposed contracts with the school board unless the union allows them to do so. Where the service fee is equivalent to dues, some teachers become union members and pay the full amount of union dues.

Interestingly enough, in Table 3.3 the 1993-94 NEA budgets show 23,000 agency fee payers, and estimate union income therefrom to be $2,208,000. This comes to $96 per payor, just to the NEA; inasmuch as the service fees must also be paid to state and local associations, the total amounts extracted from nonmembers is several times this amount. Needless to say, the AFT also relies on service fees to generate a significant amount of union income.

In the NEA budget, agency fees provide 1.3 percent of the NEA's membership income. What this means, however, is that service fees are a much higher proportion of union income in the states that allow or require such fees. The NEA figures on revenues from service fees are for all of the states combined; if, as is the case, almost half the states do not allow service fees, the fees must be a substantially higher percentage of NEA income in the states that allow them.

The union rationale for service fees is that members of the bargaining unit should not receive the benefits of representation without paying their "fair share" of its costs. This rationale is based on the fact that when a union becomes the exclusive representative, it must represent everyone in the bargaining unit, whether or not the individuals are members of the union. Thus the interests of the employees are to be "free riders," that is, to receive the benefits of representation without paying for the union services that supposedly were responsible for them.

There are several objections to this rationale. Obviously, if a union did not seek exclusive representation, it would have no right to force nonmembers to pay for the union's services. In practice, the unions demanded the right to represent everyone, and then, having achieved this right, cited it as a reason to force nonmembers to pay the service fee. It is as if someone painted your house against your wishes, and then demanded that you pay for the service so that you would not be a "free rider."

The most basic objection to service fees is that they violate the rights of individuals to contract for their labor. In effect, collective bargaining forces individuals to accept representation they may not want and terms and conditions of employment that may not be as good as those that could be negotiated individually. Unquestionably, many individuals are worse off as a result of union representation; for example, mathematics and science teachers could often negotiate higher salaries for themselves if they were not tied to the salary schedule for all teachers. In any event, the vast majority of persons would strenuously object to being compelled to buy a service because the vendor insisted that the benefits outweighed the costs. Benefits are supposed to be evaluated by the potential buyer, not by the party who compels the alleged beneficiary to pay for them.

At bargaining tables, school boards face strong temptations to agree to service fees. The teacher unions accord such clauses a high priority and will typically offer valuable concessions for board agreement to a service fee. Such quid pro quo's are very attractive to school boards because individual teachers, not the boards, pay for the concession. Furthermore, by agreeing to a service fee, the board is discouraging support for a rival union which might challenge the incumbent union for not extracting enough concessions from the board. With a service fee, incumbent unions need not fear defections so much if they agree to board proposals that are highly unpopular among the teachers. If teachers have to pay a service fee regardless of other considerations, the union does not lose so much revenue by agreeing to unpopular board proposals.

In states which do not mandate or prohibit service fees, the public policy issues must be faced at the district level. The local district is faced with a dilemma: It can protect the rights of individual teachers or it can sacrifice them for union concessions on other matters. Whatever one's view of the dilemma, many boards have opted for the concessions from the union instead of protection for all teachers in the bargaining unit.

What are the employee's options at this point? To put it mildly, they are not very attractive. The U.S. Supreme Court has upheld the constitutionality of service fees, but it has also held that the fees must be limited to the employee's pro rata share of the costs of bargaining and processing grievances. It has also upheld the union position that nonmembers can be charged for the costs incurred by the state and national organization for these purposes. Clearly, the Modesto contractual language quoted above requires nonmembers to pay more than is constitutionally permissible. In practice, however, the teacher must initiate a grievance or lawsuit to get a rebate of the excess deduction.

For purposes of discussion, let us assume that a teacher would be entitled to $150 if his or her objection to the service fee were legally sustained. The teacher union has an enormous stake in defeating or minimizing the rebate; thus it employs a phalanx of attorneys prepared to argue the union position at every step of the case. Meanwhile, the teacher faces a quandary. How much time and money should be invested in getting the rebate? At least from a financial point of view, it does not make sense to invest $5,000 or $1,000 or even $150 in the chance to regain the $150 that has been wrongfully deducted from the teacher's paycheck. Without access to pro bono legal services, the teacher is extremely unlikely to challenge the excessive deduction even though it would be invalidated if carried to a definitive legal decision. The National Right To Work Committee (NRTWC) provides such legal services upon request. NRTWC attorneys experienced in California agency shop litigation estimate that 7-10,000 California teachers are not members of AFT or NEA; of these, only about 1,500-2,000 initiate grievances or lawsuits to get a rebate.

The foregoing analysis actually understates the obstacles for nonpayment of union dues or service fees. For instance, California school boards can agree to a maintenance of membership clause. Under such a clause, teachers who are members of the union must maintain their membership in it until a certain number of days before the expiration of the contract; 30 days before the contract expires would be the window in California. In districts that have agreed to maintenance of membership, teachers cannot resign from membership until the window period. If a teacher has just been employed and joins the union, the teacher must remain a member until the window period, which may be almost three years in the future; the teacher cannot avoid payment of union dues and assessments prior to the window period.

School boards that accept service fees face complex problems of implementation. One is the amount of the fee. The U.S. Supreme Court has held that the fee must be the individual's pro rata share of the costs of bargaining and processing grievances; in theory, nonmembers cannot be assessed for other union activities. Logically, this means that the service fees must be less than regular union dues and assessments, but teacher unions nevertheless still collect regular dues and assessments as a "service fee" in many school districts. Needless to say, the unions have a very expansive view of what expenditures are for bargaining and grievance handling; opponents of service fees have a more restrictive view of these matters. Understandably, litigation over this issue is widespread, especially since the proportion of union expenditures for bargaining and grievance handling can vary widely from time to time and district to district.

Implementation of service fee agreements raises several other issues which cannot be discussed here. Among them are the following:

1. The procedures for assessing the amount of the service fees.
2. The procedures for challenging the fees and seeking review for fees already paid.
3. The use that can be made of fees that have been paid but challenged.
4. Who bears the cost of challenges to service fees.
5. School board liability for service fees that violate employees' constitutional rights.

6. The information that unions must provide upon request to payors of service fees.
7. Whether the service fees apply only to the local union that is the exclusive representative, or may also include the teacher's share of the costs of the state and national affiliates that provide bargaining assistance to the local unions.
8. Who has the burden of proof on which issues in litigation involving service fees.

To illustrate the complexity of these matters, the U.S. Supreme Court has held that the costs of preparation for an illegal strike can be counted as expenditures requiring payment of a "fair share" by nonmembers under a service fee. Given such decisions, it is hardly any wonder that service fees are a source of continuing confusion and litigation among all parties interested in the issue. As the foregoing discussion indicates, however, the stakes in this litigation are very large indeed for the teacher unions. Membership dues and service fees for 1993-94 just for the NEA, exclusive of the much larger amounts going to its state and local affiliates and other unions such as the AFT, were estimated to generate $172,756,000, almost $18 million more than the 1991-92 revenues from these sources. Needless to say, the larger the revenue stream from service fees, the more difficult it will be to limit the union income from this source.

External Recoveries
In addition to dues from members and service fees from nonmembers, the NEA also receives income from sources outside the Association. For 1993-94 these funds were reflected in the budget as reimbursements from state affiliates for jointly funded executive director positions, advertising in NEA publications, rebates, sales of library materials, and exhibit booth and conference center rentals. Specific budget items are:

Communications	$ 15,500.
Conference and facility rent, rebate	42,000.
Data processing	1,400,000.
Governance (Convention income)	185,000.
Human resources, Retirement Trust	11,321.
Membership and affiliate reimbursement	2,664.590.
Publishing sales, advertising income	3,733,000.
Total:	$8,186,411.

Delegates at the 1993 Representative Assembly in San Francisco approved the 1993-1994 general fund budget of $173,206,000, an amount far exceed-

40

ing the income and expenditures of any other professional organization. However, the $8 million income from sources outside the NEA as shown above was not included as part of the general fund income; instead, NEA accounting procedures show the external recovery funds as an offset to program costs. In short, both the NEA's total income and total expenditure figures omitted the amounts from external recoveries. Clearly, however, the 1993-94 NEA general fund income budget was over $181 million.

NEA GENERAL FUND EXPENDITURES

NEA programs and administration are carried out by union executives and approximately 550 employees in the Washington, D.C. area and in NEA's six regional offices.

The 1993-94 NEA programs and respective budgets were as follows:

NEA Program and Administration

A. Center for Advocacy	$36,939,207.
Collective Bargaining/Compensation	1,473,104.
Human & Civil Rights	5,256,623.
Legal Services	23,493,241.
Research	6,461,546.
Office for Advocacy	254,693.
B. Center for Membership and Affiliates	$60,808,420.
Center for Revitalization of Urban Ed.	1,338,790.
Constituent Group Relations	7,652,140.
State Relations	48,631,161.
Training & Organizational Development	2,641,039.
Office for Membership & Affiliates	545,290.
C. Center for Policy and Strategic Planning	$14,644,295.
Center for Strategic Planning	351,720.
Governance	10,197,448.
International Relations	458,991.
Office for Policy & Strategic Planning	3,636,136.
D. Center for Public Affairs	$24,716,531.
Communications	7,131,783.
Government Relations (incl. NEA-PAC admin.)	9,423,589.
Health Information Network	479,213.
Publishing	7,447,253.
Office for Public Affairs	234,693.

E. Center for Teaching & Learning $ <u>7,136,012.</u>
National Center for Innovation   1,873,219.
National Foundation for the Improvement of Ed.   500,000.
Professional Standards & Practices   4,484,174.
Office for Teaching & Learning   278,619.

F. Center for Administration & Finance $ <u>27,229,475.</u>
Business & Finance   12,376,130.
Conference & Facilities Management   5,785,453.
Data Processing   6,125,600.
Human Resources   2,435,008.
Office for Administration & Finance   507,284.

Contingency $ <u>1,732,060.</u>

NEA 1993-94 administration/program
budget expenditures   Total: $<u>173,206,000.</u>

According to the "Financial Reports" of the NEA secretary-treasurer and independent auditors, contingency fund expenditures are approved by the NEA Executive Committee or the NEA Board of Directors. In 1992-93, 13 contingency fund expenditures were authorized, including: 1) $150,000, approved by the NEA Board, December 11-12, 1992, "To assist Michigan EA (Education Association) in fighting State Ballot Initiatives on Tax Limitations, Cutting Education Taxes and Term Limitations"; 2) $50,000, approved by the NEA Executive Committee, March 29-30, 1993, "To assist TSTA (Texas State Teachers Association) in defeating a State Constitutional Amendment which would impede TSTA's ability to achieve salary and other financial benefits for its members"; and 3) $200,000, approved by the NEA Board, April 30-May 1, 1993, "To support Connecticut EA's Quality, Integrated Education Project" (NEA, 1993).

In addition for 1993-94, the $8 million of external recoveries income was allocated as follows:

Publishing $3,733,000.
Membership and Affiliates   2,664,590.
Data Processing   1,400,000.
Governance   185,000.
Human Resources   111,321.
Conference and Facilities   42,000.
Business and Finance   35,000.
Communications   <u>15,500.</u>

NEA 1993-94 additional budget expenditures $8,186,411.

NEA estimates that approximately 36 percent of its budget is returned to state and local affiliates through the UniServ Program (20 percent); Unified Legal Services Program (9.8 percent) and other projects (6.2 percent). It should be noted that the NEA receives funds from state and local affiliates and also allocates funds to them for programs that are cooperatively administered.

The usefulness of these figures is highly debatable; our view is that they are not informative for several reasons. One is that certain objectives are funded from several budget lines. Collective bargaining services to local affiliates may require expenditures by legal counsel, research, communications, and several other programs and services. Another problem is that budget information is often presented in ways that obscure rather than reveal information members might wish to have. For instance, most NEA members probably believe that the salaries of the NEA executive officers in 1993-94 were as follows:

President	$165,410.
Vice-President	$145,410.
Secretary/Treasurer	$145,410.

However, in addition, the executive officers receive the following:

1. *A living allowance based on 20 percent of salary.* The justification for this is not clear. It may have originated when NEA officers were elected for one year terms but would hardly be applicable to officers who may spend six or more years in Washington. Justification aside, inasmuch as the allowance is provided without restriction, it seems misleading to exclude it from the salary figures.
2. *A 20 percent fringe benefit allowance.* The fringe benefit allowance is in addition to the living allowance. The NEA executive officers can but are not required to participate in the NEA's health insurance plan; the $20,000 allowance is supposed to enable them to make their own arrangements for health insurance. Here again, the issue being raised is member knowledge about the situation.

If an NEA president gives up his or her position in the individual's home state, there is no reason why the individual should receive a living allowance. If the president maintains his or her position in the individual's school district, the president is likely to be covered by the district's health insurance and retirement system. For that matter, the NEA president and president's family may be covered by spousal health insurance.

In addition to the 40 percent additional ($66,000 in 1993-94) the NEA president receives several other benefits.

1. Tax preparation at NEA expense
2. Travel for a companion to the annual convention and to one international conference
3. Moving expenses

The point to be made is not whether the NEA president should receive these benefits; it is that the members simply do not know the total compensation paid to their officers. The additional items cited above may not be exhaustive, but add about $75,000 in toto to presidential compensation, which can be treated as ordinary income. We do not know whether NEA members care what the NEA president receives annually in salary and benefits; our point is that unless the members know, there is no way to assess their reactions. Parenthetically, we note that in a paid advertisement in the *Washington Post*, NEA President Keith Geiger repeatedly urged the nation "to move beyond the profit motive," to enact gun control. Geiger went on to approve Martin Luther King's statement that *"our economy must become more person centered and less profit centered "* (Geiger, 1994).

Similarly, the budget documents given to NEA convention delegates show that just over $152 million has been set aside for retirement benefits for NEA staff. These benefits ordinarily vest after five years of NEA service. Is $152 million appropriate? To answer this question, members need to know the number of beneficiaries of the $152 million, but this information (about 1,200) is not provided in the budget documents. Indeed, even knowing the number of beneficiaries and how much in toto has been set aside for their retirement benefits is not sufficient information for budgetary purposes. Information about the trends in retirement costs and the projections would also appear to be essential for informed judgment. Will the NEA have an entitlement problem, similar to the entitlement problems of Medicare and Social Security? The NEA's budget documents do not provide adequate information for the delegate who is or may be concerned about the issue.

NEA SPECIAL PURPOSE FUNDS

NEA has special purpose funds in addition to the General Fund. Restricted funds are designated for specific projects and purposes for members and employees. The special purpose funds vary in the extent of direct NEA control, their magnitude, tax status, beneficiaries and funding mechanisms. In addition to the funds which support the UniServ operation, the follow-

44

ing eight special purpose funds illustrate the complexity of NEA financial operations.

1. *NEA-Retired Program Fund*
   For over 10 years the NEA has offered retired life memberships through a special purpose fund known as the NEA-Retired Program. Payments to the fund qualify retired members for several services such as pre-retirement seminars and publications. The NEA-Retired Program Fund for members records payments to the fund as deferred income when received and amortizes them over the estimated life expectancy of its NEA retired members. As of August 31, 1992 the balance in this fund was $2,710,882.

2. *The Member Benefits Corporation (MBC)*
   The Member Benefits Corporation, a wholly-owned subsidiary of NEA, administers several special membership services. As of August 31, 1992, MBC had total assets of $2,163,663.

3. *NEA Members Insurance Trust*
   As part of NEA Special Services, the NEA Members Insurance Trust is a separate tax exempt organization, which also reports income and expenditures. For the year ended August 31, 1992, the NEA Members Insurance Trust had total assets of $88,159,667.

4. *Defined Benefit Retirement Plan*
   Substantially all NEA permanent employees are covered by its Defined Benefit Retirement Plan which includes some employees from state and local affiliates. The defined benefit retirement fund had net assets available for benefits of $152,232,340 as of January 1, 1992.

5. *401(k) Salary Reduction Plan*
   NEA contributes to a 401(k) salary reduction plan based on a set percentage of employee contributions. For the years ended August 31, 1992, NEA contributed $903,131.

6. *NEA Post-Retirement Health Care Benefits*
   As of August 31, 1992, NEA had accrued approximately $7,900,000 to provide post-retirement health care benefits for its present retirees and eligible active employees upon retirement.

7. *NEA Foundation Funds*
   In 1969 NEA created the National Foundation for the Improvement in Education (NFIE). As a tax-exempt, nonprofit organization, NFIE receives gifts and grants from private foundations, individuals, corporations, and the government. In the 1980s NFIE's board of directors converted it from a grant-seeking organization to an endowed foundation now engaged in grant-giving. With NEA and substantial corporate support, NFIE has accumulated assets of nearly $11,000,000.

45

NFIE's Annual Report lists contributions from NEA, corporations, individuals and private foundations; a partial list includes:

Apple Computer, Inc.
ARCO Foundation
Ashland Oil Foundation
The Bell Atlantic Charitable
  Foundation
The BellSouth Foundation
The Bristol-Meyers Squibb Foundation
Citibank
The Danforth Foundation
Digital Equipment Corporation
Edison Electric Institute
The Edna McConnell Clark
  Foundation
GTE Service Corporation
The Hitachi Foundation
The Horace Mann Ins. Companies
IBM Corporation

The Johnson Foundation
MBNA American Bank, NA
New England Telephone.
NIKE Inc.
The NYNEX Foundation
The Pacific Telesis Foundation
The Prudential Foundation
The RJR/Nabisco Foundation
Sega Youth Ed. and Health
  Foundation
Student Loan Marketing Assn
Southern New England
  Telephone
Time Warner, Inc.
United Resources
The US West Foundation
Xerox Corporation

These funds are used to sponsor regional conferences, state instructional and professional development conferences, publications, television programming, video programs, media efforts, and other outreach programs in every region of the country. NFIE is governed by an 18 member board of directors that includes the NEA president, the NEA past president, the NEA executive director, other academics and corporate executives.

8. *NEA-PAC*

In 1972, the NEA established the National Education Association Political Action Committee (NEA-PAC) as a separate fund to support its endorsed candidates for national office. NEA-PAC generated over $4 million in 1991-92 and spent almost $6 million during the 1992 election cycle. We discuss NEA-PAC funding, political activities and details of state and local teacher union PACs in Chapter 4.

In practice, it is impossible to determine from budget figures how much the NEA spends on various activities and programs. This is due partly to the fact that the budgeted amounts often refer to expenses incurred by one unit to facilitate the objectives or operations of several others. For example, legal counsel may be called upon for collective bargaining with staff unions, NEA's tax exemptions, contracts with vendors, drafting legislation, and a host of other activities shown as receiving specified budget amounts. In addition, several NEA activities are carried on by its wholly owned subsidiaries, such as the Member Benefits Corporation. Without the budgetary information from these subsidiaries, it is impossible to ascertain the amounts actually spent for certain programs. On the other hand, the reason for their exclusion from the regular budget may be to avoid full disclosure of their operations. We shall come back to this issue in the next chapter, but it is a major obstacle to full understanding of NEA governance and financial operations.

AFT GENERAL FUND/UNION DUES AND FEES

Table 3.5 shows the AFT's cash receipts and disbursements for the year ending June 30, 1992, as shown on Form LM-2.

Like the NEA, over 90 percent of the AFT's annual revenues are derived from a per capita tax and service fees which totaled $67,740,516 for the fiscal year ending June 30, 1992. In 1992 the AFT convention approved a $.40 per-capita, per month increase, beginning September 1, 1992 and an additional $.40 per member per month, beginning September 1, 1993. These increases raised the per capita tax to $8.55 per month per member. AFT's other income is derived from sources similar to NEA's sources of additional revenues:

Publications Income	$ 212,900.
Subscription service	201,339.
Locals' insurance	3,652.231.
Insurance administration	1,701,716.
Grant income	710,188.
Distribution from limited partnership	648,213.
Travel plan commissions	140,745.
Exhibit income	407,216.
COPE contributions	1,944,479.
Total	$9,619,027.

Table 3.6 shows the AFT assets and liabilities as reported on Form LM-2.

AFT SEPARATE FUNDS

Pursuant to the bylaws, the AFT Executive Council is charged with preparing and adopting the annual budget. The AFT allocates specific per capita amounts to several separate funds, each separately administered. Table 3.7 shows the 1992-93 AFT budget with amounts allocated and budgeted expenses for these separate funds.

Table 3.5

American Federation of Teachers, AFL-CIO
Period Covered 7/1/91-6/30/92
Schedule B   Form LM-2

Receipts

Per Capita Tax	$56,452,144.
Fees	1,215.
On Behalf of Affiliates for Transmittal to Them	11,288,372.
Sale of Supplies	123,360.
Interest	914,048.
Rents	1,017,152.
Repayment of Loans Made	148,342.
From Other Sources	9,619,027.
TOTAL RECEIPTS	$79,563,660.

Disbursements

Per Capita Tax	$ 3,280,650.
To Affiliates of Funds Collected on Their Behalf	11,132,732.
To Officers	681,339.
To Employees	9,553,795.
Office and Administrative Expense	6,828,636.
Educational and Publicity Expense	3,148,413.
Professional Fees	1,995,069.
Benefits	5,267,489.
Loans Made	120,966.
Contributions, Gifts and Grants	1,982,295.
Supplies for Resale	265,132.
Purchase of Investments and Fixed Assets	209,068.
Direct Taxes	864,124.
Withholding Taxes	4,860,449.
For Other Purposes	18,549,420.
TOTAL DISBURSEMENTS	$68,739,577.

Table 3.6

American Federation of Teachers, AFL-CIO
Period Covered 7/1/91-6/30/92
Statement A   Form LM-2

Assets

Cash on hand	$ 4,640.
Cash in banks	28,206,675.
Accounts Receivable	9,854,064.
Loans Receivable	176,951.
Other Investments	1,273,467.
Fixed Assets	2,192,559.
Other Assets	463,314.
TOTAL ASSETS	$ 42,171,670.

Liabilities

Accounts Payable	$ 2,421,828.
Other Liabilities	11,693,138.
TOTAL LIABILITIES	$ 28,056,704.

1. *AFT Militancy Fund*
The AFT militancy fund provides assistance by 1) paying interest on strike loans (made by the member) made on the first payday missed because of the strike, provided the strike has lasted at least five days, and member is unable to pay; 2) helping the local pay legal fees incurred as a result of a strike; and 3) helping to appeal if fines are assessed.
2. *AFT Defense Fund*
The AFT defense fund provides assistance to locals and state federations to help protect members' rights relating to job security and due process. The fund also provides assistance in arbitration cases when the arbitration involves job security.
3. *AFT Building Fund*
The AFT building fund was established pursuant to bylaws requiring that $.25 of each member's per-capita tax shall be set aside each month to finance the purchase of an AFT building. The fund shall continue until such time as the purchase has been completed and

49

Table 3.7

American Federation of Teachers, AFL-CIO
1992-1993 Budget

Income

General Fund	1992-93 Budget
Per Capita Dues	$57,145,000.
Less Militancy Fund Allocation	(1,800,000.)*
Less Defense Fund Allocation	(700,000.)**
Less Building Fund Allocation	(1,800,000.)***
General Fund Per Capita	$52,845,000.
Less State Federation Rebate	(1,440,000.)
Net General Fund Per Capita	$51,405,000.
Subscriptions, Advertising & Literature	417,000.
Locals Insurance	3,500,000.
Program Administration	900,000.
Investment Income	400,000.
Grants	100,000.
Other	696,000.
TOTAL INCOME	$57,418,000.

Expenses

National Office (Operational)	$10,049,022.
Administrative and Departmental	16,330,770.
Organizing and Servicing	23,939,227.
Affiliation Fees	3,685,712.
Conventions, Meetings and Conferences	900,000.
Locals Insurance	3,500,000.
Other Expenses	1,155,000.
TOTAL EXPENSES	$59,559,731.

* Militancy Fund	
Income	$1,800,000.
Strike Assistance Expenses	1,800,000.
** Defense Fund	
Income	$700,000.
Legal Fee Expenses	700,000.
*** Building Fund	
Income	$1,800,000.
Rental expenses, audit, legal, other	1,800,000.

50

any additional costs of the building not covered by income from the building have been met. In 1992, the AFT Executive Council approved the purchase of the remaining one-third share of the AFT building in Washington; in 1994 AFT will be the sole owner of the building, which includes four floors rented by the U.S. Department of Education; two floors house the Office of Education Research and Improvement Library (OERI).

4. *AFT Educational Foundation*
   The American Federation of Teachers Educational Foundation is an AFT subsidiary which conducts and sponsors educational research. As with AFT/COPE, the foundation shares the same executive council that presides over it and the AFT. Financial operations of the foundation are included in the budget funds discussed above.

5. *The American Nurses Foundation, Inc.*
   The American Nurses Foundation, Inc. represents more than 50,000 nurses and other health professionals, the Federation of Nurses and Health Professionals (FNHP) and is an affiliate of the AFT. Receipts and disbursements of FNHP are included in the budget information already discussed. However, a separate not-for-profit corporation was established to educate its members and leaders on all new health care proposals before Congress, as well as health and safety standards, and administer grant funds. Health care workshops and seminars, training and organizing assistance programs are targeted and budgeted separately. Five members of the Foundation's nine-member board of trustees were also members of the American Nurses Association, which provides staff and other support for the foundation. In addition, the group has a separate PAC which contributed $288,498 to political candidates in the 1991-92 election cycle.

6. *AFT/COPE*
   Funds for the AFT Committee on Political Education (COPE) must be kept separate from union funds. As its political action committee, AFT/COPE funds are the union's political vehicle operating at the local, state, and national levels of government. Two types of funds may be used for political action: union treasury funds (soft money) and political action funds (hard money). Generally, union treasury funds (dues and fees, sometimes called "soft money") can be used to raise money for COPE, to communicate political endorsements and other candidate information to members, and for direct contributions to candidates for local and state offices. Some state laws limit political expenditures to candidates and require COPE committee reports. Federal law considers the COPE committees of

51

AFT locals, state federations and the AFT itself, to be related committees and limits the combined expenditures of all three in federal contests. Therefore, any affiliate COPE committee which becomes involved
in campaigns for federal office must coordinate contributions through
AFT/COPE to comply with campaign contribution limits. This procedure also eliminates the necessity of separate filing requirements for
the affiliates, as AFT/COPE files the required federal reports.

We have included a discussion of AFT/COPE in the political activities of the teacher unions in Chapter 4.

UNION REVENUES AND MERGER

Historically, the strength of the NEA was in its state affiliates; they received
and spent most of the dues income. In the AFT most of the dues revenue
stayed in the local, relatively little went to the state and national offices. This
reflected the fact that the AFT was predominantly a large city union, and
unions in large cities require substantial funds. Meanwhile, AFT state affiliates
typically lacked the local affiliates and revenues to be a major player in the state
legislatures.

For 1993-94, the national dues of the two unions were $99 for the NEA and
from $100 to $135 for the AFT, a difference that would not pose any merger
problem. State dues might constitute a problem if the AFT's high local dues
were combined with the high state dues of some of NEA state affiliates. In all
likelihood, the emerging dues structure will be a compromise between the
NEA emphasis on the state and the AFT emphasis on local dues.

We do not have comprehensive data on the finances of the state and local
teacher unions, especially of state teacher union PACs. In view of the tremendous amounts raised by some, and their inadequate reporting and disclosure
requirements, the annual income of local, state, and national teacher unions
from all sources is probably over $1 billion, but it may be a long way from
having reached its peak.

A major legislative thrust, with or without merger, will be the enactment of
legislation that requires automatic payment of service fees to the exclusive representative, instead of having to negotiate such fees district by district. The
teacher unions, in conjunction with other unions representing state and local
employees will try, and often succeed in enacting mandatory service fees. In
that case, school districts will lose the leverage of being able to grant or with-
hold agency shop, and the school district employees will lose the leverage associated with nonpayment of dues or service fees. School districts will have to
deduct the service fee from the first paycheck to the last one, and we can expect
a quantum increase in union revenues.

CHAPTER FOUR

TEACHER UNION ORGANIZATION FOR POLITICAL ACTION

What are the political objectives of the teacher unions? How do they try to achieve their political objectives? How effective are their political operations? This chapter and the next one attempt to answer these questions. In many respects, they are among the most important questions raised in this book. As will be evident, our analysis is not comprehensive, but it may serve to demonstrate the impressive political influence of teacher unions.

THE NEA'S LEGISLATIVE PROGRAM

The NEA's legislative program is prepared by its Standing Committee on Legislation after an extensive process of eliciting member views. The Committee conducts open hearings at regional leadership conferences and solicits the views of various sub-units, such as the National Council of Urban Education Associations, the Education Support Personnel, and Higher Education. The 11-member Standing Committee on Legislation submits its recommendations to the Executive Committee and the Board of Directors; the latter is responsible for recommending the legislative program to the Representative Assembly, which considers, amends, and adopts the program as it deems appropriate. The Committee is then responsible for monitoring implementation of the program throughout the year.

The legislative program is categorized into three tiers that reflect the levels of resources to be utilized within each category (*NEA Handbook*, 1993-94).

First Tier
NEA Priority Legislative Initiatives are legislative issues initiated by NEA "that require continuing high activity levels to accomplish the goal." The two items in the First Tier, increased federal funding for public schools and postsecondary education and collective bargaining rights for NEA members at all levels of education, can be characterized as issues on which NEA is the principal advocate.

53

Second Tier

Current Priority Congressional Issues are "legislative issues requiring NEA, singly or through coalitions, to initiate intensive activity to advance NEA's objectives." These second tier priorities include federal funding in 18 of 20 targeted legislative areas, such as early childhood programs, HIV research, a tax-supported single payer health care plan, statehood for the District of Columbia, sustained Medicare/Medicaid benefits, full funding for federally mandated educational services for individuals with disabilities, improved Social Security benefits, expanded drug treatment and rehabilitation programs, and partial public funding of federal election campaigns.

Third Tier

NEA Ongoing Legislative Concerns are "legislative issues constantly monitored by NEA that require appropriate NEA activity" as developments occur. Federal funding of assistance to local school districts for computer equipment and software purchases, adequate public financing for public broadcasting, continuation of the U.S. Department of Education, and repeal of the right-to-work provision of federal labor law are included in the third tier agenda.

The NEA's legislative program serves as a guide for planning and action by NEA in lobbying Congress, presenting the views of the membership to federal agencies, and working in coalition with like-minded national organizations to attain NEA legislative goals. Moreover, the legislative program provides the core of the NEA-PAC questionnaire used to evaluate candidates for federal office, and it serves as the basis for the NEA Legislative Report Card assessing the voting record of federal officeholders (*Reports of Committees,* 1993).

NEA STRUCTURE FOR POLITICAL ACTION

Formally at least, the NEA's legislative objectives are set by the Representative Assembly (RA). Practically, it is impossible for the RA to set all the priorities, allocate funds for each objective, assign staff to lobby as circumstances change, and to perform all the other tasks required to implement the NEA's legislative program. These tasks are distributed to various units within the NEA along the following lines.

The NEA operates with an executive director who supervises the work of six assistant executive directors. Political activities generally are the responsibility of the assistant executive director of the Center for Public Affairs, who administers and coordinates the following NEA units:

Communications
Government Relations
NEA-PAC
Publishing
Health Information Network

Although their political activities vary, all are essential to effective political operations. For example, Communications prepares news releases, arranges press conferences, handles requests for interviews and information, and operates a broadcast studio for video productions and teleconferences.

The NEA's Government Relations Program
Government Relations is the NEA unit most directly responsible for advancing the NEA's legislative program. According to the NEA Handbook,

> Government Relations carries lead responsibility for organizing and training NEA members to elect pro-education candidates to federal office, influencing the executive branch in its development of legislative proposals and its regulation of programs of interest to NEA; working with organizations of education policymakers at the state, regional and local levels to adopt positions compatible with NEA's, and advancing NEA's Legislative Program in Congress. To implement its broad agenda, Government Relations comprises the following sections: Federal Relations, Political Advocacy, Information Services, Field Services, and Administration.

In addition to a staff of 31 at NEA headquarters, Government Relations operates field offices in Washington, DC and Colorado. Essentially, Government Relations is directly responsible for lobbying, identifying and supporting candidates for federal office who support NEA policies, training state and local staff and members on political issues, strategy, and tactics, tracking the progress of legislation of interest to NEA, polling, research and information. Government Relations is also responsible for NEA relations with the Democratic and Republican parties and for implementing NEA positions on issues that cut across party lines, such as redistricting. It is also responsible for developing a unified government relations program in each state and for consultant services to state and local affiliates on political matters. In addition, Government Relations also administers NEA-PAC, the association's political action arm nationwide. We turn next to this extremely important dimension of NEA political operations.

The NEA Political Action Committee (NEA-PAC)

Political action committees emerged in the 1940s when labor unions were prohibited from spending regular union funds for candidates for federal office. Instead, the practice of pooling political contributions from members and presenting the funds to the candidates became the conventional way to contribute cash to candidates endorsed by the unions. Even though federal restrictions discouraged many groups from setting up their own committees, the idea appealed not only to labor unions, but to business and ideological groups as well. With the establishment of NEA-PAC in 1972, the NEA became the first education association to organize a national political action committee.

In 1974 Congress passed several amendments to the Federal Election Campaign Act, officially sanctioning the concept of political committees. Soon thereafter, the great PAC rush began, and endorsements, contributions, and volunteers began flowing to favored candidates and causes. In recent years, the number of national political action committees (about 4,000 as of July, 1993) has stabilized, and even begun to decline. Although total PAC dollars have also stabilized, the amounts going to incumbents continues to rise with each new election (Makinson, 1990). NEA-PAC participated in this trend. By 1988 annual contributions to NEA-PAC reached $3.1 million; only the National Association of Realtors, the American Medical Association, and the Teamsters had larger PAC funds. In the 1991-92 federal election cycle NEA-PAC raised almost $4.5 million.

NEA-PAC's objective is to elect candidates who support federal legislation consistent with the policies established by the Representative Assembly. To achieve this objective, NEA-PAC contributes financially to endorsed candidates and encourages members to volunteer services to the campaigns. NEA-PAC endorsement may be given only to a congressional candidate whose endorsement is recommended by the appropriate body in the state affiliate. Establishing separate state PACs for the same purposes at the state and local level is encouraged and supported by the national organization. In 1992 virtually all of the NEA's state organizations and many of its 13,000 local affiliates made campaign contributions through political action committees.

Each state affiliate is represented on NEA-PAC. Other members of NEA-PAC are representatives of the Board of Directors, the Executive Committee, minority caucuses, the Higher Education Caucus, the Women's Caucus, the Caucus of Educators of Exceptional Children (CEEC), Advisory Committee of Student Members, educational support personnel, NEA-Retired, and the National Council of Urban Education Associations (NCUEA).

NEA-PAC is responsible for screening U.S. presidential candidates and recommending endorsement of candidates to the Representative Assembly. The RA then decides which candidates, if any, to endorse in presidential elections. The NEA has been a major supporter of Democratic presidential candidates since 1976, when it played a leading role in the Carter-Mondale campaign. Carter thereupon vigorously supported legislation creating a U.S. Department of Education, a longtime NEA goal. Significantly, NEA members have been the single largest block of delegates at every Democratic convention since 1980. At the 1992 Democratic convention, 512 of 4,288 delegates were NEA or AFT members.

NEA-PAC Fundraising Procedures and Results. Initially, NEA-PAC was supported by a "reverse checkoff" system. Essentially, under the reverse checkoff, a certain amount is deducted from teacher paychecks for the teacher PAC. The teacher who does not want to contribute to it must take some action to avoid the deduction or to have the money refunded. In other words, instead of requiring teacher assent to a deduction from teacher paychecks, the reverse checkoff forces teachers to take action to avoid the deduction.

At the time NEA-PAC was established, unions were prohibited from using the reverse checkoff procedure. The NEA, however, claimed that it was a "professional" organization, not a union, and was therefore free from the restrictions placed on unions with regard to PACs. However, on July 20, 1978, the Federal Elections Commission brought suit against the NEA, NEA-PAC, and eighteen of NEA's affiliates to enjoin them from collecting political contributions by means of a reverse checkoff. For PAC purposes at least, the NEA was held to be a union, and as such, not eligible to utilize the reverse checkoff. The court set April 1, 1979, as the deadline for obtaining each member's written consent to the contributions they had made through the reverse checkoff. NEA was also to return the deductions to individuals who did not submit the affirmation.

In his oral argument before the U.S. District Court NEA General Counsel Robert H. Chanin asserted:

> . . . [I]t is well recognized that if you take away the mechanism of payroll deduction you won't collect a penny from these people, and it has nothing to do with voluntary or involuntary. I think it has to do with the nature of the beast, and the beasts who are our teachers who are dispersed all over cities who simply don't come up with money regardless of the purpose. Transcript at 19-20.

Federal district judge Oliver Gasch commented on Chanin's startling assertion (because of its candor) as follows:

57

This additional element thus appears to be a curtain of indifference that envelops the NEA's members when finances are involved. With respect to their dues, defendants raise this curtain through payroll deduction. While it is still up, they add to the deduction the additional dollar for their political action fund. Then through reverse check-off, they lower the curtain back around its members to cause that indifference to insulate the union from requested refunds. The Supreme Court said in *Pipefitters* that the essence of whether a contribution is actually or effectively required for union membership in violation of the state "is whether the method of solicitation for the fund was calculated to result in knowing free-choice donations." 407 U.S. at 439, 92 S.Ct. at 2276. In this Court's view, "knowing free-choice" means an act intentionally taken and not the result of inaction when confronted with an obstacle (*Federal Election Commission v. National Education Association*, 1978).

Despite its setback on the reverse checkoff, NEA-PAC has been extremely successful in raising campaign funds for its endorsed candidates. NEA has persuaded many members to contribute to NEA-PAC by: 1) signing an authorization for withdrawal (payroll deduction) for monthly contribution, 2) authorizing a lump sum contribution, and 3) contributing funds during special NEA-PAC fund raising activities. These procedures bring in millions of dollars annually to the NEA-PAC account. For instance in 1992, NEA-PAC received almost $2.3 million from state and local affiliates.

To help raise funds for federal campaigns, NEA-PAC sponsors fundraising activities at NEA conventions; at the 1993 convention, these activities generated $500,000. Characterized by NEA publications as "Education's Defense Fund," NEA-PAC has compiled one of the most impressive fundraising and win/loss records of any major organization in American politics. Since its formation in 1972, almost 80% of federal candidates endorsed and supported by NEA-PAC have subsequently been elected to national office. NEA-PAC funds are raised by person to person appeals (NEA brochures suggest organizing the appeal around payday for maximum contributions), direct mail appeals, telephone solicitation, special events such as bikeathons, fundraising dinners or dances and giveaways (raffles) and auctions. The NEA Strategic Plan and Budget for Fiscal Year 1993-94, approved by the Representative Assembly, included $268,767 allocated to accounting services for NEA-PAC and state affiliate PAC accounting services. These services to state PACs are provided by NEA's Government Relations department and funded from members' dues. By having the NEA pay for the expenses of PAC fundraisers, NEA-PAC ends up with more cash for its candidates for federal office. This practice is explicitly recommended in *How to Set Up a PAC*, one in a series of booklets published by NEA-PAC. The booklet, which outlines step by step procedures to support NEA-PAC, or start a state or local PAC, suggests that "for maximum political effectiveness, use

PAC funds solely for making contributions to candidates. Pay PAC administrative costs from the association budget, if possible, but check the state laws first" (NEA, 1985).

Based on FEC reports, a total of 104,552,736 citizens voted in the 1992 presidential general election. These voters represented 55.9 percent of the estimated 187 million Americans who were 18 years or older as of July 1, 1991. The low voter turnout has been duly noticed by the teacher union PACs, which emphasize the need to get out the vote.

PAC contributions to candidates for political office are euphemistically said to "gain access to politicians and the political process," as opposed to buying votes by special interest groups. Accordingly, in 1992 NEA gained access to Democrat presidential candidate Bill Clinton, 375 Democratic House and Senate candidates, 32 Republican House and Senate candidates, and two candidates in third parties. In 1991-92 NEA-PAC raised $4,427,266, ranking among the top ten PAC fund raisers in the nation for that year.

In 1992, for the first time since 1977, many of the over 4,000 registered PACs, including NEA-PAC drew on surplus funds generated from previous years' activities to spend more than they raised. Using unspent funds remaining from the previous year, NEA-PAC contributions of $5,817,975 made it the third highest PAC spender in 1992, behind the American Medical Association PAC and the Democratic/Republican/and/ Independent Voter Education Committee, also known as the Teamsters PAC. Of NEA-PAC's total, $2,323,122 in cash was given to federal candidates, while $3,494,853 was spent on campaign activities, such as those described in Chapter 5.

NEA-PAC Endorsement Procedures. In addition to establishing its legislative objectives, the NEA naturally tries to elect lawmakers who will support these objectives. The NEA's endorsement procedures play a crucial role in this process. For Congressional candidates, these procedures are spelled out in the NEA-PAC Endorsement Kit, which goes to every interview team and included the following documents in 1994:

1. *NEA's "How To Endorse Candidates" Training Book and Guide.* This book is used to train members of the interview teams. Affiliate guidelines determine how interview team members are selected and the number of NEA members on the team. Team members may include NEA UniServ staff, some of whom are employed specifically to organize political operations for the affiliate. The training program covers both the substantive policy issues and the techniques to be utilized by the interview teams.
2. *Candidate Questionnaires.* Each candidate receives the questionnaire with a suggested cover letter. The NEA interview team that evalu-

59

ates the candidates is supposed to have at least one week to review the responses to the questionnaires before the candidates are interviewed. This schedule enables the interview team to prepare its questions for the interviews. Candidates were asked to agree or disagree with 25 NEA position statements and to identify and rank the candidate's top five priorities for the nation.

3. *1994 Addendum to the Congressional Candidate Questionnaire.* For those House incumbents with an 80 percent or better record of support for NEA-identified issues during the 103rd Congress, positions on previously stated positions were verified and only two questions were asked on this questionnaire:

"NEA supports the goal of a national, tax-supported, single-payer health care system for all residents of the U.S., its territories, and the Commonwealth of Puerto Rico. NEA will support health care reform measures that move closer to this goal and that will bring about universal coverage, quality assurance, significant cost reduction, and address the needs of children and education employees."

"NEA opposes the taxation of Social Security benefits."

For each question, the House incumbent can either agree with NEA's position (to support legislation which reflects NEA's position), or disagree with NEA's position (oppose legislation which reflects NEA's position). From the Report Card, 217 House incumbents received an NEA rating of 80 percent or higher.

4. *NEA Legislative Report Card.* The "Report Card" shows how the candidate voted on issues of importance to the NEA. Interview teams are cautioned against accepting candidate statements of support for NEA positions without checking their actual voting records.

5. *NEA Legislative Program for the 103rd Congress.* Copies of the legislative program are utilized to train members of the interview team as well as to elicit the positions of the candidates. Interview teams are urged to follow a consistent practice in interviewing candidates.

6. *Background on NEA Issues.* This document sets forth the NEA rationale for its legislative proposals. The rationale for the NEA position includes its emphasis on federal guarantees of basic rights—for meaningful collective bargaining, for substantial federal funds, for a single-payer health care system built on the foundation of social insurance established in such programs as Medicare and Social Security.

7. *Interview Team Worksheet.* These worksheets are used to facilitate orderly comprehensive candidate interview. The actual questioning of the candidates is done by the interview team chair.

8. *Incumbent Profile.* The profile includes whatever information about the candidate that may be available from a variety of sources: Correspondence to or from the candidate, reports of NEA lobbyists and Congressional Contact Teams, assessments of election prospects, and so on.
9. *Election District Profile.* This profile provides demographic and economic data about the election district.
10. *Tally Sheet.* The tally sheet summarizes the information from the Candidate Questionnaire and the interview. It must be completed and returned with the Endorsement Recommendation Form for recommended candidates, and is used later for lobbying as well as for endorsement purposes.
11. *NEA-PAC Endorsement Recommendation Form.* The recommendation form is generally signed by the president of the affiliate who verifies compliance with the endorsement procedure, after which NEA-PAC determines its endorsement and support.

The 1994 NEA-PAC endorsement kit for Congressional candidates included a list of high-priority legislative issues and the NEA's position on each. The ratings of candidates who had voted on these issues were shown. Generally, a score of 80 percent was the minimum acceptable for endorsement. "Friendly incumbents" are candidates who supported the NEA position on 80 percent or more of the votes.

Appendix D in this volume consists of worksheets recommended by NEA-PAC for interview team members. Clearly, the entire interview and endorsement process reflects a highly sophisticated approach to achieving political influence; when combined with the enormous resources available to the NEA, the process poses difficult problems for candidates who do not espouse most NEA positions.

NEA-PAC's political orientation may fairly be characterized as reflective of the left wing of the Democratic Party. Significantly, NEA-PAC can and does contribute to other PACs that share this orientation. This is evident from the following NEA-PAC contributions to other PACS in 1991-92:

Democrat Candidate's Fund (Tip O'Neill's PAC)	$5,000
Democrats 2000	5,000
Effective Government Committee	10,000
Emily's List	5,000
House Leadership Fund (Tom Foley's PAC)	5,000
Independent Action PAC (for progressive Democratic candidates)	10,000
Keep Hope Alive PAC	5,000

National Committee for an Effective Congress (for progressive candidates)	10,000
National Women's Political Caucus	8,000
Voters for Choice	4,225
Women's Campaign Fund	10,000

The freedom to contribute to several PACs which can in turn contribute to individual candidates enables NEA-PAC, as it does other PACs, to contribute more than the legal maximums to its favored candidates.

PARTY CAUCUSES IN THE NEA

Despite its overwhelming support for Democratic candidates, there is a Republican Educators Caucus (REC) in the NEA. In 1994, the REC enrolled about 500 members who paid $10 each in caucus dues. The caucus meets only at the NEA convention. Out of approximately 9,000 delegates to the NEA conventions, about 20 have attended recent meetings of the REC. In view of the fact that membership is open to any Republican who is an NEA member, and about 35 percent of NEA members identify themselves as Republicans, active caucus membership is not very impressive.

The REC constitution lists support for Republican candidates, both within the NEA and for public office generally, as a caucus objective, but there is no explicit statement that promoting the Republican agenda in the NEA is such an objective. Interestingly enough, the REC statement of objectives implicitly assumes that the Republicans will be a minority within the NEA; the statement calls for "equal and fair Republican representation" on all association governance bodies.

Although one member of NEA's Executive Committee, Kathy Bell of Florida, was a member of the caucus in 1994, the REC is essentially a paper organization, with little if any influence in either the NEA or the Republican Party. It is fair to say the REC is much more useful to the NEA than to the Republican Party. By providing minimal if not token representation to Republicans, the NEA is able to claim that its political activities are "bipartisan." In view of the NEA's overwhelming support for Democratic candidates, the claim is grossly misleading. For all practical purposes, the leadership of the REC is identical to that of the Teacher Advisory Council (TAC), an official affiliate of the Republican National Committee (RNC). The REC chairperson in 1994 is Laura Fortune of Virginia, who also chairs the RNC's Teacher Advisory Council. When the TAC held a national meeting on January 8, 1994, the meeting was held at the NEA building. The NEA paid for the air travel of attendees, and NEA affiliates paid for their hotel accommodations. The RNC paid the NEA for use of the meeting space and paid for the lunch. The only action taken at the meeting was a vote to reiterate opposition to vouchers, a vote taken without advance notice that the issue would be on the agenda. An NEA official who has been intimately involved with NEA-PAC since its inception in 1972 could not identify a single instance in which a candidate who supported NEA positions on education was denied support on non-educational grounds. Furthermore, TAC/REC members did not object to or raise any questions about the NEA's overwhelming preponderance of Democratic endorsements. Everything considered, the REC is not a significant Republican effort to influence the NEA; it is primarily an NEA effort to influence the Republican Party. Of course, the caucus could and perhaps should serve both functions to some extent, but the NEA effort to influence the Republican party clearly overshadows caucus efforts to influence the union.

The NEA has a Democratic as well as a Republican caucus. The main purpose of the Democratic Caucus is to persuade Democratic legislators to support teacher union positions. Surprisingly, the Democratic Caucus was founded partly in response to the formation of the Republican Educators Caucus in the NEA. Although it appears that the leaders of the Democratic Caucus are more active in party affairs than their Republican counterparts, there is no teacher unit in the Democratic National Committee comparable to the Teacher Advisory Council in the Republican National Committee, perhaps because the NEA overwhelmingly supports Democratic candidates regardless. Whereas the Republican Educators Caucus is impotent, the Democratic Caucus is redundant.

AFT LEGISLATIVE PROGRAM

Despite a much simpler structure for developing its legislative program, the AFT supports essentially the same legislative objectives as the NEA. Some differences result from the fact that the AFT is more sensitive to issues of concern to the AFL-CIO. Even this difference is narrowing, however, as the public sector unions play a more prominent role in the AFL-CIO and as the NEA moves toward closer cooperation with it. Occasionally delegates to either the AFT or NEA convention propose legislation for internal political reasons, hence differences in proposed legislation can result from a variety of idiosyncratic factors. Realistically both unions commit their resources to the same legislative objectives, such as defeating the North American Free Trade Agreement (NAFTA).

AFT Rates Congress is an AFT legislative report to its members, prepared by its Department of Legislation. Education, health care and other social service programs have dominated the AFT agenda. Opposition to vouch-

63

ers, to direct aid to private schools, and to privatization of public services are all prominent agenda items. As the AFT characterized the matter, most of its efforts were directed against presidential vetoes and attacks on critical programs rather than advancing AFT initiatives during the Bush adminisration.

> Whether the issue was preventing the permanent replacement of striking workers, stopping American companies from taking jobs to Mexico, redirecting savings in the defense budget to short-changed domestic programs or funding education, health care and public services, the AFT and organized labor consistently faced a battle in Congress and a like veto from the White House (*AFT Rates Congress,* 1992).

In 1992 the AFT took credit for federal legislation which permitted payment of off-season unemployment benefits to paraprofessionals and school-related personnel. The AFT was also active in the successful effort to extend the tax-free status of several union-negotiated employee benefits programs, including group legal services, employer-paid education, and tax-sheltered annuities. Mandatory HIV testing of health care workers was defeated, in part because of AFT opposition. Campaign finance reform was a major topic in the 102nd Congress (1990-92) during which time AFT vigorously opposed a measure which would have reduced PAC contributions from $5,000 to $1,000 and which would have required that the majority of individual campaign contributions come from within the congressional district. AFT supports public financing of elections and supports the retention of PACs and PAC contributions.

Despite its opposition to the North American Free Trade Agreement (NAFTA), the AFT was highly supportive of the Clinton administration's legislative program, especially its health care proposals. The AFT secretary-treasurer met regularly in 1993 with the administration's health care policy adviser to advocate the AFT's position on the issue. Because health care benefits were coming under severe fiscal pressures at teacher bargaining tables, the AFT formed the AFT Health Care Reform Committee to analyze reform proposals and to make recommendations for the benefit of its members. As did the NEA, the AFT downplayed the fact that the Clinton administration's health care plan would enable school employers to pay higher salaries if the federal government absorbed a larger share of the costs of health care.

AFT COMMITTEE ON POLITICAL EDUCATION (COPE)

To support the AFT legislative programs through lobbying and direct contributions to candidates, AFT members are encouraged to support the AFT's

Committee on Political Education, widely referred to as AFT/COPE. COPE is the AFT political action committee operating at local, state and national levels of government. Like NEA-PAC, AFT/COPE is overwhelmingly supportive of Democratic candidates for federal office. Obviously, AFT/COPE does not support candidates opposed by the AFL-CIO, so we can expect AFT/COPE to be at least as supportive of Democrats as the AFL-CIO. Inasmuch as the AFL-CIO is relatively weak in some states where the state associations affiliated with the NEA are a major interest group, NEA-PAC is more likely than AFT/COPE to support a few Republican candidates for federal office. In 1989-90, AFT/COPE was the 9th largest contributor of "soft money," that is, funds that are contributed to party organizations, usually for activities not related to a specific candidacy. The entire AFT/COPE contribution of $170,000 went to Democratic party organizations. In that same year, NEA-PAC contributed $285,000 to Democratic, $5,000 to Republican party organizations. Despite the AFT's much smaller membership, AFT/COPE raises significant amounts; for example, in 1991-92, NEA-PAC contributed $2.3 million, and AFT/COPE $1.1 million to candidates for federal office. Significantly, their combined contributions were considerably higher than the contributions of any other political action committee.

Unlike NEA-PAC however, COPE contributors must be informed that their COPE chapter is engaged in joint fundraising efforts with the AFL-CIO and that the money contributed to COPE will be used in connection with federal, state and local elections.

Not surprisingly, one of President Clinton's first campaign appearances after receiving the Democratic nomination for president was at the 1992 AFT Convention. At the convention, delegates received AFT/COPE packets which included Clinton and Gore fact sheets, camera-ready letters for local leaders to send to members, phone bank scripts and other campaign materials. Subsequently, AFT staff were assigned to campaign activities in Illinois, Michigan, Ohio, New York, Pennsylvania, Georgia, Missouri, Louisiana, Connecticut, Oregon and Minnesota. The AFT/COPE director has estimated that 75 percent of the AFT membership supported Clinton. AFT activists volunteered for phone banks, organized get out the vote efforts, held rallies, distributed literature, displayed yard signs, campaigned door to door and voted.

THE POLITICAL ROLE OF TEACHER UNIONS AT THE LOCAL LEVEL

In seeking bargaining rights, the teacher unions argued that "equity" required it. Private sector workers had the right to bargain collectively whereas

65

teachers did not. The fact that teachers could play an important role in the election of the public officials who constitute management was simply dismissed. As AFT president Albert Shanker asserted, "If teachers control both sides of the bargaining table in a substantial number of school districts, we should find many teachers with huge salaries, greatly reduced class sizes, longer holidays and vacations than ever before—you name it" (Shanker, 1979). According to Shanker, since there do not appear to be such districts, objections to teacher bargaining based on the teacher role in electing management must be fallacious. Such is the union rebuttal to the argument that their opportunity to affect the election of school board members justifies some restrictions on their bargaining rights.

Perhaps the most appropriate commentary on the issue is to be found in the literature disseminated by the teacher unions. An AFT brochure published in 1993 for school related personnel describes in glowing terms how AFT locals managed to elect supportive school boards in various school districts. For all practical purposes, there is no counterpart to this situation in the private sector. It should be emphasized that the teacher union presence in local school board elections does not imply that the teacher unions have unfettered power over both sides of the bargaining table. It means that they have enough influence on the managerial side to achieve concessions at the expense of citizens and groups which do not bargain collectively with school boards.

There are approximately 15,000 local school districts in the United States. Understandably, no one knows the extent of union influence in each and every district. On the face of it, however, it would be irrational for the teacher unions to create an effective political capability and then store it in mothballs during local school board elections. In practice, the same resources, practices and techniques that are employed in federal and state elections are brought to bear on school board elections. For example, candidates for school board are frequently asked to complete a questionnaire which is then scored by the local union. Quite often, the questions are taken from questionnaires prepared by the state association for state office.

Union influence at the local level is extremely variable. Where school board elections are held separately from general elections, voter turnout is usually very low, perhaps two to three percent of the turnout at general elections. Teacher union support is frequently the key to victory as voter turnout declines. This point was dramatically illustrated by the teacher union campaign to defeat Proposition 174, the California voucher initiative. The California Teachers Association successfully opposed the effort to have the initiative on the ballot in a general election, and then was by far the most influential interest group active in the special state election on the initiative. Coincidentally, it was easy for CTA telephone banks established to defeat Proposition 174 to support union endorsed candidates in the school board elections held concurrently with the state ballot on Proposition 174.

In some metropolitan areas, teachers in suburban districts or outlying areas live in the central cities. Although teacher union influence does not necessarily depend on teachers being voters in the districts where they teach, some large districts have an unusually large teacher constituency while neighboring districts may have practically none. At all levels of government, however, the immense NEA/AFT political capability underscores a paradoxical fact. Unquestionably, the growing political power of teacher unions has been due to teacher bargaining, especially on organizational security clauses that maximize union revenues and contributions to union controlled political funds. The paradox is that teacher bargaining was initially justified on the grounds that political and legislative procedures were inadequate to resolve terms and conditions of teacher employment. In the pre-bargaining era, teachers often had to enact state legislation to achieve benefits; since the benefits could often have been achieved at the local level with strong local organizations, the need for a stronger local presence was understandable. The upshot, however, was that the legislative framework intended to strengthen teacher influence at the local level turned out to be the basis for their unprecedented political power. It would be difficult to think of a more unexpected turn of events in either education or politics.

STATE AND LOCAL TEACHER UNION PACS

State and local political affiliates of the NEA have established political action committees that support state and local candidates and issues. In addition, state and local PACs collect most of the funds which are subsequently submitted to NEA-PAC.

Federal restrictions on PAC funds do not apply to elections for state and local office or ballot measures. The latter are governed by state statutes that vary widely. One important difference is that the "reverse checkoff" is prohibited by federal, but is permitted by some state statutes. In any event, each state must comply with the federal campaign finance laws applicable to candidates for federal offices. Federal law specifies that (1) money contributed to federal candidates must be collected separately from dues; (2) voluntary contributions must be kept in a separate account; and (3) members must not be coerced into contributing to the PAC fund. Nevertheless, unions that collect funds for national PACs can contribute to candidates for state and local offices. In addition, the unions can use general funds, or dues revenue to pay political staff, to publish articles or to purchase materials used to collect PAC funds. Unions can also legally employ political directors who direct political campaigns and coordinate fundraising and are paid from dues revenues. Such revenues can also be used to print and distribute literature asking for PAC contributions, although agency fee payors must not be charged for this.

Although comprehensive data on the income and expenditures of the state association PACs are not available, the following examples are probably representative of the others.

Colorado—NEA-PAC and two PACs associated with NEA affiliates in Colorado were among the largest political action committees active in the 1992 elections in Colorado. CEA Ed-PAC, the state PAC of the Colorado Education Association, was the leading contributor at $533,957. Of that, $180,000 was spent to defeat the school voucher issue, $18,300 was given to the Colorado Democratic State Central Committee (none to the Republican party), $65,000 to the Colorado Democratic Coordinated Campaign and 47 contributions ranging from $100 to $2,000, went to individual state candidates.

The NEA (not NEA-PAC) was the third largest cash contributor to Colorado political contests in 1992, with contributions of $100,000 or more to No on Vouchers, the Colorado Democratic State Central Committee, and the Colorado Education Association.

The Jefferson County Education Association, an affiliate of CEA/NEA was the fifteenth largest contributor in Colorado, spending over $78,000 for various candidates, the Democratic party agencies and the NEA and state affiliates. In contrast, supporters of the 1992 Colorado voucher initiative contributed at most only $106,000 to the voucher campaign.

Wisconsin—WEAC-PAC, the Wisconsin Education Association political action committee, received $578,309, primarily from member contributions just for the 1992 primary election. Disbursements of $441,061 were spent for voter/survey research, television production, lease-back for phone banks, wages for phone bank operators, endorsement/member communications, travel and lodging expenses, literature drop, and other expenses associated with political campaigns. In addition, pre-election WEAC-PAC independent disbursements for staff time, television production and advertisements were estimated to be over $38,000.

The political assistance provided by state teacher union PACs is often underestimated in several ways. First, it is easy to overlook their importance in the entire election cycle, including contested primaries. Teacher union support may persuade some candidates not to run, thereby enabling the union endorsed candidate an uncontested path to the nomination. The availability of teacher union support may render its utilization unnecessary in the early stages of an election cycle.

Beyond any doubt, the noncash contributions of teacher unions are vastly underestimated, even in states where they are legally required to be reported. First, states vary in what they require to be reported. Second, it is practically impossible to monitor some categories that are required to be reported such as telephone time, meals and mileage, folding envelopes, postage used, whatever; it is virtually certain that all such contributions will be underreported. Furthermore, the contributors are often the ones who place the valuation on the contribution and they have a strong political interest in minimizing it. Some interesting data on the opposition to Proposition 174 suggests the importance of the source as well as the amount of PAC contributions. Citizens Against 174, a coalition PAC opposing the initiative, received over $10 million in cash and $6.9 million in noncash contributions. Only 16 individuals contributed $100 or more to it; five labor unions provided 95 percent of the contributions. The total union contributions were about $15.7 million, or 92.7 percent of the total contributions. Cash contributions from unions usually are accompanied by many more contributions in-kind than are cash contributions from individuals. This point is emphasized in the following chapter.

THE IMPLICATIONS OF UNION POLITICAL CONVERGENCE

The fact that the NEA and AFT (including their PACs) agree overwhelmingly on which candidates to support raises some interesting questions about their endorsement procedures. For example, the NEA emphasizes the fact that its legislative program is the result of an extensive effort to elicit member views on legislative issues and candidates. The AFT seems to arrive at the same positions on candidates and issues, albeit as the result of a different and less extensive process. Whatever the differences in positions ultimately adopted, they do not appear to be based on any significant difference in political philosophy or union structure. Whether teachers are members of the NEA or AFT, their unions overwhelmingly support the same candidates and positions. Similarly, the widespread perception that the AFT is more reform oriented than the NEA can be attributed more to AFT President Albert Shanker's media skills than to any significant differences between the NEA and AFT on educational issues.

The convergence of NEA and AFT positions on a wide spectrum of candidates and issues suggests that the importance of some organizational differences is greatly exaggerated. Second, the convergence highlights the importance of leadership control of union communications. In the 1970s, NEA leadership was opposed to merger, hence NEA publications and conferences were directed at stirring up rank and file opposition to it. Just as clearly, NEA leadership in 1994 is striving to produce a favorable climate of opinion concerning merger. Our point is not to support or oppose any position on merger; it is to emphasize that governance procedures that are formally democratic may nevertheless be dominated politically by incumbent union leadership. What teachers want their unions to support does not emerge out of a vacuum; more often than not, union leaders who control union communications have played a major role in shaping the teacher objectives.

CHAPTER FIVE

TEACHER UNION POLITICAL OPERATIONS: THREE CASE STUDIES

This chapter presents some anecdotal evidence on the political influence of the teacher unions. This evidence suggests that an NEA/AFT merger would probably result in the formation of the most powerful political interest group in American politics. The evidence that follows does not establish this conclusion, but it certainly points in that direction.

THE 1993 CALIFORNIA VOUCHER INITIATIVE (PROPOSITION 174)

In recent years, legislation providing financial assistance to parents who wish to enroll their children in private schools has been introduced in several state legislatures and ballot initiatives. Chiefly because of teacher union opposition, such legislation has never been enacted in a statewide election. The most striking example of this opposition was the defeat of Proposition 174, a California voucher initiative that lost on November 2, 1993 by 1,451,322 (30.3%) (Yes) to 3,334,678 (69.7%) (No). Under the initiative proposal, parents would have been entitled to a voucher worth $2,600 (about half of the $5,200 that the state supposedly spends annually per elementary and secondary pupil) to enroll a child in any public or private school of their choosing, including parochial schools. In view of the fact that a majority of voters appeared to support school choice at the outset of the campaign, the overwhelming defeat of the initiative obviously suggests an aggressive well financed campaign to defeat it. As we shall see, this inference understates the CTA's successful efforts in this regard.

About 15 percent of all school children in the United States live in California. Of California's nearly six million students, 550,000 of them were enrolled in some 3,839 private and religious schools where the average tuition charged was about $7,000 per year; however, a large number of California private schools, especially Catholic schools, charged much less for tuition (*New York Times*, 1993). Both proponents and opponents of Proposition 174 agreed that its enactment could set off a chain reaction of school choice laws across the nation. Understandably, the initiative ignited what may have been the most intensive campaign over a state educational initiative in U.S. history.

Proponents of Proposition 174 contended that its enactment would eventually result in huge savings in state expenditures for education while simultaneously raising achievement levels. Meanwhile, the CTA contended that enactment of Proposition 174 would result in large tax increases because (1) there would be large new expenditures for pupils already enrolled in private schools; and (2) private schools did not have the capacity to absorb enough transfers from the public schools to offset the additional expenditures for pupils already enrolled in private schools. The CTA emphasized this argument very effectively with tax conscious voters, especially retirees concerned about tax increases. The union also argued that 174 was "a risk that we can't afford," since it included no provisions prohibiting extremist groups from establishing taxpayer funded private schools (*CTA, Election News*, 1993).

Proposition 174 raised a host of such issues that are outside the scope of this book. Obviously, the teacher unions were adamantly opposed to it, but our concern here is not with the merits or demerits of their position, but with their efforts to defeat it. To convey some idea of the massive resources that the teacher unions can utilize for political purposes, let us look briefly at how they reacted to Proposition 174.

The NEA Role
The NEA's opposition to parental choice plans such as Proposition 174 is spelled out in its official resolution on the issue:

A-28. Federally or State-Mandated Choice/Parental Option Plans
The National Education Association believes that federally or state-mandated parental option or choice plans compromise the Association's commitment to free, equitable, universal, and quality public education for every student. Therefore, the Association opposes such federally or state-mandated choice or parental option plans.
The Association believes that local districts, in partnership with state and federal governments, must provide a quality education for every student by securing sufficient funding to maintain and to enhance excellence in each local public school district.
The Association continues to support alternative programs in the public schools for specific purposes (*NEA Today*, 1993).

Calling the defeat of Proposition 174 its top political priority, the NEA contributed $1 million in cash to assist the CTA defeat Proposition 174. Its cash contribution was supplemented by a wide variety of supportive activities. Referring specifically to Proposition 174, NEA President Keith Geiger publicly called for the members to "repel this assault—just as we did in Colorado. This November, we must not—we will not—permit our nation's most populous state to be ruled by the ideology we repudiated last November when we elected President Clinton" (*NEA Today*, 1993). In accordance with these sentiments, NEA publications launched a heavy barrage of criticisms of Proposition 174 over several months prior to the election. For example, *NEA Today*, the NEA's monthly publication sent to members, repeatedly warned NEA members of the dire consequences that would follow passage of Proposition 174. *NEA NOW*, a weekly newsletter disseminated to NEA leaders nationwide, featured "The Voucher Battle" and set forth the NEA's intention to "mobilize every friend of public education in the state by election day—and deliver the drive to privatize public education a blow that will end voucher as a live threat to improving public education" (*NEA NOW*, 1993).

Nationwide attacks on Proposition 174 were crucial to NEA's efforts to enlist support from union members outside of California to defeat the perceived threat to public education. The importance of defeating Proposition 174 was effectively disseminated throughout the United States through no fewer than ten national publications targeted to students, active members, retired members and opinion leaders. Chapters 6 and 7 take up in more detail NEA-PAC, the NEA's political action committee. Officially at least, NEA-PAC contributes only to candidates for federal office and was not directly involved in the campaign to defeat Proposition 174.

The Role of the California Teachers Association (CTA)
Indisputably, the CTA, the state affiliate of the NEA, was the major source of opposition to Proposition 174. For starters, the CTA assessed its 225,783 members $57 each as part of a plan to raise and spend from $12-15 million to defeat Proposition 174 (*New York Times*, 1993). Although some membership categories were not required to pay the full assessment, it appears that over 200,000 CTA members were subject to it. The assessment was in addition to CTA/NEA dues ($475 per year in 1993-94), some of which was spent on various staff activities devoted to defeating Proposition 174.

CTA Political Action Committees. In addition to national political action committees, state PACs exist to collect and spend funds on state ballot issues and candidates for state offices. Regulations governing contributors, contribution limits, reporting requirements, and disclosure are enacted and implemented on a state by state basis.

Several state political action committees opposed Proposition 174: Citizens Against 174, CTA Issues PAC, CTA/Association for Better Citizenship PAC and the Committee to Protect the Political Rights of Minorities, headed by a CTA associate executive director. In 1993 there were no dollar limit restrictions on contributions to California PACs. Individuals, businesses, corporations, organizations, political parties or other PACs could legally contribute to state PACs in California, hence the CTA PACs were virtually unrestricted in their ability to accept contributions. As of November 2, 1993, the CTA PACs had raised $18,000,000. In contrast, the proponents of Proposition 174 had established only one PAC, Yes on 174, A Better Choice, which had raised only $2.7 million by election day.

CTA Advertising. Most CTA funds were funnelled through the PACs established to defeat Proposition 174 and thereafter spent on advertising. By mid-summer, with the election months away, the CTA had spent $1.9 million for a six-week series of radio and TV advertisements telling Californians that Proposition 174 would result in higher taxes while gambling with children's futures. By late September the CTA had spent another $4.7 million for radio and television advertising, whereas the Yes on 174 campaign had not even begun advertising as of October 1. By mid October "No" spots aired six to ten times as often as the "Yes" spots (*No on Vouchers*, 1993).

The CTA also funded weeks of paid newspaper advertisements. In addition, press releases, news items, editorial commentaries, and letters to the editors of California daily and weekly newspapers were disseminated frequently. During the summer, the CTA scored a media coup with a story about a coven of witches who would supposedly establish their own voucher-redeeming school if Proposition 174 were enacted. It is somewhat surprising that the proponents of Proposition 174 did not raise the question of what schools these witches had attended.

In addition, a variety of CTA publications sent to members, such as *No on Vouchers, Chalk Talk, Election News* and *Liaison News* (the CTA weekly newsletter), included updates about the union's activities and membership responsibilities relating to Proposition 174. Meanwhile, the CTA's Government Relations Division distributed one-page flyers opposed to Proposition 174 in at least seven languages. And if readers were literate in languages other than Armenian, Chinese, English, Korean, Russian, Spanish, Tagalog ("Filipino"), or Vietnamese, the CTA was prepared to draft and disseminate flyers in other languages as well. In addition, the CTA's Ethnic Minority Affairs Committee successfully arranged denunciations of Proposition 174 as "racist" by prominent elected black leaders, and actively solicited statements of opposition from other ethnic leaders in the Hispanic and Asian communities, among others.

CTA Consultants. Professional advisors (consultants) were hired by the CTA to develop strategies, create images, and deliver a targeted message to key voter groups. Polling data indicated where the money should be spent and which attacks would produce the desired results. Tactical trends made it possible to respond rapidly to attacks while using the most effective appeals to undecided voters. Since most voters make up their minds in the 10 days before an election, final media messages, direct mail appeals, and get out the vote efforts were carefully crafted for maximum results.

It should be emphasized that the CTA resources devoted to the actual election on November 2, 1993 were not all of the CTA resources devoted to defeating Proposition 174. As early as 1991, the CTA had contributed $430,000 in an effort to keep the voucher initiative off the ballot. Proposition 174 was originally scheduled to appear on the June 1994 California primary ballot with the following title: "Education. Scholarships. Parental Choice." This had been the proposal's working title for 18 months, but after CTA attorneys argued that it was inappropriate, the state attorney general and secretary of state accepted the CTA's recommended title: "Education. Vouchers. Initiative Constitutional Amendment." In a post-election assessment, pollsters for Proposition 174 stated that the change in the title resulted in a 10 percent drop in support for Proposition 174. Unquestionably, if Proposition 174 had passed, CTA attorneys would have challenged it constitutionally on the grounds that it constituted state support of religion.

CTA efforts to prevent Proposition 174 from being on the ballot were unique in the annals of California politics. As Proposition 174 supporters circulated petitions to get the measure on the ballot, they were often challenged by anti-174 forces employed by the CTA at sites where the petitions were being made available for signatures (Weber, 1992). In fact, the measure first failed to qualify for the November 1992 general election ballot for highly controversial legal reasons. The president of one of the two companies in California that specializes in collecting signatures for initiative petitions submitted a sworn statement to a California court, asserting that he had been offered $400,000 to refrain from gathering signatures for the initiative. The offer was allegedly made by the signature-gathering firm employed by the CTA. In a statement disseminated at the 1992 NEA convention, CTA president D.A. Weber explained the union's efforts to dissuade voters from signing the petition as follows:

> And you and I, the California Teachers Association, decided to do something very dramatic, something nobody had ever tried in the nine decades that the initiative has existed in this state. We decided to create an organized campaign to block an initiative from getting enough signatures to qualify for the ballot.
>
> We realized that we would be accused of acting in an "undemocratic" manner. What was wrong, after all, with letting the people vote on an issue?

Our answer was firm: There are some proposals that are so evil that they should never even be presented to the voters. We do not believe, for example, that we should hold an election on "empowering" the Ku Klux Klan. And we would not think it's "undemocratic" to oppose voting on legalizing child prostitution.

Destroying public education, in our view, belongs in that category (Weber, 1992).

CTA Voter Registration/Absentee Ballots. Voter registration by mail in California is a process in which a non-registered resident may request an application for registration, complete the form and return it to the election officer at the county auditor's office, who in turn advises the individual of the voter's precinct, polling place and confirmed registration.

Voting by mail is a procedure similar to voter registration by mail. In 1992 almost 2 million Californians voted absentee ballots, the highest number recorded since the enactment of a 1978 law allowing absentee voting (*Campaign*, 1993). In 1993, all CTA members were encouraged to vote by mail against Proposition 174 so they would have extra time on election day to volunteer for other political activities.

Absentee ballots have the potential to change the outcome of an election and are an important aspect of campaign strategy. Prime targets for absentee ballots include senior citizens, disabled persons and out-of-town students. The request for an absentee ballot is a public record; therefore, the CTA assigned individuals, county by county, to monitor the absentee ballot requests. Each voter requesting a ballot then also received a letter and brochure explaining CTA's opposition to Proposition 174. Dedicated volunteers, such as retired CTA members, as well as paid personnel were utilized in these efforts.

The CTA also conducted extensive, sophisticated voter identification and get out the vote drives. Of the 500 phone banks being operated by the coalition, nearly 100 were in CTA offices. The majority of the phone bank volunteers were CTA members and staff who had called more than 500,000 voters by the end of September (*CTA Action*, 1993). The week before the election, phone bank operators called 25,000 registered voters each day to determine how the voter intended to vote on election day. Teachers were urged to volunteer for two to six hours work on the phone banks; however, some workers were paid to supplement the volunteers. The CTA phone banks utilized phones and phone lines purchased by the CTA or other unions, ostensibly for union business. This is a common technique to avoid paying the higher rates charged political campaigns. Working from a carefully crafted script which covered all likely responses, the voter's responses were tallied by phone bank personnel. The valuable information obtained this way was used to identify and activate those voters who supported the CTA position. Starting the night before election day, follow-up calls reminding the voter to vote were made to all voters who had indicated support for the CTA position. If the voter had not yet been to the polls but remained favorable to CTA's position, a second reminder call would be made if time permitted. In the campaign against Proposition 174, the CTA exceeded its goal of one million telephone calls, directed mainly to voters who had presumably voted Democratic in the past four elections. Obviously, maintaining such lists and preparing effective responses for the campaign against Proposition 174 required substantial funds and political expertise.

CTA Report Card. CTA monitors the votes of all California lawmakers, especially those who have received union contributions. The results are set forth in the *CTA's Report Card*, a summary that utilizes a point system to grade legislators and candidates. In 1991-92 legislators had until October 15 to respond to the CTA questionnaire, but even non-responding legislators were monitored to determine whether they had endorsed the initiative.

Using computer technology, CTA staff tracked key votes cast by every state senator and assembly member. In scoring the results, the CTA included committee votes and activities on various issues deemed important by the CTA. However even those scores were adjusted to reflect positions taken for or against Proposition 174 (*NEA/CTA Making the Grade*, 1992). In fact, Tom Campbell, a prominent candidate for the state senate who had supported the initiative, changed his position after the CTA threatened to run one of its officers and mount an all-out campaign against him. After CTA announced that it would "saturate the area" with money and campaign workers (*Los Angeles Times*, 1993), Campbell, a Stanford University law professor, let it be known that after reading the initiative more carefully, he had decided to oppose it.

The CTA is widely regarded as the most powerful and biggest spending lobby in California. Insofar as cash contributions foster influence, this conclusion is obvious. According to the California Secretary of State, the CTA spent $2,125,472 lobbying in first quarter of 1993, four times the amount spent by the next highest special interest group, the California Medical Association. In 1991-92, the CTA spent over $7.4 million on political campaigns and lobbying. Legislators who support the NEA/CTA positions are typically rewarded with contributions in the next election cycle.

In 1990 CTA-endorsed candidates won in 95 percent of their primary races with the highest winning percentages in state legislative and Congressional candidate races. CTA-endorsed candidates for state senate won 16 of 16 races, and Assembly candidates won 52 of 53. In the 1990 June primary 83 percent of ballot measures endorsed and supported by CTA were approved (*CTA Action*, 1990).

According to California Common Cause, in the 1989-1990 election cycle, the top ten PACs gave more than $6,000,000 to legislative candidates and causes. CTA PAC was the top contributor, giving more than $1,000,000 to legislative candidates and key ballot measures (*American School Board Journal*, 1991). PACs representing trial lawyers, real estate agents, hospitals, labor unions, dentists, optometrists, and restaurant owners were among the other top contributors. Quantifying how much influence the contributions buy is very difficult, but CTA opponents as well as supporters agree that legislation opposed by the CTA is very unlikely to be enacted.

CTA In-Kind Contributions. In addition to direct contributions California requires that the fair market value of any goods or services provided to or on behalf of a committee, including a description of the goods and services provided, be disclosed and filed with the Secretary of State. In-kind contributions and/or non-monetary contributions from CTA included: staff time, consultant time and travel, printing, duplicating, postage, photography, meetings, legal consultations, advertising, buttons, or specific projects, such as the CTA Vote-By-Mail Project. Even so, volunteer CTA staff time, routine advertising and endorsements in CTA publications, union sponsored newspaper columns, CTA phone bank operations, CTA petition solicitations, precinct walking, rallies, and CTA leadership training are only some of the influential campaign activities that are not recorded.

CTA Independent Expenditures. According to California Form 420, an "independent expenditure" is an expenditure made in connection with a communication that expressly advocates the election or defeat of a clearly identified candidate, or the qualification, passage, or defeat of a clearly identified ballot measure, but is not made to, or at the behest of, the affected candidate or any committee primarily formed to support or oppose the candidate or measure. Made "at the behest of" means made under the control of, or at the direction of, in cooperation, consultation or concert with, or at the request or suggestions of the candidate or committee. An expenditure that is made to, or at the behest of, a candidate or committee is a "contribution."

When independent expenditures exceed $500, the parties responsible for them must file a return disclosing the expenditures. The latter may include or be associated with:

• The preparation, production and distribution of campaign literature and printed solicitations, including expenditures for mailing lists, postage, design, copy and layout, printing and reproduction.
• The production and purchase of radio and television advertising.
• The production and purchase of advertising in newspapers, periodicals and other publications.

- The production and purchase of advertising on billboards or other campaign signs, and campaign paraphernalia such as buttons, bumper stickers, potholders, etc.
- Designing or conducting polls, reports on election trends, voter surveys, etc., including payment to signature gatherers for qualification drives, and door-to-door solicitors.
- The holding of a fundraising event, including payments to restaurants, hotels or halls, caterers and other food and refreshment vendors, entertainers and speakers,
- And for travel within or out of California.

CTA efforts to defeat Proposition 174 also included independent expenditures. In addition, press reports alleged that several CTA members had engaged in anti-Proposition 174 independent expenditure activities.

CTA Coalitions. Coalition building is usually essential to any successful campaign, hence it is not surprising that the anti-Proposition 174 steering committee included virtually the entire California public education establishment. Seven anti-voucher coalition groups comprised the Executive Steering Committee of the Citizens Against 174 committee. See Table 5.1 for the member groups and the funds contributed by each for the defeat of Proposition 174. Prior to changing its name in late August, the group was known as the Committee to Educate Against Vouchers or CEAV. By far the largest membership organization represented on the steering committee, the California Teachers Association contributed over 80 percent ($12.3 million) of the coalition budget and provided the organizational structure, staff and office space for its efforts. Although each of the other six organizations on the Executive Steering Committee of Citizens Against 174 has its own organizational structure, the CTA messages were evident in the activities of coalition members. Coalitions offered speakers' bureaus, voter registration/information drives, phone banks, and election day precinct walks to help promote the No on 174 campaign.

The preceding discussion has not presented a complete account of the CTA campaign to defeat Proposition 174, and it may not be possible to do so for years to come. It is especially important to recognize that CTA played a critical role in fostering and orchestrating the local teacher union efforts to defeat it. For example, CTA prepared the telephone messages used at the local level to guide teachers who worked on the telephone banks. It prepared the various translations of the "No on 174" flyers distributed at the local level to different ethnic groups by CTA's local affiliates. Similarly, a host of other campaign activities were carried out by CTA's local affiliates with CTA resources under CTA guidance and leadership. Although we lack a comprehensive summary of campaign activities at any level, the pre-

79

Table 5.1

Executive Steering Committee
Citizens Against Proposition 174 Coalition

Funds - No on 174 *

California Teachers Association (CTA) $12.3 million
230,000 members;
1 million including retirees

California School Employees Association $1.3 million
Represents 170,000 secretaries,
teachers aides, bus drivers, gardeners,
and other classified public school employees

California Federation of Teachers (CFT) $1.1 million
An AFT AFL-CIO affiliate, the 40,000
member teacher union helped enlist trade
union support

Association of California School Administrators $ 450,700.
Represents 14,000 school administrators
many of whom volunteered in the campaign
and spoke at local forums and debates

California State Council of Service Employees $ 310,000.
Affiliated with Service Employees Inter-
national Union (SEIU) an AFL-CIO affiliate.
The 350,000 member union represents 40,000
classified school employees.

California School Boards Association $ 257,800.
Represents 950 public school districts,
provided representation at forums

California Parent Teacher Association (PTA)
A non-profit tax-exempt group with
approximately 1 million members. Provided
volunteers, but no significant funding

* Some of the figures in Table 5.1 were subsequently revised upward.

80

ceding comments obviously reveal an impressive political operation that left nothing to chance or to lack of resources.

American Federation of Teachers (AFT)

By June 1992, the AFT had contributed $8,500 to defeat Proposition 174 and its state affiliate was also a member of the steering committee of Citizens Against 174. Although AFT efforts to defeat Proposition 174 were similar to NEA's in many respects, its efforts should not be considered merely additive. AFT President Albert Shanker was an early and perhaps the most effective national opponent of vouchers and privatization. For several years, Shanker has criticized such plans in AFT sponsored advertisements in the *New York Times*. In this forum as well as several others which are open to him, Shanker has disseminated criticisms of school choice to millions of readers and television viewers. He is especially skillful at presenting his criticisms to the academic and policy communities; one can only wonder how or why the Bush administration appointed Shanker to the National Council on Competitiveness, a federally sponsored policy group that is supposed to enhance the nation's ability to compete economically.

Having referred to Proposition 174 as the likely coup de grâce of public education, it is hardly surprising that Shanker was instrumental in arranging AFL-CIO opposition to it. This opposition was expressed in AFL-CIO publications disseminated to millions of AFL-CIO members. In addition, President Clinton and Secretary of Labor Robert Reich announced their opposition to Proposition 174 at the October 1993 meeting of the AFL-CIO Executive Council in San Francisco. Following an earlier appeal by the AFT, the AFL-CIO Executive Council launched an aggressive campaign against Proposition 174, charging that if enacted it would undermine support for public services throughout the nation (*American Teacher*, 1993).

California Federation of Teachers (CFT)

The AFT state affiliate, the California Federation of Teachers (CFT), raised $1.1 million from its 40,000 members to defeat Proposition 174. Federation funds were collected and disseminated through its Committee on Political Education (CFT/COPE). In addition, CFT/COPE trained and organized activist opponents county by county to disseminate the CFT message of opposition to Proposition 174 throughout the state. Non-cash contributions also included payment for direct mail, paid and unpaid media, phone banks, coalition building, voter registration drives and get-out-the-vote activities.

In this study we have not tried to track the role of the nonteacher unions in the campaign against Proposition 174. In California, educational support staff have been organized by several unions, including the following:

American Federation of State, County, and Municipal Employees (AFSCME) (AFL-CIO)
Service Employees International Union (SEIU) (AFL-CIO)
Teamsters (AFL-CIO)
California School Employees Association (CSEA)

Although these unions were represented on the steering committee of Citizens Against 174, they were not major players in the campaign to defeat it. Undoubtedly one reason was the expectation that the teacher union effort, along with AFL-CIO support, would be sufficient to defeat the initiative. The likelihood is, however, that the members and unions of school related personnel would have been more active politically as members of the NEA or AFT; inasmuch as support personnel are likely to be organized by the NEA or AFT, especially if these unions effectuate a merger, teacher union political influence may increase considerably in the near future.

ALABAMA: THE HUBBERT CAMPAIGN*

Like the CTA, the Alabama Education Association (AEA) is the state's largest and most powerful special interest group. Like other NEA state affiliates, AEA political activities are designed to influence legislation, elect candidates, and promote or defeat legislation. But in Alabama teachers do more than influence legislation—they propose and vote on it. An Alabama ethics commission reported that by 1987, 58 of 140 members of the state legislature were teachers, former teachers, or spouses of teachers. AEA Executive Director Paul R. Hubbert is the dominant power in the state legislature on educational issues, and is credited with creating a powerful alliance that includes teachers, blacks and unions. As early as the 1960s, when Hubbert had been a classroom teacher in rural north Alabama, and before he received his doctorate, he looked for politically effective ways to mobilize the state's 40,000 teachers. In 1969 Hubbert moved to Montgomery as executive secretary of the AEA. Since then, Hubbert has transformed the AEA into the strongest single interest group in Alabama politics. According to one recent study, Hubbert has been a dominant force in the state Democratic party since 1982 (Ehrenhalt, 1991).

---

*The discussion of the Hubbert campaign is based largly on Alan Ehrenhalt, *The United States of Ambition* (New York: Random House, 1991).

In June 1993, for the second time in three years, the steering committee of A-VOTE, the political action committee of the Alabama Education Association, voted to set aside $1 million dollars for a Hubbert gubernatorial campaign. Hubbert, still the executive director of the association, also received $1 million from the same PAC in 1990, when he ran and lost a close race for governor to Republican incumbent Guy Hunt. NEA-PAC contributed $150,000 to the Alabama Democratic Party in 1990; this was the largest NEA-PAC contribution to an organization in that year.

The 1992-1993 NEA Handbook lists AEA membership in toto at 65,644; annual dues for active teachers are $147.50 and includes $80 for support personnel. These amounts include $12 for A-VOTE, thus ensuring substantial funding for AEA-endorsed candidates throughout the state each election year.

A "negative dues check-off" applicable to members of the Alabama Education Association was approved by the 1986 Alabama legislature after support from Hubbert and AEA members. Under this procedure, PAC funds are deducted from each teacher's paycheck and transferred to the AEA political action committee unless the teacher directs otherwise in writing. This mechanism enables the AEA to raise money, provide talent and organization, and generate effective voter turnout.

In Hubbert's 1990 campaign for governor, AEA managers asked the Association's full-time field representatives (UniServ directors), to help with additional fund raising in their districts for Hubbert's campaign. Goals were set within each district, with the total AEA A-VOTE goal set at $1 million, or $20 more per member. Although not every member was supporting Hubbert in the primary, some UniServ directors saw the directive as a mandated quota from the executive secretary who was now the gubernatorial candidate, Paul Hubbert (*Huntsville Times*, 1991).

Hubbert's salary in 1991 was $122,000, making him the second highest paid executive director of any state teacher organization (*Florence Times*, 1991). During his campaign for governor in 1990 and again in 1994, Hubbert continued to receive his AEA salary, as well as AEA PAC contributions to his gubernatorial campaign. In addition to providing PAC funds, the Alabama Education Association was a major source of campaign volunteers, as is likely to be the case if and when Hubbert runs for elective office again.

NEW YORK: THE CUOMO CAMPAIGNS

New York is home to 183,000 teachers, most of whom are members of the New York State United Teachers (NYSUT), the state affiliate of the AFT. One quarter of the entire AFT membership is concentrated there, mainly in New York City; in 1993 state membership was about 150,000.

Like the state affiliates of the NEA, NYSUT is a major player in New York state politics. Its influence was dramatically evident in Mario Cuomo's gubernatorial campaigns in New York. When Cuomo did not have NYSUT support in 1978, he lost to an opponent who had been endorsed by the teacher unions.

When both NEA and AFT have members in a state, they usually endorse the same candidates, even though the decisions are made independently. Shortly before the 1982 primary, the much smaller New York affiliate of the NEA contributed $10,000 in cash to gubernatorial candidate Cuomo. As Cuomo himself recognized, however, the key to his election prospects was NYSUT's endorsement and support.

In 1982, Cuomo's opponent in the Democratic primary was New York City Mayor Ed Koch, who was a strong favorite to win the nomination. In his diary entry for Wednesday, March 10, 1982, Cuomo wrote that he had been approached by a representative of the United Federation of Teachers (UFT) indicating that UFT president Albert Shanker (who was also AFT president) wanted to confer with him. Cuomo's diary notes the crucial importance of a NYSUT endorsement. "Teachers are perhaps the most effective of all the State's unions. If they go all out, it will mean telephones and vigorous statewide support. It will also mean some money. I would have had them in 1977 if it had not been for a clumsy meeting I had with Shanker. I must see that I don't make the same mistake again" (Cuomo, 1984).

Later that year, NYSUT convention delegates gave Cuomo a standing ovation following his speech emphasizing the importance of fundamental skills, discipline and respect, especially for teachers, and the primacy of public schools. Still, Cuomo was concerned that NYSUT might remain neutral in the primary. With less than three weeks before the September 23, 1982 primary, Cuomo addressed some 2,000 AFL-CIO Convention delegates. His speech "turned them upside down" and there seemed to be little doubt that he would be endorsed over Koch.

That morning, before and after his speech, there were rumors about what the teachers would do. By themselves they represented 20 percent of the AFL-CIO delegates. Koch was still maneuvering for union neutrality, which would have been a major victory for him. Meanwhile, Cuomo was concerned that Shanker would recommend neutrality at the teacher caucus the day before the full vote was scheduled. One reason for Cuomo's concern was that to retain teacher union support, or at least their neutrality, Koch was reported to be interested in restoring the UFT's right to the check-off of union dues directly out of teacher paychecks. This possibility was based on the fact that the New York Public Employment Relations Board (PERB) had barred the UFT from utilizing the checkoff as a penalty for engaging in illegal strike activity. This penalty had forced the union to collect union dues by other more expensive and time consuming procedures. As governor, Koch could have restored the checkoff by not appealing a PERB proposal to lift the ban. Despite Cuomo's concern, the teachers voted to endorse him, in spite of the fact that the New York City delegation was sympathetic to neutrality in the primary. Instead, NYSUT gave Cuomo a critical convention victory. Even better for Cuomo, the Service Employees International Union (SEIU), disendorsed Koch and then endorsed Cuomo.

With NYSUT and AFL-CIO endorsements, activities, funds, and votes, Cuomo emerged victorious over Koch by a narrow margin in the Democratic primary and went on to win the governorship, also by a narrow margin. Shortly thereafter, a quid pro quo emerged. Cuomo, now governor, supported legislation that required state aid for New York City schools to be spent only for teacher salaries. Over the objections of Mayor Koch, this legislation was enacted despite the fact that the New York City schools were in deplorable, even wretched condition as the result of unrelenting pressures to skimp on maintenance and allocate school funds to teacher salaries and benefits.

TEACHER UNIONS AND POLITICAL PARTIES

Teacher unions overwhelmingly support Democratic candidates at all three levels of government: local, state and national. The Federal Election Commission (FEC) reports show who supports the candidates who run for the 435 seats every two years in the United States House of Representatives. In the 1992 election 398 congressional candidates were endorsed and supported by total NEA-PAC contributions of $2,340,796. Of those endorsed by NEA-PAC 369 or 92 percent were Democrats, 29 or 7 percent were Republicans. NEA-PAC endorsed candidates for the House of Representatives won 71 percent of their races in the 1992 election cycle.

The NEA's pro-Democratic tilt is just as evident in the elections to the U.S. Senate. With one-third of the 100 Senators up for election every two years, NEA-PAC endorses and contributes to senate candidates, while carefully monitoring each senator's votes during the six-year term. In 1992 NEA-PAC endorsed or supported 39 senate candidates with contributions of $279,831. Of those Senate candidates supported by NEA-PAC, 38 or 97 percent were Democrats; one, Arlen Specter of Pennsylvania, was a Republican. NEA-PAC contributed $2,000 to Specter's primary campaign, none to his campaign in the general election; meanwhile, his Democratic opponent, Lynn Yeakel, received $5,000 for the Democratic primary and $5,000 for the general election against Specter. The $2,000 contribution to Specter's primary campaign was unusual; although NEA-PAC also supports Congressional candidates in primary elections; such support also goes almost exclusively to Democratic candidates. NEA-PAC endorsed candidates for the United States Senate in 1992 won in 68 percent of their races.

Endorsements and contributions are not the only way in which the NEA and NEA-PAC influences lawmakers. In 1989 it spent $7.4 million on a computerized system for sending letters to Congress from 300,000 NEA members who pre-authorized the use of their names (Toch, 1991). Congressional Contact Teams, consisting of two NEA members from each congressional district are encouraged to serve on the campaign staff of candidates endorsed by the NEA. These individuals are specially trained as lobbyists and flown to and from Washington to encourage the successful candidates to support NEA objectives. A satellite linkup between the NEA's television studio in Washington and its state affiliates is available, and a full time lobbying staff is on duty throughout the year.

Clearly, the NEA has evolved into one of the most powerful special interest organizations in the political arena. Its influence extends to every state and community where teachers and support personnel live or work, which means just about everywhere in the United States.

If one were merely to add the political resources of the NEA and AFT and their state and local affiliates, the result would be an immense organization that is certain to tilt a wide range of public policies toward union and liberal Democratic positions. The fact is, however, that an additive process tends to underestimate the political potential of NEA/AFT. One reason is that the NEA/AFT will probably organize a much larger proportion of school related personnel than the two unions have organized separately up to this time. It would not be surprising if NEA/AFT organized at least one million support personnel within a few years after merger. If the actual numbers turn out to be anywhere close to this figure, or even higher, the NEA/AFT will be a political behemoth indeed.

Politically, the NEA and AFT are affiliates of the Democratic Party, complete with the ethnic, victim, and special interest caucuses that dominate that party. About one in ten delegates to the 1992 Democratic National Convention was a member of the NEA or AFT. When NEA-PAC rated members of Congress on 14 votes of special interest to the NEA, 23 Democratic senators received a perfect score and 11 others voted the NEA's position 90 percent or more of the time. No Republican senator voted the NEA's position on 90 percent or more of the votes. No Democratic senator voted against the NEA's position on more than 40 percent of the votes, whereas 32 Republican senators did so, with two never supporting the NEA's position and seven others supporting it less than 10 percent of the time. The AFT pattern was very similar, as was the AFL-CIO's.

Unquestionably, the cash contributions were overshadowed by the value of the noncash contributions, such as manpower for demonstrations, mailings, telephone banks, transportation to the polls, publicity in union media, and so on. Teachers as well as union staff have much more time than most citizens to serve as campaign volunteers; for many, it is a social outlet as well as a responsibility. Right to life partisans are the only conservative presence in both NEA and AFT conventions, but their influence is negligible. There is no Republican caucus in the AFT; the NEA Republican caucus, discussed in Chapter 4, is a paper organization bereft of program, strategy, or sense of mission, as well as of members who play an active role in NEA affairs. The Republican caucus was much stronger in 1974, when some Republican members of the House of Representatives as well as the Assistant Secretary of Education (under the Secretary for Health, Education and Welfare) took an active interest in it. It was clear then that the teacher unions would be a major player in national politics and that they would be controlled by the Democratic Party by default unless action was taken to avert this outcome. The Republican Educational Caucus in the 1970s got off to an excellent start, but floundered and sank into oblivion as a result of Watergate and the Republican National Committee (RNC) preoccupation with other matters. It became practically impossible to persuade teachers to work with the Republican party while President Nixon was being hammered daily in the media and facing impeachment. The existing Republican caucus in the NEA has the formal blessing of the Republican National Committee, but no meaningful support or leadership from it.

Merger will render it impossible for conservative forces to ignore the teacher unions. Of course, these forces already realize that the teacher unions support anti-conservative positions, but they lack any program or strategy to change the situation. This is partly due to their ignorance about teacher union structure, leadership, revenues, governance documents, dynamics—just about everything that matters. With merger, or closer cooperation between the NEA and AFT, this situation is unlikely to continue. The conservative forces will have to focus on the teacher unions as they have never done before. It will take a while and some expensive adult education, but the change from not so benign neglect to a conservative focus on teacher unions is inevitable.

CHAPTER SIX

UNION SPONSORED MEMBER BENEFIT PROGRAMS

The primary function of most unions is the negotiation of favorable terms and conditions of employment for employees represented by the union. This function also includes ensuring that the employer live up to the terms of the contract negotiated with the union; the most common way to do this is to negotiate a grievance procedure culminating in binding arbitration of claims that the employer has failed to abide by the terms of the contract.

Although the union's ability to negotiate benefits paid by the employer is paramount, most unions also sponsor benefit programs paid by the union or by union members. Teacher unions are especially active in this regard; both the NEA and AFT offer a wide range of products and services to their members. These operations have not received the attention they deserve, perhaps because they seem so familiar to the educational community. Whatever the reason, union sponsored benefit programs can play an important role in building union membership. Because of their large membership base, the teacher unions can often take advantage of economies of scale in buying goods or services. Also, because teachers are relatively attractive to vendors from a demographic and economic point of view, the unions can sometimes negotiate lower prices for various services. To be sure, unions, including teacher unions have sometimes sponsored benefit programs of dubious value to union members. First, however, let us note the range of services provided by union sponsored programs. Including services offered by the state as well as the national teacher unions, the list includes the following:

Insurance Programs:
    accidental death and dismemberment insurance
    automobile insurance
    dental insurance
    health insurance
    homeowners insurance
    liability insurance
    life insurance
    strike benefit protection

term life insurance
vision insurance
Financial Programs:
  credit cards
  credit plans
  mortgages
Investment Programs:
  annuities
  money market accounts
  mutual funds
  securities
Discount Programs:
  travel discounts
  auto purchase/lease
  book clubs/magazine subscriptions
  legal services

These services are provided in different ways. Some are provided directly by the unions. Some are provided by independent contractors who may or may not have secured a contract through a competitive bidding process. The extent of union involvement may also vary widely. In the following discussion, we focus mainly on the member benefit operations of the two national unions, but we believe that the member benefit operations of their state and local affiliates deserve more scrutiny than they have received in the past.

NEA member benefits operations consists of a complex arrangement of subsidiaries, funds, and fund transfers which provide revenue and services to help support the NEA, its programs, and its political operations. To the majority of members, the NEA political agenda is of secondary concern; most members join the NEA primarily for the job protection and teacher welfare benefits that accompany membership. Legal protection and/or legal representation are provided to NEA members in matters relating to teacher/student conduct or terms and conditions of employment. In addition, NEA members are automatically covered by NEA Dues-Tab Insurance (underwritten by Prudential Insurance Company of America, Inc.), which provides up to $1,000 life insurance, $5,000 accidental death and dismemberment insurance and up to $50,000 job related accidental death and dismemberment. At the same time, however, most NEA subsidiary operations provide millions of dollars in union revenue. In addition, the property holdings and assets of the subsidiaries provide the NEA with even greater resources to utilize for a variety of purposes. Although not all subsidiary operations are member benefits, the collective purchasing power of the more than two million NEA members obviously offers unique opportunities for member benefits. Understandably, as benefit opportunities have expanded, so has the organizational structure necessary to provide the requisite special services.

NEA SPECIAL SERVICES

The NEA Special Services area includes contracts for 1) investment services (annuity, money market account); 2) financial services (credit card, credit plans); 3) personal services (discount rental car programs, magazine service, and computer marketing); and 4) insurance through the National Education Association Members Insurance Trust (life, accidental death and dismemberment, health, homeowners, etc).

NEA Member Benefits Corporation

As a wholly owned subsidiary of the NEA, the Member Benefits Corporation (MBC) is retained by the NEA to administer the contracts held by the National Education Association's Special Services area. In order to market these special services to NEA members, the NEA created the MBC, a for-profit corporation which recovers its costs for administration, marketing, research and development, training, member service, and affiliate service support for NEA Special Services through written agreements between NEA Special Services and NEA's Member Benefits Corporation. The MBC is governed by three executive officers, each of whom also serves on the NEA Board of Directors and who receive annual payments from $67,000 to over $100,000. MBC total assets for the period ended August 31, 1992 exceeded $2 million.

NEA Members Insurance Trust

The NEA Members Insurance Trust (the Trust) is a separate, tax-exempt organization under Section 501(c)(9) of the Internal Revenue Code of 1954, as amended. Prudential Insurance Company of America, Inc. underwrites life insurance and accidental death, dismemberment and disability insurance. Washington National Insurance Company underwrites a more comprehensive program of disability insurance. Both programs, which entitle NEA members to purchase group life and other insurance benefits, are classified as employee benefit plans. The Trust also provides an all-member life insurance benefit known as the "Dues-Tab Program" at no cost to the members. As mentioned above, the Trust is a part of the Special Services area and is therefore administered by the Members Benefit Corporation which provides administrative and promotional services for the Trust programs. For the year ended August 31, 1992, the NEA Members Insurance Trust had total assets of $88,159,667.

Further, the Trust has entered into an agreement with NEA to provide data processing services for the maintenance of the Dues-Tab membership files. Under this agreement, the Trust reimburses NEA $75,000 per year or $.04 per member, whichever is greater. In addition, during 1992, the Trust remitted $500,000 to NEA for a portion of the costs associated with the NEA Systems 2000 project, a software development project. NEA officers, directors and members hold all of the five trustee positions which direct the activities of the NEA Members Insurance Trust.

NEA LEGAL ASSISTANCE FUNDS AND PROGRAMS

NEA Employees Assistance Fund, Inc.

The National Education Employees Assistance Fund, Inc. (NEEAF) is another nonprofit corporation providing assistance to NEA members. NEEAF was incorporated in 1970 to provide a vehicle for interest-free loans through lending institutions to the NEA members of the 38 NEA state affiliates who are members of NEEAF. The program is implemented and administered as a strike loan program. In this connection, NEEAF has guaranteed loans made by lending institutions to teachers who were involved in such disputes. These loans are secured by letters of credit from those state affiliates which are members of NEEAF and also by NEA's line of credit.

Two-thirds of the interest on the loans to members is paid by the state association and one-third is paid by NEEAF. In the event of default, all loans provided by the lending institutions are guaranteed by NEEAF up to one-half of the loan amount; the balance of the loans is guaranteed by the respective state associations. NEEAF's financial activities are included in the special purpose funds of NEA and are budgeted by the Representative Assembly. Under provisions of Section 501(c)(5) of the Internal Revenue Code and the applicable income tax regulations of the District of Columbia, NEEAF is exempt from income taxes.

NEA provides both accounting and management services to the National Education Employee Assistance Fund at no charge, and appropriated $100,000 to the Fund in 1992. As a member of NEEAF, the NEA maintains a letter of credit, which accounts for approximately 50 percent of the NEEAF's available letters of credit. Currently, combined letters of credit exceed $4 million; NEEAF is contingently liable in the event of default for just over $1.5 million. Between December 18, 1989 and February 28, 1990, NEEAF loaned a total of $1,282,000 to the TerreBonne Education Association Federal Credit Union for use in loans to striking teachers who were members of the Louisiana Education Association. By June 30, 1992, although most of the note had been paid off; $27,236 in loan defaults were written off.

NEA Kate Frank/DuShane Fund
Another benefit of NEA membership is the availability of legal assistance from the Kate Frank/DuShane Fund (the "Fund") which was established by the Representative Assembly to protect the human, civil and professional rights of educators. The major program of the Fund is the Unified Legal Services Program, which provides legal assistance to members of the teaching profession in matters related to their employment. An educator may request assistance from the NEA Office of Legal Services by first contacting the local UniServ representative or the legal services office of the state affiliate. The 1993 RA voted to pay up to 46% of state costs of legal representation to guarantee adherence to local contracts and collective bargaining agreements; to uphold state fair dismissal laws; to protect constitutionally guaranteed free expression rights, including academic freedom and political association; and to fight job discrimination on the basis of age, sex, race, or ethnic or cultural origins. For 1993-94 almost $17 million was budgeted for the DuShane Unified Legal Services Program.

Educators Employment Liability Program
The Educators Employment Liability Program provides coverage for up to $4 million in damages and additional payments for legal fees for most civil and some criminal lawsuits. This program provides protection for members from personal financial liability when NEA members are sued as a result of employment related activities, such as accidents occurring to students while members are teaching or supervising educational activities. NEA fully funds the insurance premium for this program.

Association Professional Liability Program
The Association Professional Liability Program protects local, state, and national association officers and staff from personal financial liability in lawsuits resulting from their advocacy on behalf of NEA and its members. All funds are administered at the National Education Association Washington, D.C. office.

NEA Attorney Referral Program
Through the Attorney Referral Program, members have access to a national panel of NEA-approved attorneys for personal legal matters such as preparation of wills, real estate matters, divorce proceedings, and consumer complaints. Participant attorneys may provide advice and consultation at

no charge and discount their usual fees by 30 percent as a service to NEA members.

DIRECT SERVICES TO MEMBERS

From an NEA standpoint, the member services available for purchase are overshadowed by those made available to members and affiliates without charge directly through NEA administrative units. For instance, NEA publishes several periodicals for the general membership as well as others for interest groups within the NEA, such as for higher education and educational support personnel. Advertising in member publications often includes the NEA Member Benefits and Special Services.

The programs offering direct services to members typically reflect the NEA's political and social orientation. Thus the union's programs focus on such topics as "women's and girls issues," "equal access and minority leadership training," or "women's leadership training." In this connection, it is instructive to note how the NEA's transformation from professional association to union impacted its programmatic orientation. Prior to unionization, the NEA was the organizational base for several national organizations devoted to curriculum and instruction. These organizations, such as the National Science Teachers Association and National Council of Teachers of Mathematics, had their own organizational structure but were affiliated with NEA and housed in the NEA building. The NEA's Research Division was a rich source of information on virtually all aspects of education. With the emergence of teacher bargaining, however, the curriculum and instruction organizations withdrew from the NEA as did organizations of principals and school administrators. Meanwhile, the NEA's Research Division focused on school finance, cost of living, and other topics primarily related to teacher bargaining. Most of its work is backup for NEA and its affiliates on bargaining or compensation or revenue issues.

NEA STATE ASSOCIATION BENEFIT PROGRAMS

The NEA's state affiliates often sponsor member benefit plans of their own. We do not have systematic data on the number, scope, resources or administration of these plans, but there is at least one overriding reason to scrutinize their operations more carefully than in the past. As previously noted, the state and local affiliates of the NEA and AFT are not subject to federal regulation of union activities. Appendix E sets forth the reporting and disclosure requirements in federal statutes that are not applicable to state and local teacher unions. The inapplicability of the federal statutes is compounded by the fact that the state bargaining laws typically omit the reporting and disclosure requirements as well as the union member rights incorporated in the federal statutes. In the absence of such reporting and disclosure requirements, union officials are more likely to abuse their positions, to the detriment of their members and/or their employers.

A recent case in point emerged in November 1993, when The Mackinac Center for Public Policy published a report entitled *Michigan Education Special Services Association: The MEA's Money Machine.* According to the Mackinac Center report, the Michigan Education Association owns and controls three subsidiary corporations: the Michigan Education Special Services Association (MESSA), the Michigan Education Association Financial Services, and the Michigan Education Data Network Association (MEDNA).

In 1960 MESSA was incorporated by the MEA as a wholly-owned, not-for-profit subsidiary to administer insurance benefit programs to participating MEA members. Life, accidental death and dismemberment, disability, health, dental, and vision coverage are included in the insurance programs. Local affiliate unions of the MEA are encouraged to bargain MESSA insurance plans into their labor contracts with their respective school districts. In such cases, the corporation which administers insurance benefits to the school district's employees is also a part of the organization which represents the school district's employees during contract negotiations. When this occurs, the MEA has unprecedented leverage in controlling the compensatory benefits received by its members. In 1962 MESSA received $360 million from approximately 60 percent of Michigan's school districts for insurance coverage of school district employees, including teachers, support staff, and administrators.

Similar to NEA subsidiary governance, the two most recent appointees to the MESSA Board of Trustees are the incumbent president and vice-president of the MEA. In addition, six of the trustees are elected from and by the MEA Board of Directors.

In 1973, the MEA created the Michigan Education Financial Services Association. Now known as MEA Financial Services, this subsidiary provides MEA members with numerous investment services, including annuities, investment retirement accounts, credit cards, mutual funds, auto owners insurance, and home owners insurance, again, much like the NEA Special Services program.

In 1982, The Michigan Education Data Network Association (MEDNA) was established as a wholly-owned, for profit subsidiary of the MEA. Unlike the other subsidiaries, but comparable to the NEA's MBC, MEDNA's purpose is to service the MEA rather than MEA's members. MEDNA provides a wide range of clerical and administrative services to the MEA and its

94

other subsidiaries, including data processing, communications, and accounting. And like the MBC at the national level, MEDNA receives compensation from the MEA and its other subsidiaries, forming a lucrative resource pool for the whole MEA conglomerate.

In regard to the relationship between the MEA and its subsidiaries (see Table 6.1), the Mackinac Center report concluded that "Both the Michigan Education Special Services Association (MESSA) and the Michigan Education Association (MEA) have the necessary resources to fight any attempt at restraining the MESSA operation. The MEA can manipulate many public officials through campaign contributions and political pressure, and MESSA has enough financial reserves to pay for legal services, lobbying staff, and other programs necessary to combat its opposition. Moreover, MESSA can recuperate the costs of self-defense by increasing premium rates, inducing more illegitimate taxpayer support" (Bockelman and Overton, 1993).

It is only fair to point out that the MEA and MESSA have vigorously denied the validity of the Mackinac Center report, nor have the authors of this book had the time or opportunity to conduct their own assessment of the charges in the report. We will say, however, that the abuses set forth in the report are likely to exist in some of the state associations; in fact, it would be surprising if they did not exist in some states.

AFT MEMBER BENEFIT PROGRAMS

AFT Plus includes nine AFT officially sponsored group insurance plans for its members. Programs and coverage appear to be similar to the NEA options. The AFT office of the secretary-treasurer is responsible for monitoring and negotiating national AFT member benefits.

Union Privilege, AFL-CIO was created by the AFL-CIO in 1986 to bring union members and their families high quality consumer benefits and services. When adopted by the American Federation of Teachers (or any other affiliated union) these programs are designed to help make the dollars union members earn go further and to make the union a more vital part of members' daily lives.

Union Privilege benefits include a low-interest credit card, discounts on such services as travel, car rentals, moving vans, and theme park admissions and the mortgage program for buying or refinancing a home, music and video discounts. By endorsing programs which are specially designed for union members and which offer genuine value and superior member service, the collective purchasing strength of over 14 million union members can be utilized to benefit union members.

THE MEA TRIANGLE:

How tax dollars intended for education end up supporting MEA political activity

Mackinac Center for
Public Policy, 1993

(1) Parents and other citizens provide school districts money to educate children.

(2) MEA bargaining representatives pressure school districts to purchase unusually generous MESSA insurance packages. School Boards face the threat of illegal teacher strikes that disrupt children's education.

(3) School districts that give in to MEA demands pay premiums to MESSA.

(4) MESSA pays the MEA for "marketing" services, i.e., to pressure school districts to purchase MESSA insurance.

(5) MESSA holds tens of millions of dollars in "reserves," and shares facilities, equipment and personnel with the MEA.

(6) After withholding unusually high administration fees, MESSA forwards premiums to Blue Cross/ Blue Shield, the actual insurance underwriter.

(7) MESSA pays MEDNA for data processing and other services.

(8) MEDNA sells data processing and other services to the MEA for administration and political action.

(9) Both the MEA and MESSA provide money and personnel to lobby the Michigan Legislature. The MEA also channels millions of dollars to legislative candidates through various political action committees.

Parents and other Taxpayers (1)

Revenue from School Taxes

SCHOOL DISTRICTS (3)

BLUE CROSS/ BLUE SHIELD (6)

$$$ for Insurance Premiums

MESSA (5)
Michigan Education Special Services Association

(Wholly-owned by the MEA)

(2) Bargainers work to obtain MESSA contracts.

$$$ and Bargaining Agents

$$$ for Bargaining Services

$$$ and Lobbyists (4)

MEA
Michigan Education Association

$ and Lobbyists (9)

Political Candidates

MICHIGAN LEGISLATURE
Both the MEA and MESSA provide money and personnel to lobby the Michigan Legislature

Data Processing and Other Services (7)

$ $ $

Data Processing and Other Services (8)

$ $ $

MEDNA
Michigan Education Data Network Association

(For-Profit Corporation Wholly-owned by the MEA)

Table 6.1

AFT LEGAL ASSISTANCE FUNDS

AFT Defense Fund

The AFT Defense Fund provides assistance to locals and state federations to help protect the rights of AFT members. Applications of less than $2,000 may be approved by the five member defense committee. In most states, the defense committee recommends that AFT locals and state federation share the legal costs on a one-third each basis. Cases most often involve AFT member job security and the necessity to protect the members' right to due process. In addition, the defense fund provides grants in arbitration cases when the arbitration involves job security. If a request is for more than $2,000, the defense committee makes recommendations to the executive council for approval. For 1992-93, $700,000 had been budgeted for the Defense Fund (1990-92 Report of AFT Officers).

AFT Militancy Fund

The AFT Militancy Fund provides assistance to member affiliates in three ways:

1. The AFT will pay interest on strike loans made on the first payday missed because of the strike, provided the strike has lasted at least five days. The member secures a loan and files a form with the local. The local and the AFT will help to secure a loan when the member is unable to do so.
2. The AFT helps the local pay legal fees incurred as result of a strike.
3. If fines are assessed, the local may apply for help in appealing the fines.

Three AFT vice presidents are the militancy fund trustees, overseeing the almost $2 million budget allocation for 1992-93.

POLICY ISSUES IN MEMBER BENEFITS

The preceding discussion has not analyzed teacher union benefit programs in detail; our purpose was mainly to invite attention to an important dimension of union activity that is widely ignored in the literature on teacher unions. It seems apparent, however, that union sponsored benefit programs raise several significant policy issues.

The rationale for these programs is that by using their large membership base, the unions can enable their members to buy products and services more efficiently and at a lower cost than they could otherwise. We have no

97

quarrel with this rationale, but we do have some reservations about the way it is being implemented. Our major reservations are as follows:

1. Clearly, union sponsored benefit programs constitute a conflict of interest in some situations. Consider the example of the Michigan Education Special Services Association (MESSA), which is a wholly owned nonprofit subsidiary of the Michigan Education Association (MEA). MESSA sells insurance plans (most often health insurance plans) to school districts.

   In 1992, MESSA received over $360 million in revenues and provided insurance plan administration for over 300 of the 523 K-12 school districts in Michigan. Inasmuch as the identity of the insurance carrier is a mandatory subject of bargaining in Michigan, negotiators for MEA affiliates are likely to recommend MESSA insurance plans, even if benefit costs and costs of administration are excessive. Typically, the union cares more about benefits than costs. Realistically, neither the average teacher nor the school district is in a position to challenge the MEA representative who negotiates scores of school district contracts every year, and who may threaten a teacher strike if the school district resists the union program.

   If the MEA itself had opened the insurance program to competitive bidding, there would not necessarily be a conflict of interest. However, if and when the administrator, such as MESSA, is a union subsidiary that faces potential competition from other vendors, the conflict exists, regardless of whether the union subsidiary is nonprofit or for profit.

2. By using wholly owned subsidiaries, the teacher unions may be able to take advantage of legal freedoms that apply to one organizational entity but not to others.

Because unions, nonprofit organizations and for profit organizations operate under different statutes, the member benefit corporations can be used to shift or transfer funds to avoid disclosure that would be embarrassing or even illegal if reported accurately. For example, the in-kind contributions of subsidiaries in political campaigns may come under less stringent requirements than those pertaining directly to the unions per se.

Actually, the unions often have a stake in avoiding disclosure of certain practices that are commendable but do not conform to union ideology. For instance, the unions sometimes do invite competitive bidding on their member benefit programs. In other words, they use the same practice that they would deny to governments when the latter seek providers for government services, such as health insurance plans for public school teachers.

In view of the many transfers of funds between the NEA, the AFT, and their state and local affiliates, it is often impossible even for members to understand union operations. The NEA's UniServ program is a striking example of a "local" operation that is actually financed in large part from national union funds.

CHAPTER SEVEN

NEA/AFT MERGER: A HISTORICAL PERSPECTIVE

In both the NEA and AFT, interest in merger talks has waxed and waned since 1960. In that year, Myron Lieberman published *The Future of Public Education*, a book that proposed merger on the basis of no affiliation with the AFL-CIO and the expulsion of administrators from the NEA. At the time, Lieberman believed that affiliation with the AFL-CIO was the major organizing obstacle to the AFT; also, that administrator membership in the NEA was incompatible with teacher bargaining, which he believed to be imminent (Lieberman, 1960).

Although some activists in both the NEA and AFT agreed with this analysis, they were not well organized in either union. During the 1960s and early 1970s the NEA could probably have forced a merger by cutting a deal with AFT leaders who were not enamored of affiliation with the AFL-CIO. There were a sizable number of such leaders; after all, despite having just published a book urging disaffiliation with the AFL-CIO and despite an inept campaign, Lieberman received one third of the votes for the AFT presidency at its 1962 convention.

In the early 1970s, the NEA might have achieved merger by offering inducements to AFT leaders to bring their locals with them if and when these leaders switched over to the NEA. To effectuate a merger, the strategy need not have been successful with all or even most AFT locals; only enough of them to force the others to the table to salvage what they could from a deteriorating situation. Although some of its strategists wanted to adopt this strategy, the NEA did not do so; instead it focused upon defeating AFT locals in representation elections. This strategy naturally led the NEA to portray the AFT and AFL-CIO as evil forces to be avoided at all costs, a posture the NEA is now trying to change with the advent of merger talks.

Merger talks did take place in 1973 and 1974, but they broke down very quickly, and the unions lapsed back into their combat modes (Selden, 1985). According to Selden, the talks ostensibly broke down over affiliation with the AFL-CIO and the guarantee of minority participation. Selden, however, believed that these might have been resolved if Shanker had not privately been opposed to merger. During the time in 1972-74 when the merger talks were going on, Shanker had amassed enough support in the AFT to replace Selden as president. In Selden's view, Shanker feared that merger would have forced Shanker to give up his control over the AFT and to take his chances in a newly merged organization in which his AFT supporters would be vastly outnumbered. Paradoxically, there was also a fear in some NEA quarters at the time that a merger would lead to a "Shanker takeover" of the merged organization. In this connection, it is interesting that Shanker tried to remove Selden from office as AFT president in 1973 for allegedly exceeding his authority in discussing merger with NEA leaders (Selden, 1985).

From time to time, however, mergers have taken place at the local level, usually on the basis of dual membership in the NEA and AFT and affiliation with the AFL-CIO. This solution did not attract much support and because of the costs involved, it is unlikely to be widely adopted in the 1990s. New York was the only state in which there was a merger at the state level, but the merger there did not survive the anti-merger sentiment that pervaded the NEA in the 1970s.

It should be kept in mind, however, that the long-time existence of rival unions competing for the same members is the exception, not the usual outcome in the labor movement. During the time when sophisticated leadership might have averted the organizational stalemate that eventually emerged, the NEA was a badly divided organization with an extremely diffuse governance structure. Survival, not principle, drove the NEA to embrace teacher bargaining; indeed, the NEA's initial response to AFT victories in representation elections was to establish an "urban project," in the naive belief that collective bargaining was an issue limited to urban areas. The NEA did not explicitly accept union status or terminology or philosophy until the window of opportunity to merge without affiliation had closed, and merger talks were the only way to achieve a unified teacher organization. Today, however, there is no practical difference between the two unions regarding the desirability of teacher bargaining. The extent to which affiliation with the AFL-CIO remains as an issue remains to be seen and is discussed later in this chapter.

NEW BUSINESS ITEMS 1993-A AND 1993-B: THE 1993 CONVENTION BACKGROUND

The NEA's interest in merger and the possibility of a change in its position on affiliation with the AFL-CIO, was evident in New Business Items 1993-A and 1993-B, adopted by the Representative Assembly at the 1993 NEA convention.

New Business Items A and B were submitted to the Representative Assembly by the NEA's Board of Directors. The items were originally recommended by a Board of Directors Special Committee, which had been directed to review NEA policies on merger and report back to the board. When the Special Committee did so, the Board of Directors approved the report, including the recommendations that merger talks and moratoriums on merger talks at the state and local levels and on representation challenges be submitted to the 1993 Representative Assembly. The vote on the Board of Directors to do so foreshadowed the substantial majority that the items received in the Representative Assembly vote on July 2 (Geiger, 1993).

Significantly, there had been growing interest in merger talks in the NEA prior to the establishment of the Special Committee of the Board of Directors. In several states characterized by costly competition for bargaining rights and members, merger talks had been initiated or considered in recent years: Minnesota, Wisconsin, Michigan, New Mexico, Florida, and California are among these states. In these states, NEA affiliates wanted to explore merger possibilities but were unable to do so because of the NEA's restrictions on affiliation with the AFL-CIO. The situation brought some pressure to bear on the NEA to avoid an organizational free for all in which its state affiliates might negotiate merger agreements that were not in the best interests of the national organization. At the 1993 NEA convention, a small group was opposed to merger except through a total AFT capitulation to the NEA; a larger group was predisposed to merger and to make significant concessions to achieve it; and a still larger group will undoubtedly be heavily influenced by the proposals and arguments that are submitted to the Representative Assembly in 1994. Of course, even the parties favoring merger do not support it regardless of the arrangements, but they are more likely to make concessions to bring it about.

On its face, the moratoriums on merger talks below the national level and on representation challenges appear only to recognize the fact that the NEA and AFT are firmly entrenched in their respective domains. The possibility of a few successful challenges by either union was deemed not worth the risk that such challenges might disrupt the merger talks. Even apart from this consideration, however, the two moratoriums are extremely significant. In effect, they centralize control of the merger talks in the national leadership of the two unions. (It is possible that other unions, especially unions of support personnel, will be involved in the talks, but because the critical issues are those dividing the AFT and NEA, our analysis will be limited to these two unions.) To be sure, the negotiating teams for the NEA and AFT will confer with their key constituencies during the talks; a great deal of emphasis was placed on this point during the debate in the

Representative Assembly. NEA President Keith Geiger assured the delegates that there would be adequate communication between the NEA's team and various constituencies within the NEA. Nevertheless it should be noted that the moratoriums rule out initiatives by state or local affiliates in both unions. For this reason, the moratoriums place tremendous power in the national leadership of the two unions.

The debate preceding the vote on the merger talks was spirited but essentially irrelevant to the outcome. The proposals for merger talks had been disseminated over a month before the convention, and they were discussed in the various caucuses before the convention vote. It is unlikely that many votes were changed by the debate; clearly, the proponents, led by Geiger, who had just been reelected to a three year term as NEA president, were prepared to defeat maneuvers to block or weaken the merger talks. Organized opposition to the talks emerged in state delegations from New Jersey, New York, Massachusetts, and Illinois, but it was clear at the outset of the debate that the opponents of the talks could not block them on a straight up and down vote. Although many delegates voted for the talks with reservations ("Why oppose talks with the AFT?"), many others felt that merger talks would develop a momentum of their own leading to a merger. In their view, voting for merger talks was tantamount to voting for merger. Some of this thinking was based upon the fact that the new business items authorizing the talks explicitly questioned NEA policies prohibiting affiliation with the AFL-CIO, a major obstacle to merger in the past.

Less than a week after the NEA authorized merger talks, the AFT held its annual convention on educational issues in Washington. Interestingly enough, the NEA's actions were a non-event at the AFT convention; the overwhelming majority of delegates seemed not to care, or even to know about the NEA's actions. Even AFT President Shanker disclaimed detailed prior knowledge or discussions with NEA leaders on merger issues; however, when asked how the NEA leaders could be so confident that the AFT would accept the moratoriums, Shanker conceded that he had indicated that the moratoriums would not be a problem. Obviously, the leaders in both unions have been very careful to avoid opposition to merger based on failure to follow proper organizational procedures. Whether or not they had reached any informal agreement before New Business Items 1993-A and 1993-B were adopted, they probably have some common reasons to believe the talks will be more productive than previous merger talks.

Teacher affiliation with the AFL-CIO is a major difference between the NEA and AFT; obviously, it is a major issue in the merger talks. In our view, the issue is a practical, not a moral or professional one. By "practical," we mean that the issue will be resolved on the basis of whether teachers believe that they will be better off if affiliated with the AFL-CIO. Of course, the answer to this question does not necessarily answer the question of whether teacher affiliation with the AFL-CIO is in the public interest, or whether the public interest is or should be a factor in how the issue is resolved.

Although affiliation is a merger issue, affiliation or non-affiliation should not be grounds for opposing merger if one accords the highest priority to a unified teacher organization. That is, regardless of whether one favors or opposes affiliation, it should not be grounds for opposing merger if one's highest priority is a unified teacher union.

We do not believe that affiliation with the AFL-CIO will be a make or break issue in the merger talks. Our point is not that all teachers will be required to affiliate, or prohibited from doing so. Our thought is only that the issue will be resolved in a mutually satisfactory way in the merger talks. The resolution may be only a short-term one, but merger will not be held up over the issue.

Conceptually, there are at least two ways to approach the affiliation issue. One is to examine the AFL-CIO constitution to ascertain the implications of "affiliation," at least as they are evident from it. The other way is to analyze the arguments for and against affiliation without regard to the AFL-CIO constitution or any other document. In this case, however, both approaches lead to the same conclusions.

A perusal of its constitution reveals a surprising fact about affiliation with the AFL-CIO. Except for payment of per capita taxes (dues) to the AFL-CIO there does not appear to be any significant substantive commitment involved in affiliation with the Federation. Of course, there are several organizational requirements and procedures, such as the determination of voting strength at conventions and procedures for becoming affiliated, but there is no restriction on policy positions that can be adopted or taken. The AFL-CIO constitution does provide for the investigative and disciplinary procedures relating to corrupt affiliates, or to affiliates whose policies or activities "are consistently directed toward the advocacy, support, advancement or achievement of the program or of the purposes of the Communist Party, any fascist organization or other totalitarian movement" (Article 8, Section 7, AFL-CIO Constitution). It is unlikely that a significant number of NEA members would take exception to these provisions, at least to the extent of insisting that they be eliminated or amended as a condition of merger.

Despite the concerns over teacher union autonomy under affiliation, the AFL-CIO constitution emphasizes the autonomy of its constituent unions; its ability to act for all is much more problematic than any danger of infringing on the autonomy of an affiliated union. The following provisions illustrate this point:

> The objects and principles of this Federation are:
> . . . To preserve and maintain the integrity of each affiliated union in the organization to the end that each affiliate shall respect the established bargaining relationships of every other affiliate and that each affiliate shall refrain from raiding the established bargaining relationship of any other affiliate and, at the same time, to encourage the elimination of conflicting and duplicating organizations and jurisdictions through the process of voluntary agreement or voluntary merger in consultation with the appropriate officials of the Federation, to preserve, subject to the foregoing, the organizing jurisdiction of each affiliate.
> . . . To safeguard the democratic character of the labor movement and to protect the autonomy of each affiliated national and international union (Article II, Section 8,11, AFL-CIO Constitution).
> . . . The Federation shall be composed of: (1) national and international unions which are affiliated with, but are not subordinate to, or subject to the general direction and control of, the Federation . . . (Article III, Section 1, AFL-CIO Constitution).

The financial obligations of affiliation are significant but not especially onerous. AFT dues are $8.55 per month ($102.60 annually) for regular full-time teachers. State Federation dues vary but are almost always much less than state association dues in the NEA. Local dues also vary, but are comparable or even higher than local association dues in the NEA. Beginning in January 1993, each national affiliate of the AFL-CIO is obligated to pay 40 cents per month per member, payable on or before the 15th of the month for the preceding month. The per capita tax for members who are not "regular members" or who "receive less than the full range of the union's representation services is two-thirds of the regular per capita to the nearest whole cent," or 26 cents per month per member. Under certain circumstances not likely to be applicable to the NEA, the AFL-CIO's Executive Council can raise the per capita one cent per member per month.

The 1993-94 NEA budget is based on the equivalent of 2,208,000 regular members. At $.40 per member per month, its annual financial obligation to the AFL-CIO would be $4.80 per member, or almost $10,600,000 annually. This figure does not include the per capita paid to local and state central labor bodies. These figures will vary, but would not be a major obstacle to merger.

The AFL-CIO was established on the basis that the economic interests of workers in various industries necessarily outweigh their conflicting or divergent interests. This is a fallacy sustained by faulty economics. For example, when the auto workers receive wage increases, the popular view is that their "employers" pay for them. Actually, the wage increases are passed on to car buyers in the form of higher prices, paid by the members of other unions in the AFL-CIO as well as by the public generally.

The counter argument is that the mutual assistance unions in the AFL-CIO receive outweighs the costs they inflict on each other. Thus the question is whether the union members give up more as consumers than they gain as producers through their affiliation with the AFL-CIO. It is not at all clear that the benefits outweigh the costs, at least all of the time to all of the unions in the AFL-CIO. The issue is really an empirical, not an ideological one. One can argue that the gains due to affiliation clearly outweigh the costs because parties outside the AFL-CIO, such as the unorganized, absorb most of the costs of the gains achieved through affiliation.

Nevertheless, there is a significant and growing conflict of interest between the public and private sector unions in the AFL-CIO. The private sector unions are more likely to be hurt by high taxes and government expenditures, whereas public sector unions are strongly opposed to limits on taxes and government expenditures (Troy, 1993). Of course, it might also be argued that affiliation is imperative precisely to avoid such a split in the labor movement.

The opponents of affiliation in the NEA fear that the AFL-CIO will restrict the NEA's independence or autonomy. As previously pointed out, this is about as likely as the NEA interfering with the autonomy or independence of the airline pilots or autoworkers, which is to say it is extremely unlikely. The basic issue is whether the teachers are willing to help other unions inflict higher costs on the rest of the population, including the disadvantaged, in exchange for the help these unions give the NEA to achieve its objectives. Many, perhaps most, teachers are willing to do so. The problem is that the teachers are being urged to accept affiliation on the basis of its benefits, while its real costs are totally ignored in the irrelevant debate over "autonomy" or "independence." The teachers might well conclude that the benefits are worth the real costs, including the cost of giving up their cherished belief that teachers are much concerned about the disadvantaged; the latter are the largest group disadvantaged by the AFL-CIO policies generally. In any event, affiliation is not a moral issue or one of high principle, as it is made out to be by partisans on both sides of the issue.

From a public interest point of view, teacher affiliation with the AFL-CIO would have some benefits. No one takes seriously the idea that unions of autoworkers or teamsters or restaurant workers, for example, exist to protect the consumers. The legal and practical role of unions is to advance the interests of their members, regardless of whether the unions label themselves "professional associations" or some other self-serving title. This is not a pejorative comment. People have the right to be represented by organizations that advance their interests, and most people belong to such organizations. Affiliation with the AFL-CIO would help to remove the veneer of dedication to children that still permeates NEA rhetoric and obscures clear thinking about public policies toward teacher unions.

In any event, the wording of the NEA resolutions on merger talks demonstrates NEA willingness to move away from rigid opposition to affiliation. Inasmuch as the NEA is not likely to impose affiliation on all of its state and local affiliates, affiliation is likely to be a state and/or local option. Such an option, however, is likely to be only an interim solution. Over time, the state organizations with mandatory affiliation will become a majority and be able to coerce or persuade the remaining state organizations to accept affiliation. This will happen when and if the pro-affiliation forces can require affiliation without substantial defections from the merged organization. In the meantime, anyone who opposes merger because affiliation with the AFL-CIO is mandatory, or because it is not mandatory, probably has an agenda that does not accord a high priority to an NEA/AFT merger.

In this connection, it is doubtful whether a large majority within the AFT strongly supports affiliation with the AFL-CIO; in our view, it is an open question whether rank and file AFT members care deeply about the issue, one way or the other. AFT members support affiliation with varying degrees of commitment, or tolerate it, but most probably would not require much persuasion or major concessions to change their position. Significantly, more than two years after proposing merger on the basis of no affiliation with the AFL-CIO and the exclusion of administrative personnel from the merged organization, Lieberman received one-third of the votes for AFT president at its 1962 national convention. In addition:

1. David Selden, AFT president before Shanker, was willing to move away from a rigid affiliation requirement in the 1974 merger talks. Selden wanted to propose an opt-out provision, whereby members of the merged organization would have the option not to have any of their dues go to the AFL-CIO. Because he was a lame duck president in a union that had come under Shanker's control, Selden was not able to make this offer to the NEA merger team (Selden, 1985).
2. Many AFT locals are in communities where there is no central trades and labor council affiliated with the AFL-CIO. Affiliation is a state and federal, but not local relationship in many of these communities.
3. Evidence from many sources supports the conclusion that the single most important factor keeping affiliation alive as an issue is Shanker's

undeviating insistence upon it in a merger. Of course, affiliation must appeal to some in the AFT or Shanker could not sustain his commitment to it; in many cases, however, the office seekers in the AFT support affiliation out of political expediency, not principle or even organizational welfare. In saying this, we are not passing judgment on the merits, but on the support it has in the AFT. In the large urban centers, affiliation tends to be more useful than in the suburbs, but since the urban school districts are so influential in the AFT, affiliation receives more support than it would according to membership sentiment.

At the 1993 NEA convention, the Illinois Education Association (IEA) raised several serious questions about the advisability of affiliation. For example, the IEA pointed out that most legislative activity affecting private sector unions is at the federal level, but the state level is the critical arena in education. Thus the IEA questioned the value of NEA affiliation with a predominantly private sector organization, especially in view of the fact that the state affiliates of the NEA are usually among the most effective lobbies in the state capitals. The IEA objections, however, failed to recognize the dramatic increase in public sector unions and decline in private sector ones; furthermore, its argument did not mention the possibility of federal legislation that would require state and local governments to bargain collectively, an objective of both the NEA and AFT.

The fact is that the private sector unions no longer overwhelmingly dominate the labor movement. Significantly, about 40 percent of public sector workers are organized, whereas the highest level of union penetration in the private sector was 36 percent in 1953. In 1992, less than 12 percent of private sector workers were unionized, a lower figure than was the case in 1929. If these trends continue, even at a slower pace, the strongest argument for affiliation will be the common interests of NEA members and the members of the AFL-CIO.

The IEA also pointed out that the NEA could affiliate without merger; however, the AFL-CIO, which does not want its constituent federations to compete against each other, is not likely to accept the NEA separately. AFL-CIO unions sometimes do compete for the same workers, but it is something to be avoided if at all possible. Separate affiliation would create internal problems for the AFL-CIO; for example, if the NEA supports ethnic quotas and the AFT opposes them, the AFL-CIO could get involved in controversies between the separate unions. With a single organization, the issue would have to be resolved before it reached the AFL-CIO.

The IEA analysis leaves the impression that affiliation is a mixed bag, which probably is the correct view of it from a teacher perspective. If affiliation is a mixed bag, however, merger should not be hostage to it. Granted, some principles are more important than unification in a single teacher organization. For instance, neither union would or should agree to a merger if certain ethnic groups were denied membership in the merged organization. The fact that the merged organization could and would eliminate the discrimination would not be justification for merger with this restriction, even if it were specifically stated to be in effect for only a short time.

It is difficult, however, to see justification for treating affiliation as this kind of an issue. Theoretically, it would be possible to propose disaffiliation immediately after a merged organization with affiliation comes into existence, but there are likely to be time limits before disaffiliation can be raised. It can be argued that it would be foolish to launch a new organization with an unresolved issue that will divide it from the outset, but how long should the moratorium on this issue be?

THE ROLE OF ALBERT SHANKER

The foregoing discussion highlights the role that AFT President Albert Shanker will play in the merger talks. Shanker is a vice-president of the AFL-CIO and a member of the Executive Council, its governing body. The AFL-CIO constitution requires that union representatives on the Executive Council must be one of the "principal officers" of the union. The phrase has never been defined, but in the past, there have only been two exceptions to the tradition of presidents only on the Executive Council. One was Shanker's acceptance as the 1st vice-president of the AFT. This was made possible only because Shanker had the strong support of AFL-CIO President George Meany, who supported Shanker's inclusion over the objections of several members of the Executive Council. One factor underlying the opposition to Shanker was the fear that allowing membership on the Executive Council to officers below the rank of president would or could lead to the ascendancy of rivals to the union presidents. It is interesting that Shanker was elected to the position of 1st vice-president of the AFT, a position specifically created to elevate him over the other AFT presidents and thus to strengthen his accession to the Executive Council (Troy, 1993, Selden, 1985).

Minimally, therefore, Shanker would need the vice presidency of NEA/AFT to retain his seat on the AFL-CIO Executive Council. Unquestionably retention of it would be a sine qua non of any merger agreement. Shanker is vice-president of the AFL-CIO, vice-chairman of its Executive Council, the chairman of the General Board of its Department of Professional Employers, and chairman of its International Affairs Committee.

Shanker's enormous personal and professional stake in his AFL-CIO role is also evidenced by his longtime support of its policies, his avoidance of any public criticisms of them or its leaders, and his continual stroking of AFL-CIO causes and leaders in his weekly advertisement in the *New York Times*. These are only a small part of the evidence that merger is subordinate to affiliation with the AFL-CIO in Shanker's thinking. Furthermore, it would hardly make sense for NEA/AFT to be represented by a new person when it has available someone with real influence on the AFL-CIO Executive Council. Indeed, the pro-merger forces in the NEA can cite Shanker's role in the AFL-CIO to justify offering him the vice presidency of NEA/AFT. In any case, it is unthinkable that Shanker would agree to any arrangement that terminated or weakened his role in the AFL-CIO. To be fair about it, however, the AFT has an organizational claim here that is at least as strong as any NEA claim that the top executive officer of the NEA/AFT come from the ranks of the NEA.

There is a problem with this solution. The existing NEA constitution prohibits its executive officers from holding office for more than two consecutive three-year terms. The top three NEA officers were reelected to a second term in 1993. This means that they will no longer be eligible for reelection in 1996, just about the time the constitution of NEA/AFT may go into effect. NEA officers who are adversely affected by the limits on their reelection may try to eliminate them; officers and candidates for office who benefit from the term limits will contend that these term limits should carry over to the governance policies of the merged organization. In both cases the "principle" invoked will be a rationalization of the interests involved. Ultimately NEA leaders will abandon a principle that was adopted for short range reasons. Imagine a candidate for political office who runs on a platform calling for term limits, and then abandons the platform when the term limits would be applicable to the candidate as an officeholder. This is likely to be the picture in the NEA when the merger agreement is presented to its Representative Assembly for approval.

None of this fully answers the question of Shanker's role in NEA/AFT. Most NEA members feel that because the NEA is the much larger of the two unions, the president of the merged organization should come from the ranks of the NEA. Second, in view of the unclear governance structure of the new organization, it would be difficult for Shanker to organize support within the NEA, even assuming (which we do not) that his immediate objective is the presidency of NEA/AFT. Third, some of the forces within the NEA opposed to merger assert that their opposition is based on their antipathy to Shanker and to his anticipated role in the NEA/AFT. This attitude is probably confined to a small group in the NEA, but an overt power grab by Shanker at the outset would run a significant risk, even though he commands the respect of an influential leadership strata in the NEA. In our opinion, the logic of the situation leads to the conclusion that Shanker will be the sole or 1st vice-president of NEA/AFT in its initial stages, so that he can remain on the AFL-CIO Executive Council and enhance his leadership position in the AFL-CIO. However, the vice-presidency of NEA/AFT will not solve the problem if NEA/AFT retains term limits on its executive officers. Eliminating the term limits for only the vice presidency would be difficult to defend; eliminating them for all the executive offices would upset a host of plans to run for these offices, and for the offices that would become open if their incumbents run for executive office. These interests are likely to clash with the logic of a Shanker presence on the AFL-CIO Executive Council. In any event, the interrelatedness of term limits on NEA/AFT executive offices and representation of the AFL-CIO Executive Council are sure to be important considerations in the merger talks.

CHAPTER EIGHT

MERGER ISSUES

This chapter is devoted to various organizational and governance differences between the NEA and AFT. These differences must be resolved to effectuate a merger. It must be emphasized, however, that the differences to be discussed may be overshadowed by many others as serious merger talks proceed. Obviously, one of the most critical issues will be who gets what job in NEA/AFT, but the resolution of this issue will undoubtedly be deferred until a basic agreement on structure and governance is in sight. After all, it would be foolish to negotiate personnel issues before there was any likelihood that the organizational issues had been resolved, or were near solution. In fact, without prior agreement on the structure and governance issues, the negotiating teams would not know what positions were to be filled, let alone who would fill them.

PROFESSIONALISM AS A MERGER ISSUE

Long before the 1993 NEA convention, many NEA members regarded affiliation with the AFL-CIO as incompatible with professional status. In fact, although most NEA members accept the fact that the NEA is a union, some NEA members still oppose merger on the supposition that the NEA would lose its character as a "professional" organization by merging with the AFT. To understand the relevant issues, we must first clarify the different meanings of "professional" (Lieberman, 1956).

The term "professional" is frequently applied to or denotes expertise, regardless of other considerations. The term is also often applied to individuals who exhibit a strong devotion to clients or consumers. In these contexts, "professional" refers to individual characteristics that are not necessarily related to any particular occupation or organizational structure. Thus one might refer to an editor as a "professional," meaning that the individual resolves editorial and business issues promptly and efficiently.

For most practical purposes, merger is irrelevant to these definitions of "professional." If an individual teacher is highly competent, the term "professional" applies, merger or no merger. Similarly, if a teacher shows a deep concern for pupil welfare, the term would be applicable independently of

112

organizational issues. In practice, however, the concept of dedicated teachers as "true professionals" has occasionally come into disrepute within the teacher unions; in some situations, "professional" is a pejorative term, especially in the AFT. Thus at the 1981 Annual Convention, AFT President Albert Shanker commented that "a professional is the closest thing to a propped up dead body that I know of." Shanker's comment illustrates the union tendency to equate "professionalism" with meek acceptance of administrative edicts, especially on terms and conditions of employment.

Despite Shanker's denigration of "professional," teacher union publications, conferences and policy statements often express a teacher yearning to be considered "professional" in one sense or another. Thus, referring to a brochure entitled *How Collective Bargaining Works,* the AFT Publications catalog states that "special emphasis is placed on the AFT's use of collective bargaining to improve professionalism." Referring to a brochure on the obstacles teachers face, the catalog mentions "commitment to education reform and professionalism for teachers" (*AFT Publications Catalog,* 1992). These sentiments may simply reflect a vague wish to be a prestigious well-paid occupational group. In any event, we shall adopt and follow the definition proposed by economic historian Richard H. Tawney, to wit, "a profession may be defined most simply as a trade which is organized, incompletely, no doubt, but genuinely, for the performance of function" (Tawney, 1920). However, it is essential to recognize that Tawney assumed that protection of clients/consumers was one of the functions of a profession.

According to the foregoing concept of the professions, a wide range of occupations could be "professions." For instance, when most citizens need automobile repairs, they must depend on the recommendations of automobile mechanics. The latter frequently have opportunities to advance their own economic interests by recommending services and parts that the car owner does not really need. The situation is similar to the one in which physicians might prescribe drugs that augment physician income but are not helpful to patients. The practical difference is (or was) that pharmacists, not physicians, sell drugs to patients, thereby lessening physician incentives to prescribe drugs on the basis of economic benefits to the physicians.

The suggested concept of professionalism is more applicable to fee takers than to salaried employees, such as teachers. With salaried employees, the employer/consumer has ample opportunities to evaluate the services and to adopt safeguards against unethical conduct. It should be emphasized, however, that under the proposed definition, there are no pejorative implications to the absence of professional status. Professional status is not related to level of education, autonomy in the workplace, or practitioner skill

113

and knowledge but only to whether the occupational group is organized to protect the consumers of the services. Teachers are highly organized, but the purpose of their organizations is to advance the interests of teachers, not of students, parents, taxpayers, or the public at large. Of course, teachers characterize (and often sincerely believe) that their organizational efforts are devoted to the welfare of students or the public, but all interest groups characterize their efforts this way.

Legally and practically, unions are organizations established to protect and defend the interests of their members, not consumers or clients. Of course, unions sometimes act to protect consumers in ways that do not conflict with their producer role, but this is not a major union activity. On this view of professionalism, affiliation with the AFL-CIO is irrelevant to professional status. It may be relevant to public perceptions of teachers as an occupational group, but it is irrelevant to professional status as we have defined it. According to the suggested concept of "profession," the NEA abandoned the rationale for professional status when it became a union (Lieberman/Hostetler 1980, 1989). Despite its code of ethics, the NEA adheres to the view that it is the employer's (school administration's) responsibility to discipline teachers who are incompetent or act unethically. The teacher unions cannot serve as prosecutor, defense attorney, and judge when teachers are accused of misconduct. The effort to do so makes more sense in the fee-taking professions, where the employment relationship is too intermittent and too limited to enable employers to protect themselves from incompetent or unethical conduct. This is not the case with full-time salaried employees who work for a single employer; the latter should be able to deal with misconduct or incompetence in appropriate ways.

Teachers, like union members generally, join unions and pay dues for protective purposes. If their protector becomes their prosecutor, to whom do teachers accused of misconduct turn for representation? For better or for worse, teacher bargaining has laid to rest the idea of education as a self-governing profession; merger and/or affiliation with the AFL-CIO are irrelevant to this issue. A small minority of teachers in the NEA will oppose merger and affiliation with the AFL-CIO on the grounds that these things are contrary to professionalism; their misplaced beliefs will be countered by the equally misplaced claim that merger and affiliation are the path to "true professional status." Be that as it may, NEA and AFT leaders as well as most union members accord the highest priority to the protective role of unions, and the dynamics of teacher bargaining and union governance would propel them in this direction even if they opposed it.

To be fully effective, a union must avoid competition to perform the work done by union members at a lower rate. For this reason, unions discourage contributed services if the union is seeking or plans to seek compensation for the kind of work involved. This is not to say unionized teachers never do more than what they are contractually required to do. Of course, some do. The point is, however, that the dynamics of unionization and collective bargaining weaken the tendency to perform beyond the legal requirements of the job. To illustrate, suppose that because of budgetary pressures, a school district cannot pay teachers to supervise various extracurricular activities. The teacher who volunteers to supervise the activities without additional compensation is likely to be criticized by other teachers for doing so. In their mind the contributed effort sets a bad example; as the administration ponders what items to cut, it will be more likely to cut the extracurricular budget if it believes that teachers will supervise extracurricular activities for nothing or for a lower stipend. Or let us assume that the union is negotiating for payment to teachers to meet with parents in the evening, or on Saturdays. The teachers will naturally feel that the way to achieve such payment is not to have the service performed without it. Teachers who agree to meet with parents without pay weaken the union's argument in this regard. In short, any time a teacher is willing to contribute his or her services, there is an erosion or potential erosion of union solidarity on getting paid more for doing less work.

As a matter of fact, the tendency of unionization to discourage contributed services applies even to services contributed by parents. To illustrate, consider an actual situation involving a union representing support personnel in a district forced to undergo severe economic retrenchment. Because of financial exigencies, the district was forced to lay off a nonteaching employee who was responsible for financial management of the student bookstore. As a result, the bookstore, which had been a source of revenue for student activities, was forced to shut down.

Upon learning of the situation, a group of parents volunteered to contribute the services that had formerly been provided by the aforesaid district employee. When the bookstore reopened with parent volunteers, however, the union representing the support personnel filed unfair labor practice charges against the district for utilizing the contributed services. The charge was that the district had contracted out unit work without first bargaining on it to impasse with the union. Among the arguments made in its defense, the district pointed out that by the time the bargaining and the impasse procedures were exhausted and the district was free to act unilaterally, it expected to have sufficient funds to rehire the bookstore clerk. The district's argument was to no avail; a hearing officer upheld the union's charges, thereby preventing the district from utilizing contributed help from the parents in operating the bookstore (*California School Employees Association and its South Lake Tahoe Chapter No. 286 v. Lake Tahoe Unified School District,* 1983).

115

The NEA's approach to professional ethics reflects its union orientation to ethical issues. Prior to its becoming a union, the NEA had a code of professional ethics, but it was largely a collection of platitudes (Lieberman, 1956). The items deemed "unethical" included such conduct as breaking one's contract to accept a better job in another district. Not only was the role of the school employer ignored but specific items in the code frequently revealed a management orientation. In the 1960s the NEA tried to draft and enforce a more meaningful code of ethics. This effort could not overcome the basic problems. First, NEA members did not want to accept any serious restrictions on their activities, and second, the practical problems of having the union exercise a role as prosecutor and judge with respect to members who have paid for defensive purposes, were insuperable.

Essentially the code underwent still another metamorphosis in 1975. Actions that weaken union discipline and unity, such as "preventing the practice of the profession by unqualified persons," became a focal point of unethical conduct (*NEA Handbook, 1993-1994*). Essentially, this is where the matter stands; to satisfy the popular view that professionals have a code of ethics, the NEA has one, but the code is little more than a rhetorical gesture to maintain the image of professional status.

GUARANTEES OF MINORITY PARTICIPATION

The resolution on merger talks adopted by the NEA provides that "any organization that is proposed shall guarantee minority group participation in the governance and operation of said organization." In contrast, the AFT's constitution includes no such provision. As a matter of fact, during the time the New York State United Teachers (NYSUT) was affiliated with both the NEA and AFT, it tried to eliminate the minority guarantees from the NEA constitution. Its failure to achieve this objective was instrumental in its withdrawal from the NEA.

Insofar as we know, the NEA has embraced ethnic quotas more extensively than any other major organization in the United States. Some of the relevant provisions in the NEA's constitution and bylaws are as follows:

- All appointive bodies of the Association except the Review Board shall be designated by the term committee. There shall be a minimum of twenty (20) percent ethnic-minority representation on each committee . . .
- If after any period of eleven (11) consecutive membership years a member of an ethnic-minority group has not served as President, the

116

Association shall take steps as may be legally permissible to elect a member of an ethnic-minority group . . .
- Members from ethnic minorities shall comprise at least twenty (20) percent of the Board. The Representative Assembly shall elect additional directors as appropriate to assure such ethnic-minority representation on the Board . . .
- Members from ethnic minorities shall comprise at least twenty (20) percent of the Executive Committee. The Representative Assembly shall elect additional Executive Committee members as appropriate to assure such ethnic-minority representation . . .
- Affiliates of the Association shall take all reasonable and legally permissible steps to achieve on their elective and appointive bodies ethnic-minority representation that is at least proportional to the ethnic-minority membership of the affiliate . . .
- Each affiliate shall apply the one-person-one-vote principle for representation on its government bodies except that the affiliate shall take such steps as are legally permissible to achieve ethnic-minority representation at least proportionate to its ethnic-minority membership . . .
- The Association shall, as vacancies arise, employ at all levels of service at least the same ratio of any ethnic minority as is the ethnic minority to the total population of the United States . . .
- Ethnic minority shall mean those persons designated as ethnic minority by statistics published by the United States Bureau of the Census. This designation shall specifically include Black, Mexican-American (Chicano), other Spanish-speaking groups, Asian-American, and Indian (NEA Constitution, Bylaws 1993).

In contrast, minority participation in AFT affairs is resolved politically, not by constitutional provisions. Even without any governance provisions on the issue, the 40-member AFT Executive Council includes a significant proportion of black members. Many if not all will oppose the guarantees in the NEA governance structure. The minorities in the NEA are more likely to support them or split sharply on the issue. NEA leadership may find itself in a quandary if there is significant minority opposition to eliminating the quotas. In that case, a vote to eliminate them runs the risk of alienating minority support within the NEA.

Note that both the Democratic and Republican parties professed to oppose quotas during the debate over the Civil Rights Act of 1991. The main issue in the debate was whether the proposed legislation would have led to quotas even though it did not explicitly require or authorize them. President Bush and the Republicans in Congress insisted that the legislation was a "quota bill"; the Democrats denied that the legislation would have this

117

effect. Thus the argument was not over the undesirability of quotas but whether the legislation would lead to them.

In the instant case, however, ethnic quotas are clearly mandated by the NEA's constitution and bylaws. As a matter of fact, one can easily visualize a situation in which the NEA convention has to grapple with such questions as "Who is black?" or "Who is a Native American?" Suppose, for example, a candidate with one black grandparent is elected to the NEA presidency. Would the election of such person fulfill the language and intent of the NEA's constitutional provision requiring that "legally permissible" steps be taken "to elect a member of an ethnic-minority group"? The prospect of an organization representing millions of teachers having to debate and resolve such issues seems appalling, but it has not been considered by the NEA or its state and local affiliates.

The NEA's vulnerability on the minority guarantees is rather obvious. Aren't NEA delegates able or willing to evaluate candidates on the basis of qualifications, not ethnicity? Why the concern over ethnic but not religious or other kinds of invidious discrimination? Is the NEA prepared to decide who is black, Hispanic, Asian-American, whatever, if someone challenges a nomination or an election outcome on the basis that individuals of mixed ancestry have not been categorized properly? And so on. The merger problem is not whether to get rid of the minority guarantees; it is how to eliminate them without appearing to be making a major concession to the AFT on what is supposed to be a nonnegotiable NEA position.

Inasmuch as the case for eliminating the guarantees is even stronger now than in the 1970s, it is difficult to see how the AFT can compromise on the issue. Strategically, it has no reason to do so; the NEA will face a media disaster unless it finds a way to eliminate the guarantees.

Aside from legal action, which would be greatly embarrassing to the NEA regardless of the outcome, the parties might simply agree to sunset any existing minority guarantees. The AFT would be foolish to concede more, since the NEA's ethnic quotas are likely to evoke widespread criticism and dismay when they are widely publicized outside the union. Perhaps even more important, AFT President Albert Shanker has expressed strong opposition to the quotas, and he would lose a great deal of external support and prestige by compromising on the issue.

THE SECRET BALLOT ISSUE

In authorizing merger talks, the NEA required that any merged organization that is proposed include "the use of the secret ballot to elect the officers and change the governance documents of said organization." This position differs from the AFT's.

Both the NEA and AFT are subject to the Landrum-Griffin Act, a federal statute that regulates the conduct of unions in the private sector. However, inasmuch as both NEA and AFT have organized some private sector employees, they are subject to the provisions of the Landrum-Griffin Act; most of their state and local affiliates are not.

The Landrum-Griffin election provisions require that national unions follow one of two procedures regarding the election of delegates to union conventions. If delegates to union conventions are elected by secret ballot, voting at the conventions can be by open ballot. If delegates to conventions are not elected by secret ballot, their votes at union conventions must be by secret ballot (U.S. Dept. of Labor, 1990).

Both the NEA and AFT require that delegates to their national convention shall be elected by secret ballot. In addition, Article VI 1(a) of the NEA Constitution provides that "The executive officers and the six (6) members of the Executive Committee shall be nominated and elected at large by the Representative Assembly by majority vote and by secret ballot for each individual office."

There is hardly any mystery why the AFT is opposed to the secret ballot at AFT conventions. After gaining bargaining rights in New York City, the United Federation of Teachers enrolled about one-third of AFT membership. Because it was practically impossible to be elected to AFT office without UFT support, the UFT preferred open voting at AFT conventions. Under open voting, it was impossible for candidates to renege on their commitments or to conceal a vote that displeased the leadership of the UFT. The use of the secret ballot in UFT elections to choose delegates to AFT conventions posed no problem for UFT officers and leaders. They controlled union publications and meetings and could otherwise render it all but impossible for dissident candidates to oust them in secret ballot elections. Thus the open ballot ensured control of the AFT by the UFT, led by Albert Shanker, its president. Although the UFT now constitutes a lower percentage of all AFT members, it is practically impossible to deviate broadly from the positions of Shanker's caucus and be elected to AFT office. This situation led some NEA leaders to fear a similar outcome if the secret ballot for NEA officers at the convention is dropped in the merger agreement. It is difficult to say precisely what impact this could have politically in NEA/ AFT; it is possible that a Shanker led caucus might gain more at the local level than it would lose at the convention level. In a large diverse merged organization, there will be considerable pressure to have a voting procedure that enables influential leaders to monitor any deals they make. In any event, although it meets federal requirements, the NEA position is likely to be dropped in any merger agreement. One reason is that even in the NEA, the use of the secret ballot at the convention is restricted to the election of officers and to constitutional amendments. Furthermore, there is an accountability problem with the secret ballot on convention issues. Imagine trying to hold a member of Congress accountable if his/her vote on constitutional amendments was by secret ballot. Or suppose that the vote for Speaker of the House of Representatives was by secret ballot. Everyone recognizes that elected representatives are not entitled to a secret ballot, if they are to be accountable to their electorate.

Although the secret ballot issue had not been resolved in the merger talks by early 1994, open voting at the convention of the merged organization appears to be the most likely outcome. Undoubtedly, delegates sometimes vote differently, depending on whether the vote is public or secret. Delegates may cut deals that would displease their constituents; this is much more likely to happen under a secret ballot. To be sure, a secret ballot also enables delegates to stand on principle when doing so would be politically risky. On balance, however, the secret ballot is much more likely to be abused than it is to be used to support principled but unpopular positions.

STAFF VS. MEMBERSHIP CONTROL

The NEA and AFT differ in their approaches to membership control. The NEA and its state affiliates have adopted term limits for Association officers. As of early 1994, the NEA limited its executive officers and executive committee to two three-year terms. At the same time, the state associations affiliated with the NEA typically imposed term limits on their elected officers; the latter are usually elected for one or two terms of one or two years and then supposedly return to their regular positions. Some state officers use their term of office to line up an organizational position but the ideal is supposed to be a return to the classroom. To provide continuity, the state associations employ an executive secretary or executive director who is nominally subordinate to the elected officers.

In contrast, the AFT, like most unions, provides for the election of full-time officers who can run for reelection as often as they wish. Albert Shanker has been AFT president since 1974, and many members of the AFT Executive Council have held that office for a decade or more.

The widespread belief in the NEA is that its structure maximizes membership control over staff, whereas the AFT structure supposedly weakens it. This belief was evident in the opposition to the merger talks at the 1993 convention. Although widely held, there is little evidence to support the belief, and there is a great deal of evidence to contradict it. In the past at least, the executive secretaries in the NEA structure have been every bit as dominant and as long lasting as union officers who are reelected for several terms of office.

In recent years, the executive secretaries have lost some of their power in the state associations. One reason is the erosion of term limits on the elected officers. Obviously, the longer elected officers can remain in office, the less influence is exercised by staff members.

Suppose a teacher is elected president of a state association for a one-year term. In many cases, the teacher does not even move to the state capital where the state association is located. The failure to be present on a daily basis obviously weakens the teacher/president's day to day control. If the teacher moves to the association headquarters, the teacher must also move back, a time-consuming process in a one or two year span. The teacher is usually inundated with a host of ceremonial duties, and his or her executive assistants, if any, owe their primary allegiance to the executive secretary, who will be present long after the teacher/president has left the scene.

It is practically impossible for such rotating presidents to conduct a sustained effort to achieve a policy objective; each president adopts a new theme on taking office or running for office, and the previous one is shunted aside, just as the incumbents will be in the future. Understandably, officers elected this way become heavily dependent on the staff they are supposed to direct and control.

This is not so true of the national NEA as it was when NEA officers were elected annually for one year terms. From 1976 to 1983, NEA presidents were limited to two two-year terms and from 1984 to 1990, to three two-year terms, and since 1991, to two three-year terms. With the increasing longevity of the elected officers, the position of Executive Secretary, now Executive Director, has receded in importance although it is still a very important one. By and large, the state associations affiliated with the NEA have also been moving to longer and more frequent terms of office for elected leaders.

In or out of education, there is no evidence that the NEA structure results in greater membership control. After all, when the elected officials come through a revolving door, it is virtually impossible for them to develop a sustained effort to achieve any substantive objective. The media and politicians prefer to deal with the executive secretaries, who are here today and will be here tomorrow. At the same time, the elective offices tend to be honorific positions handed out more to reward or honor activists than to move the association's program forward.

This is not to say that there is much membership control under either structure. Under both structures the idea of membership control is hazy to begin with. What are the criteria by which one measures it? What data demonstrates the superiority of the revolving officer structure? In practice, the issue is debated in vague generalities from which partisans on both sides draw whatever conclusions they wish. It is hardly open to dispute, however, that in most organizations with annual or biannual term limits, the executive secretaries and association staff tend to dominate or overshadow the elected officers.

THE STATUS OF SUPPORT PERSONNEL

According to an AFT brochure published in January 1993:

> For years, NEA prided itself as an elite professional association and deliberately excluded non-teaching school employees from its membership. Anyone who wasn't a classroom teacher or a school administrator was considered a "non-professional" and unworthy of membership. Faced with a declining teacher membership in the 1970s, due to layoffs and the growth of the AFT, the NEA finally began to accept some categories of school employees as limited members.
>
> NEA has a long history of disrespect and discrimination against its school employee members. NEA treated its school employee members as second-class citizens by not allowing them the right to vote in NEA elections or on NEA policy, or to hold NEA office *until* 1980. (NEA teachers, administrators, student members and *even* retired members had long enjoyed these basic union rights.) (AFT, 1993).

The AFT brochure then goes on to assert that the Federation has always offered support personnel full membership rights but that the NEA did so only under legal duress. The brochure alleges that as of September 1989:

1. State associations (Georgia, North Carolina, South Dakota, Tennessee) took dues from support personnel but did not allow them to vote or hold union office.
2. State associations in Alabama, Indiana, Iowa, Rhode Island, West Virginia sell services to organizations of support personnel in order to avoid having support personnel participate in the affairs of the teacher union.
3. State associations in California, Nevada, Nebraska, provide publications but no bargaining, legal, or insurance services for support personnel.
4. State associations in Minnesota and Utah do not allow membership to support personnel (AFT, 1989).

122

Inasmuch as the AFT brochure refers to conditions existing in 1989, the conditions referred to probably have been changed in at least some states. Otherwise, the AFT would not have referred to them in the past tense. Even so, the policies of the NEA and AFT are not fully consistent with respect to organizing support personnel. It is very doubtful that the AFT would accept a state option that might weaken the rights of its 100,000 or more school related personnel. Such an option in the merger agreement would risk defections by support personnel to other unions or to the independent associations of support personnel.

The history of the relationships between teachers and support personnel sheds some light on the organizational differences. The large cities organized by the AFT tended to have heavier concentrations of paraprofessionals. Indeed, in the late 1960s and early 1970s, the AFT and AFSCME were competing for bargaining rights for paraprofessionals in New York City. The United Federation of Teachers offered AFSCME jurisdiction over school related personnel outside the classroom while the AFT would organize the educational workers inside of them. Most of the paraprofessionals in the New York City schools were blacks. Anticipating black resentment against the UFT over its strike against the dismissal of white teachers and administrators by predominantly black community boards of education, AFSCME rejected the offer but the UFT won the representation election. Within the UFT, there was some resentment against the inclusion of the paraprofessionals in the UFT but Shanker's views on the issue prevailed.

At that time, most NEA affiliates showed little interest in organizing school related personnel. Consequently, the AFT established a large beachhead on this front. Over time, state and local affiliates of the NEA came to accept, or at least to tolerate, the inclusion of school related personnel in their organizations.

It is likely that merger will provide for little or no restriction on the inclusion of school related personnel; we expect a vigorous effort by NEA/AFT to organize them in every state where such workers are not already in the NEA or AFT. The upshot will be a vast industrial union, that is, a union that includes all the skills and crafts within a single school district. There may be some holdouts in the NEA, but it is difficult to see how they can prevail. The AFT cannot accept less than it now provides support personnel; to do so would risk their defection to a different union or association of support personnel. AFT rhetoric criticizes the alleged second class citizenship of support employees in the NEA and charges that the NEA continues to organize such personnel only because of declines in teacher members and dues revenues. Perhaps, but AFT leaders are also aware of the potential revenues and political influence provided by the inclusion of school related personnel.

123

THE NEA'S TAX EXEMPTION

The NEA is one of a small group of nonprofit organizations, such as the American Legion and the American Red Cross, that are chartered by Congress. The NEA's charter exempts its property in the District of Columbia from federal taxation provided that the exemption "not apply to any property which . . . shall not be applied to the educational purpose of the corporation."

Unquestionably, the 1907 Congress would not have exempted the 1993 NEA's property from federal taxation. The NEA that was chartered by Congress in 1907 was an organization devoted to disseminating information about education; as the AFT has pointed out, the NEA's union role and lobbying activities violate both the spirit and intent of the purposes under which the tax exemption was granted. In 1978, the Internal Revenue Service reclassified the NEA from a "professional association" to a labor union; and in 1979, a federal court held that the NEA was a labor union subject to the Landrum-Griffin Act. Nevertheless, when the AFT subsequently questioned the continuation of the NEA's tax exempt status, the Director of Finance for the District of Columbia astonishingly asserted that "the activities of the organization and the use made of the property is consistent with the purposes and objects provided in their Articles of Incorporation."

What is especially interesting here is that under President Albert Shanker, the AFT sought to remove the exemption but in a way that did not leave AFT's fingerprints on the action. Indeed, on this issue, the AFT was willing to work with "right wing" forces that both the NEA and AFT normally condemn for their alleged hostility to public education and to teacher unions.

Will the AFT merger team now try to persuade the NEA to forego its tax exemption? In view of the probability that the AFT will benefit from the exemption, this is not very likely. Clearly the NEA has protected its exemption from District of Columbia taxes; although District of Columbia officials take a benign view of the issue, District taxpayers may see it differently. Ironically, both unions have expressed opposition to tax exemptions that adversely affect school revenues, as is certainly the case regarding the NEA's exemption.

The tax exemption is not the most important merger issue, but it illustrates how little the public or the rank and file members of the NEA and AFT understand what is at stake in the merger talks. The question of who has the authority to remove the tax exemption is a complex one. As the AFT recognized, it would not be necessary to change or revoke the NEA's Charter to eliminate the exemption. Probably, it would only be necessary to have the appropriate District of Columbia officials rule that the NEA

124

was not in conformity with the conditions under which the exemption was granted. Legally, Congress could change or revoke the charter, but in view of NEA's influence in Congress, Congressional action to eliminate the exemption is extremely improbable. The NEA undoubtedly has considerable influence among the District of Columbia officials as well as among Congress, but at least the District would benefit from eliminating the exemption.

MERGER AND ORGANIZATIONAL DIFFERENCES: CONCLUDING OBSERVATIONS

As emphasized at the outset, the organizational issues that have surfaced will not necessarily be the most difficult to resolve. Furthermore, many agreements might be unacceptable in isolation but acceptable as part of a comprehensive package. As of early 1994, the NEA and AFT teams holding the merger talks seemed to be making good progress, but very little about the specifics has been made available for rank and file or media consumption. The NEA's Representative Assembly placed so much emphasis on being informed about the progress of the merger talks that it may be difficult, especially for the NEA team, to continue in this mode before the talks have concluded. Until that time, however, the resolution of specific differences must take into account the possibility that any agreements may be modified by others not yet reached or announced. Similarly, any conclusions about the merger should be based on an analysis of the entire merger agreement. We surmise that, as in most situations of this nature, the career interests of leading parties to the merger will play a significant role in its provisions, but the specifics may not be known for years to come, if they become known at all.

CHAPTER NINE

THE NEA/AFT MERGER:
UNIONISM'S NEW CENTER OF GRAVITY

The merger of the National Education Association and the American Federation of Teachers–AFL-CIO, would be the capstone of the shift from a predominantly private to a predominantly public sector union movement. Public employee unionism has moved from back to center stage in union affairs, as the balance of power within the union movement has shifted steadily from the private to the public sector unions. Because of its magnitude and because professional employees are involved, the NEA/AFT merger would be a climactic step in this historic transformation. The NEA is already the largest union in North America, and perhaps the world. The merged teacher union would surge to a membership never before attained by a union anywhere. It would be the Goliath of labor. On an average annual full-time dues-paying basis, its combined membership would range from about 2.5 to 2.7 million members in the short run, and perhaps an additional million or more in five to ten years.

The NEA/AFT's massive size alone would command attention. But when coupled with the policies it is certain to support, the merger becomes even more important for organized labor and for the American economy and society. The new center of gravity in the labor movement will further reorient what unions do and why. For one thing, it will highlight the transformation of unionism in the United States that began three decades ago.

From the establishment of the American Federation of Labor in 1886 to the 1960s, the union movement had been composed primarily of private sector workers. Most organized labor in the public sector was in federal employment and consisted primarily of postal employees. What we know today as the NEA was founded by school superintendents in 1857, nearly three decades before the founding of the AFL. Initially known as the National Teachers Association (NTA), it eventually changed its name to the National Education Association of the United States in 1907. Early on, the NEA shared one basic interest with organized labor. The latter tried for many years to avoid competition from firms that employed child labor. Eventually, the labor unions successfully lobbied Congress into enacting legislation that prohibited interstate commerce in goods made with child labor; shortly thereafter, however, the legislation was declared unconstitutional by the U.S. Supreme Court. Forced to find another way to prohibit child labor, the labor movement found it in the compulsory education statutes. On this issue of crucial importance to both groups, the interests of the labor movement and the public school establishment were mutually supportive. However, on other issues the NEA often adopted a different and often hostile attitude toward unionism.

Despite its initial opposition to collective bargaining, the NEA eventually embraced it wholeheartedly in the late 1960s and thereafter. Since that time, the union movement has been moving dramatically to a public sector orientation. In the early 1950s public sector unions comprised a mere 6 percent of total union membership; by 1994, labor organizations of government employees constituted more than 40 percent of total union membership. The NEA/AFT will be at the head of this transformed union movement.

In labor history, this transformation ranks in importance with the emergence of the Congress of Industrial Organizations (CIO) in the 1930s, and the founding of the American Federation of Labor (AFL) in 1886. Each marks a watershed in the development of the union movement. Although the AFL founded what is now the AFL-CIO, the establishment of the CIO marked the unionization of large-scale manufacturing and led to a fundamental change in private sector unionism. Prior to its merger with the AFL, the CIO had been dominated by the United Auto Workers (UAW), and the United Steelworkers (USW), and for most of its organizational life, the leaders of the CIO came from these two unions.

Until the rise of the CIO, most unionized private sector workers were blue collar, skilled workers in nonmanufacturing industries. The CIO changed that balance, but the private sector union movement remained essentially a blue collar movement. Unlike previous upsurges in labor organization, the emergence of public sector unionism changed the occupational and the industrial character of organized labor as never before.

The public sector unions brought large numbers of white collar workers into the labor movement for the first time. In contrast, neither the AFL nor the CIO separately, nor as a merged federation, had been able to organize the white collar occupations in the private economy. And to this day, they remain outside the union fold. The same pattern—extensive unionism among public white collar employees and nonunionism among private white collar employees—characterizes all other major industrial economies, albeit the percentage of private white collar workers unionized abroad is somewhat higher than in the United States.

Except for Canada among industrial countries, the United States has lagged in the unionization of government employees. In recent years, however, Canadian and public sector unions, aided and abetted by public policy far more pro-union than in the United States, have surpassed the U.S. lead in the unionization of government employees. As the U.S. and Canadian economies grow closer, the higher union penetration in Canada has attracted the attention of U.S. policy makers. Several have suggested that the Canadian experience should be a model for U.S. industrial relations. U.S. trends are already headed where the Canadians have already gone, so the Canadian model appeals to the conventional pro-union outlook. Indeed, since the Supreme Court's 1985 decision in *Garcia*, Congress has had the constitutional authority to enact labor law covering state and local employees (*Garcia v. San Antonio Metropolitan Transit Authority, et. al.*, 1985). If that were to happen, the public sector union movement would expand, and NEA/AFT would become increasingly important.

At the beginning of the 20th century, public sector labor organizations comprised fewer than 2 percent of all organized groups of employees; early in the 21st century however, public sector unionism, even in the absence of Congressional legislation governing state and local labor relations, will be dominant in labor membership. Abroad, labor movements in Canada, Britain (the ancestral home of unionism), France, and Italy are already composed primarily of public employees. If the 20th century was the century of private sector unionism, the 21st will be the century of public sector unionism in the United States and in the Atlantic community nations generally.

ORIGINS OF PUBLIC SECTOR UNIONISM

Despite the historic rivalry between the NEA and AFT, they share some common as well as dissimilar roots. Even their intense competition over representation rights, especially in the 1960s, was driven by the same factors. Prior to the onset of full-scale public unionism, numerous professional and civil service associations represented public employees before legislative and executive bodies. We refer to organizations that could not negotiate and strike as "proto-unions." Indeed, it was the presence of these associations like the NEA, and proto-unions like the AFT, which enabled public sector labor organization to emerge in the 1960s on a large scale and with so little of the social conflict which characterized the formative years of private sector unionism. Many proto-unions were affiliates of the AFL or CIO, either before or after their merger in 1955. In general, their labor market behavior resembled that of the professional associations like the NEA and the public employee associations prior to the 1960s.

In his classic study of public sector unions, Spero noted the distinction between proto-unions and private sector unions:

Organized labor itself has not always fully accepted the public worker. To a large extent the feeling on both sides is the result of the restrictions which government as an employer places upon the freedom of its employees to engage in political activity and strike. These restrictions mean that public employees are able to go along with fellow workers in industry only up to a certain point . . . Time and again government employee unions have had to abstain from voting on political actions in which all other unions took part (Spero, 1972).

Likewise, when it came to collective bargaining, Spero commented that "although unions in private industry have always regarded collective bargaining as the life blood of a free labor movement, unions in the public service have only recently [circa 1948] begun to show interest in the process" (Spero, 1972). While a few public sector labor organizations had taken some steps toward becoming unions during the years between the end of World War II and the 1960s, they were still far from full-scale unionism (Spero, 1972, Krislov, 1962).

Professional associations like the NEA and proto-unions like the AFT opposed strikes and overt collective bargaining. At one time, the AFT even opposed teacher strikes as a matter of policy. Local teacher organizations occasionally went on strike, but the number was small and the duration brief. For example, in 1946, a record high strike year in the private sector because of the post-war readjustments to inflation, .0034 percent of municipal work time was lost compared to 1.5 percent in the private sector (Spero, 1972). Ziskind's count of over one thousand strikes in public employment, from the end of the 19th century into the New Deal years, included 30 percent which lasted a day or less, suggesting that they should have been classified as protests, not strikes (Ziskind, 1940). In addition to the proto-unions' disapproval of the strike, public opinion at the time as well as public policy and the leadership of the nation also opposed strikes by public workers. Franklin D. Roosevelt, the president most supportive of unionism, opposed strikes by public employees and even opposed their right to organize into unions. When the National Labor Relations Act was enacted in 1935, federal employees (who could have been included) were excluded from its jurisdiction. By all the major indicators, the pre-1960s organizations of public employees were much less union oriented than the contemporary organizations that carry the same name.

The most dramatic examples of their transformation to union status were the National Education Association, and the American Federation of Teachers:

The dramatic shift in image from the milquetoast-like teacher to the militant unionist which has accompanied the adoption of collective bargaining procedures by teachers at all levels of instruction is one of the well-publicized developments in public-sector labor relations (Stern, 1988).

In the 1960s the NEA was forced to choose between unionization and diminution if not extinction. After intense internal conflict, it chose unionization. In the process, the NEA and the AFT became indistinguishable from each other (Stern, 1988), a factor which facilitates their merger. In this connection, the fact that the teacher unions are predominantly female should not be construed as an indication of unwillingness to be militant. The record of teacher strikes and job actions indicates otherwise.

For the NEA the transformation was simplified because it had the appropriate organizational profile for conversion to unionism. As Krislov concluded from his study of associations, independent associations had organized a significant number of employees, their structure and governance were similar to unions, and they engaged in membership recruitment and lobbying just as unions always have (Krislov, 1962). For proto-unions like the AFT, the conversion was even easier. The AFT was originally cast in the mold of conventional private sector unions. The Federation, an affiliate of the AFL since its founding in 1916, historically regarded itself both as a union and a professional association, and only renounced the right to strike briefly in the 1950s (Lieberman and Moskow, 1966).

The evolution of the contemporary public sector union movement was a unique development in union history. Its most distinguishing feature was the organization of the organized. In contrast, the history of private unionism is devoted to the organization of the unorganized. Moreover, the rise and spread of public sector unionism far outpaced the development of either the AFL or the CIO or any of their principal affiliates.

The absence of strong opposition to public sector unions has given them an optimistic outlook for the future. Insofar as that outlook is based on a growing labor market largely protected from competitive forces, it is justified. Public sector unionism's viability contrasts sharply with the vulnerability of private sector unionism. Manufacturing and private sector unionism as a whole are vulnerable to market forces and economic changes. Private sector unionism peaked as a percentage of employment in 1953 (at 36 percent), coincident with the birth of the service dominated labor market. Pounded by other market forces as well, private sector unionism is declining to 10 percent of the private sector working population, a figure below its 1929 market share. Its membership peaked at 17 million in 1970 and is now less than 10 million.

In sharp contrast, public sector unionism currently stands at or near record highs in both membership and market share. Indeed, public sector unions enroll more members (now approaching 7 million) than the CIO ever did, and their 40 percent share of the public labor market is higher than was ever reached by private sector unions. Moreover, public sector unions have expanded throughout all levels of government. Because of the teacher unions and the postal service organizations, public sector unions are spread more broadly across the country than private sector unions ever were.

Except for the railways, unionism among teachers is far more widespread than it is among any group of private sector employees; in government, teacher unions lag only behind the postal service (which is about 95 percent unionized), and fire fighters. The most recent census of governments (1987) reports that 61 percent of public school instructional staff employed full time were organized. Significantly, 88 percent of all township teaching staff, a small size unit, were organized. This is a remarkable contrast to the low union penetration rate among small size private employers. Among school districts, 59 percent of the teachers were organized (Bureau of Census, 1987). The high union penetration in railroad employment (around 85 to 90 percent) underscores the critical impact of government regulation on union organization over a long period of time. Like the high level of organization in the postal service, the level of organization in the railroad industry also suggests where the rest of the public sector may be headed, with the NEA/AFT leading the way.

Further gains in public sector unionization are likely because of future gains in public employment. Between 1980 and 1989, public employment in 40 of the 50 states rose more than population. The average density of public employment for all states showed state employment up 19 percent compared to a population increase of just nine percent during the 1980s. This pattern is likely to continue despite political rhetoric and promises of belt-tightening.

What accounts for the dramatic change in public sector organization between 1900 and 2000 and the likelihood of its future growth? How could public sector unions account for less than two percent of total U.S. union membership in 1900 but enroll more than 40 percent in 1993, well on the way to dominating organized labor by the next century? Public sector unionism's durability and ascending growth curve are the result of its virtual immunity from competition and government policy, which enhances its monopoly power. Its low unemployment rate is an indicator of its immunity against competition. U.S. Department of Labor statistics show that the unemployment rate of government workers is in the 2 percent range (*Employment and Earnings*, 1991), while unemployment rates in the private sector more than tripled that rate.

Naturally, the stability of public sector employment increases the relative stability of public compared to private sector unionism in membership, market share, and organizational structure. Few if any public sector unions have folded, whereas large numbers of private sector unions have disappeared over the past 30 years. These facts augur well for the future durability of public sector unionism and reinforce the expectation that it will dominate the labor movement in the next century. Even in the face of real or threatened budget cutbacks, public employment and public sector unions have increased. At most, budget cutbacks translate into a slowdown of the rate of public expenditures, not an absolute reduction; meanwhile, layoffs typically culminate in no reductions of total public employment.

The NEA/AFT's general invulnerability to competitive forces indicates that the teacher unions will not have to face the problems that have led to the decline of private sector unionism. Because of these problems, Richard Lester postulated in 1958 that the growth curve of private sector unions would level off or drift downward (Lester, 1958). In fact, private unions did peak in 1970 and have declined precipitously since, perhaps more than Lester anticipated, but he was surely on the right track.

While public policy also fortifies the monopoly power of the private sector unions, competitive markets have relentlessly undermined that power. Because the public domain is virtually immune to competition, public policy reinforces the monopoly power of public sector unions.

A MERGER UNIQUE IN LABOR HISTORY

The merged NEA/AFT will be based upon its immunity from competitive market forces and upon previous mergers. Once the professional and public employee associations became unions, mergers (and acquisitions) inevitably followed. The history of labor organization in the private labor market, like that of business enterprise, has been characterized by mergers, but also by dissolutions and disappearances.

Like the life cycle of the industries in which they are established, nearly all private sector unions are in a state of permanent decline. And this has led to numerous mergers, as it became fiscally and organizationally impractical to continue as a free-standing union. Individual unions associated with industries whose life cycle has come and gone share the fate of those industries; this is illustrated by an abbreviated roll call of unions associated with private sector industries that have dwindled or disappeared entirely: Elastic Goring Workers, Carriage Workers, Chandelier Workers, Straw and Ladies Hat Workers, Stogie Makers, Steel Plate Transferrers, Tip Printers, Glass Flatteners, Sheep Shearers, Mule Spinners, Cigar Makers, Broom and Whisk Makers, Tube Workers, Tack Makers, Sawsmiths, Gold Beaters, and Pocket Knife Grinders. Comparable developments in the public labor market are unlikely.

Major contemporary unions, like the United Auto Workers and United Steel Workers, are undergoing a long-term decline, albeit not elimination. Today these once powerful unions are less than one-half their peak size and are still shrinking as their associated industries contract. It would not be surprising to see these two unions merge with others, perhaps with each other before the end of the 1990s. In any case, union mergers in the private sector are typically the product of weakness and decline.

The record of union mergers in the public sector is different. Although there have been mergers and acquisitions for defensive reasons (to avoid raids), or reorganizations stimulated by managerial reorganizations, such as in the postal service, they have not emerged because the membership faced extinction, as in the private labor market. In this light, the NEA/AFT merger will be unique in the annals of unionism—a merger of two unions when both are at their peak in numbers, power and revenues. Theirs is a merger from strength, not weakness, and the merger will further augment their monopoly power.

To be sure, the AFT undertook some program cuts and was forced to raise its dues in 1992 and 1993, but these developments do not appear to reflect any major deterioration in the AFT's basic constituency. Unlike the NEA, AFT leadership is actively seeking union growth outside the field of education, but the moving force seems to be organizing opportunity, not internal decline. The possibility of internal financial difficulties cannot be ruled out as a factor underlying AFT interest in merger, but as we have seen, its interest in merger long antedated any existing financial problems of the AFT.

At the present time, the NEA and the AFT enroll about four of every ten public sector union members. A merger will strengthen the NEA/AFT leadership position in both the public sector and eventually in the labor movement as a whole. The concentration of membership in the new organization will also facilitate the mobilization of its political and economic powers.

If defense is not the game in an NEA/AFT merger, its strategy and its repercussions must be both precautionary and offensive. In economic terms, the NEA/AFT will seek to tighten its grip on the educational labor market. Public education is now under serious challenge from various modes of privatization. Although only in its earliest phase, the demand for a competitive educational system has picked up enough momentum to force the teacher unions to act in a precautionary manner. Their offensive strategy is, of course, to fend off competitive alternatives by political pressure, and when necessary at the ballot box (Lieberman, 1993).

Eventually, health care unions will follow in the wake of the NEA/ AFT. If the Clinton Administration succeeds in expanding the government's role in health care, another powerful branch of public sector unionism will emerge. However, none of the unions involved, irrespective of merger activity, will rival the new NEA/AFT in monopoly and political power.

IMPLICATIONS OF AN NEA/AFT MERGER
FOR THE AFL-CIO

The merger of the NEA and the AFT will have significant implications for the future of the AFL-CIO. The NEA is not now an affiliate of the AFL-CIO, but the merged organization is likely to become fully affiliated over time. Because of its size, NEA/AFT will realign the AFL-CIO power structure. The balance of power within the Federation will shift toward the public sector unions. Affiliation will be followed by a significant change in the role and importance of the Public Employees Department (PED), in the AFL-CIO. The department, established initially to represent the interests of organized public employees, has had a lackluster record. Theoretically, the PED's organizational status is the same as the Building and Construction Trades and the Industrial Union Departments. The Building Trades Department reflects the occupational basis of the original American Federation of Labor and the Industrial Union Department the industrial base of the Congress of Industrial Organizations. Together, they make up the private sector components of the AFL-CIO.

Up to this time, however, the PED has not enjoyed a power position comparable to either the Building and Construction Trades, or the Industrial Union Department of the Federation; moreover, the PED has had little impact on public policy and on public awareness. Under a more activist leadership, and with more public sector members, however, the balance of power within the AFL-CIO would swing toward public sector unionism. Significantly, the PED would outnumber the other two departments, and probably become the stepping stone to the leadership of the AFL-CIO. Early in the 21st century the Federation's leadership will pass from private to public sector union leaders, and most likely to the leaders of the NEA/AFT.

Doubtless there will be challenges to the NEA/AFT's leadership of the Federation. There will also be various controversies into which the new union will be drawn; the most important of these will be jurisdictional disputes. Many private sector unions in the AFL-CIO have reacted to their declining numbers by organizing public sector workers, and have tried to incorporate the independent employee associations still representing public employees. These efforts conflict with the established jurisdictional claims of affiliated public employee unions. Although none appear to involve professional teachers or instructional paraprofessionals, other non-instructional staff could be potential organizing targets among several unions within the AFL-CIO. Because they are already making strenuous efforts to organize educational support personnel, NEA/AFT will necessarily be involved in the resolution of such disputes. So long as there is no serious jurisdictional competition over the unorganized public employee, the relationship of public and private union movements in the Federation can be complementary, and will prevent any rupture arising from their jurisdictional differences. We believe however, that the existing jurisdictional free for all, in which several national unions seek to organize support personnel, is not likely to continue indefinitely.

In appearance, the AFL-CIO appears to be a unitary movement. In reality, it is not. The fact that private and public unions are affiliated with the same parent organization does not imply that there are no basic differences between private and public sector unions, or deny the existence of two labor movements with different philosophies. While administratively (and in other respects) a single body, the AFL-CIO today is actually a house divided between private and public unions. However, we do not expect the AFL-CIO to split into two federations, paralleling the split in the AFL and the rise of the CIO in 1937. The cost of such a split in the face of the weakening position of private sector unions and the value of the AFL-CIO label for the public sector unions point to a continuation of the existing structure that combines private and public sector unions. Moreover, the AFL-CIO has shown adaptability at various times in its history. The Federation continues to be dominated by private sector unions, but has already adjusted to the presence of a large body of public employee unions. This adjustment will facilitate any future change in leadership coming from the public sector. Such a change has already occurred in the British union movement, the oldest in the world. As in the United States, most unions in Great Britain, whether public or private, are affiliated with the same umbrella federation, the Trades Union Congress (TUC); the TUC is now dominated by membership from the public sector. Nevertheless, the affiliation of the NEA/AFT with the AFL-CIO will reveal the clash of private and public sector philosophies and policies. Conceivably, the clash could lead to the establishment of a separate federation of public employees, just as the quarrel over jurisdiction (and personal power) led to the withdrawal of unions from the AFL and the formation of the CIO during the 1930s. Certainly, the differences between private and public sector unions are sufficient and at least as important as those which led to the split within the AFL and the rise of the CIO. While the logic is there for two separate federations, the probabilities are negligible, because the union movement as a whole has been on the defensive and because of the negative outcomes of inter-union conflicts in the 1930s; a united front is a historical imperative for organized labor. Furthermore, it is important to remember that the CIO was founded in a period of rising expectations and growth for organized labor in the private labor market. This condition no longer prevails, and the growing weakness of private sector unions will inhibit their leaving the umbrella organization.

SOCIAL UNIONISM: THE NEW LABOR PHILOSOPHY

The NEA/AFT is likely to spearhead social unionism, the philosophy of the public sector union movement. Philosophically, the goal of social unionism is to redistribute an increasing share of the national income from the private to the public economy—a substitution of public for individual choice in consumption. Total government spending as a share of the national income has grown steadily since the New Deal. Today it accounts for nearly 45 percent of the national income. (National income is a more relevant measure than gross domestic or gross national product for comparative purposes because it comprises the income which the factors of production receive.) We define this development as the "socialization of income."

In contrast, the proximate goal of private sector unionism is to redistribute income from employers or consumers to organized workers. While this philosophy, historically identified as "more," is also followed by public employee unions, their pursuit of "more" *requires* the redistribution of income from the private to the public economy.

Since education is one of the largest non-defense, social expenditures of government, the NEA/AFT is understandably in the forefront of the movement to redistribute income. At the same time, a fundamental change in the structure of labor markets underscores the basic change in union philosophy; government employment now exceeds employment in manufacturing, the basic private goods industry of the economy.

The line dividing the philosophies of the private and public union movements is the mechanism for allocating resources within the economy: Private sector unions depend *primarily on markets for allocating resources*. Although private sector unions advocate government intervention in markets in several areas, the interventions are generally different from the basic approach of public sector unionism. Private sector unions promote an industrial policy (and therefore opposition to the North American Free Trade Agreement or NAFTA), more regulation of labor markets including what

136

is euphemistically termed "labor law reform," and Keynesian spending policies. In contrast public sector unionism's philosophy relies *primarily on government to allocate resources and replace market with social decisionmaking.* While it also opposes NAFTA, it has no economic stake in its opposition, which is based upon labor solidarity.

The two philosophies conflict in many policy areas, such as tax rebates on the middle class, but they are united in their advocacy of more government intervention. For that reason, and for reasons of labor solidarity, the two philosophies co-exist in the AFL-CIO, and will probably continue to co-exist under an NEA/AFT merger.

Significantly, social unionism is not the result of theorists. It is the product of experience, not of ideologues. However, the NEA/AFT will be social unionism's revolutionary vanguard. The teacher unions will provide a great deal of the intellectual leadership for social unionism, because implementation, as distinguished from conception, requires supporters whose stock in trade are ideas. Politically, the ideological bent of public sector unionism has become increasingly more radical. This surfaces in increased efforts to reduce the authority of local governments (school boards) in shaping educational methods and goals. As evidenced by the all-out effort to defeat Proposition 174 in California, the new Goliath in public education will resist even more fiercely the establishment of competitive private sector education. Indeed, since educational spending is the major outlay of local governments, the birth of a new monopoly in educational services will heighten the overall conflict between advocates of more government versus individual choice in our society.

POLICY AND POLITICAL CONSEQUENCES OF SOCIAL UNIONISM

While the overall goal of social unionism is increased government intervention in the economy and the redistribution of national income from the private to the public economy, it also has specific objectives and a political agenda as well. Social unionism is the driving force behind the NEA's commitment to a quota system based on race in staffing its organization. In fact, this is an issue in the merger talks. As noted in Chapter 8, the NEA already is committed to a racially based quota system in the staffing and governance of the Association. Indeed, Myron Lieberman has observed that, "insofar . . . as I know, the NEA has embraced racial quotas more extensively than any other major organization in the United States" (Lieberman, 1993). Unquestionably racial quotas are opposed by AFT leadership, and probably most of its membership as well.

137

Any application of the NEA's quota systems to the staffing of public education would constitute a major challenge to an open society. At a time when public education is under attack for failing to deliver quality education, social policies which rely on quotas are likely to further undermine public confidence in education.

Although the leadership of private sector unions has steadfastly endorsed Democrats for the presidency (indeed, were responsible for Mondale's nomination in 1984), the voting profiles of private and public union members differ. The majority of the private sector union members supported Reagan in 1984, but the overwhelming majority of public sector members voted for Mondale. Combined, approximately 55 percent of union households supported Mondale. As previously noted, NEA and AFT members accounted for 10 percent of the delegates at the 1992 Democratic Convention who nominated Bill Clinton for the presidency.

One of social unionism's most serious political and fiscal consequences is its tendency to skew public priorities in favor of the services provided by strong public sector unions. In fact, the increasing incidence of local governmental deficits and bankruptcies result in large part from public sector bargaining; the rising incidence of municipal insolvencies is a telling indicator of union encroachment on the fiscal stability and the sovereignty of local government (Spiotto, 1991). Currently, the power of the public sector unions to influence the size and distribution of public revenues lies at the heart of the sovereignty issue. While union power to maximize the demand for their services has been recognized, its power to weaken sovereignty with its consequences for deficits and bankruptcies has not.

Government is a labor intensive industry, so personnel costs are a major fraction of its total costs. These costs range from 60 to 75 percent of municipal budgets (Spiotto, 1991). Public sector unions have pushed up wages and fringe benefits, probably far more than statisticians have reported (Freeman, 1986). Wages in the public sector are less subject to competitive forces, and capital-for-labor substitution is more difficult than in the private sector. These factors make it difficult for local governments to limit wage increases and have contributed to their precarious fiscal status, even their insolvency in some situations.

New York City's *de facto* bankruptcy illustrates how social unionism can weaken the sovereignty of local governments. The City of New York went bankrupt in 1975 when it was unable to market its debt. Municipal officials decided that legal bankruptcy had to be avoided because under the bankruptcy laws, a proposed plan of adjustment had to show that 51 percent of the debt had been accepted by creditors. Since it was manifestly very difficult, if not impossible, to gain acceptance of a reorganization plan because of the dispersion of the debt among 160,000 creditors, an alternative to the Bankruptcy Court had to be devised (Spiotto, 1991). In addition to the administrative problems, the avoidance of bankruptcy was also a high political priority since the political costs of municipal bankruptcy would have been disastrous.

The municipal unions, including the United Federation of Teachers, were among the major contributors to the city's fiscal debacle. Although there is little if any dispute about this, two analysts of the city's financial debacle could not muster the courage to identify the unions' role. Instead, they euphemistically identified only "groups" to whom "New York's elected officials . . . found it difficult to say no" and from whom they could not obtain a *"quid pro quo"* (Spiotto, 1991 and 1993). In their explanation of the city's financial difficulties, these analysts never identified the "groups" to whom the city could not say "No" and from whom they could not demand a *"quid pro quo."* Since the word "union" never appears in their analysis of New York City's fiscal crisis, a visitor from outer space would think that New York was a nonunion city and could only speculate on the identity of these mysterious "groups." Nevertheless, the unions were clearly among the leading "groups" to whom the politicians could not say "No," and from whom increased productivity failed to materialize despite repeated assurances to the electorate. As the November 1993 election demonstrated, the theme of increased productivity from city employees remains an enduring element in New York City politics, with the city's public sector unions gearing up to oppose efforts by newly elected Mayor Rudolph Giuliani to contract out some municipal services as a cost containment measure.

As the New York City situation illustrates, the consequences of social unionism for the economy and for local government are significant. Most importantly, an NEA/AFT merger will give added political impetus for an ongoing redistribution of the national income from the private to the public economy. In all likelihood, a merger of the NEA and the AFT would be the most important development in labor relations in the 1990s. With the merger, public sector unionism will become the new center of gravity of the labor movement. Educational policy will surely become more subject to collective bargaining, hence more subject to union influence at both the legislative level and in collective bargaining.

THE FUTURE OF TEACHER UNIONS

Although much remains to be said about the past and present of teacher unions, we conclude our analysis with some comments about their future. Obviously, the possibility of an NEA/AFT merger is critical to their future. We believe that the unions will merge, hence we devote some attention to the implications of merger uncertain as it may be. Our discussion will also address the possibility of an alternative teacher organization and the concerns of various parties who oppose the growing influence of the teacher unions.

Whether or not merger materializes, we can expect a lengthy period of NEA/AFT cooperation and avoidance of actions that would jeopardize merger in the future. In some cases, the developments we anticipate under merger may also take place under a cooperative relationship that falls short of merger. We are confident however, that readers who have followed our analysis to this point will be able to distinguish the future developments that are dependent on merger from those that are not.

An NEA/AFT merger will affect education at the local, state and federal levels, but in different ways and at different times. As far as membership is concerned, merger represents a pooling of forces, but the pooling will occur more at the state and federal than at the local level. The reason is that one or the other union has organized most if not all of the teachers in any given school district; there are not many NEA members in districts where an AFT affiliate is the bargaining agent and vice versa. As previously pointed out, the tendency for membership in a given district to be exclusively NEA or AFT is especially evident in districts where the unions have negotiated agency shop clauses. Many nonmembers feel that they might as well pay regular union dues and gain the right to participate in union affairs, especially if the difference between the regular dues and the agency shop fee is not very large. Even in the absence of agency shop fees, the incumbent union typically enrolls most teachers as members; failure to do so would be a sign that the union is in danger of being ousted within a short time.

To illustrate how merger might affect state, but not local membership, we can compare the membership situation in South Dakota and Ohio. There are very few AFT affiliates and members in South Dakota, where NEA is the dominant union. In Ohio, however, although the Ohio Education Association (OEA) enrolls more members than the Ohio Federation of Teachers (OFT), several AFT locals such as those in Toledo, Cincinnati, and Cleveland, are the bargaining agents in their districts and enroll large numbers of teachers. For the sake of discussion, assume that the AFT local in Cleveland enrolls all the Cleveland teachers, and OEA affiliates enroll all the teachers in the Cleveland suburbs. Merger would not result in larger or even different membership levels at the local level, but it would result in a larger state and national organization than existed hitherto.

In practice, there may be some dual membership and/or membership in the minority union in any given school district. The extent of such membership depends on several factors but it seldom threatens the incumbent bargaining agent. Consequently, in states where bargaining laws have been in force for several years, and where local affiliates of the NEA and AFT are the minority union, they seldom challenge the incumbent union for bargaining rights.

It should be noted that management has an interest in avoiding union rivalry. The unions compete on the basis of which one can extract more benefits from management. For this reason, school management does not necessarily object to contractual provisions that render it difficult to organize or sustain a rival union.

Incumbency as the bargaining agent may not protect a union from challenge in the rare situations (1) in which a minority union represents a threat to the incumbent union and (2) when both unions are competing to be chosen as the exclusive representative. The latter situation arises when a state enacts a bargaining law and both NEA and AFT affiliates compete for bargaining rights. The first situation most often arises when either the AFT or NEA affiliate gains exclusive representation rights by a narrow margin. The winning union is monitored closely and unless it negotiates a highly favorable contract, is accused of "selling out" or failure to achieve what supposedly could have been achieved.

The common thread that runs through all of these situations is that competition for bargaining rights is conducive to union militancy; with merger, competition between the two unions will disappear. Competition between teacher unions and other unions will not necessarily disappear; both kinds may compete for rights to represent support personnel. Of course, there will always be cases of intra-union conflict, and these cases usually exacerbate union militancy. Nonetheless, unless it blunders badly, incumbent union leadership is usually able to prevail over any challengers.

The incumbents control union publications and meetings and enjoy opportunities to meet the members, opportunities that are not available to opposing candidates for union office. Despite the necessity of being reelected, union leadership positions tend to be very secure. The advantages of in-

141

cumbency in elective office in unions are very similar to their advantages in political office generally.

Because of the moratorium on representation challenges during the merger talks, incumbent unions are less likely to fear the consequences of accepting a reasonable board offer. At least until the end of the moratorium, accusations that union leadership has settled too meekly will be a management problem only in the context of internal rivalry in an incumbent union. The dynamics are the same, but the problem arises less frequently this way. One reason is that officers of incumbent unions control union media, but the dissidents must finance their challenges from personal funds. This is not the case when NEA and AFT locals are competing against each other; the challenges are financed from union, not personal funds. In the absence of an organizational rival, union negotiators can afford to be statesmen, if they are secure in their positions and do not assume the mantle too often.

At the local level union representation for nonteaching employees may become a very troublesome problem, at least in the short run. At the present time, several unions represent or seek to represent these employees. In practice, they are represented by:

- Independent state associations of support personnel, such as the California School Employees Association (CSEA).
- Local affiliates of the NEA.
- Local affiliates of the AFT.
- American Federation of State, County, and Municipal Employees (AFSCME).
- Service Employees International Union (SEIU).
- Teamsters and miscellaneous unions.

Inasmuch as school districts employ large numbers of nonteaching employees, the various unions currently seeking to organize them are not likely to allow the NEA and/or AFT to organize them without a struggle. The independent state associations of school district employees have a long history of working with the teacher unions, but it seems likely that NEA/AFT will eventually organize most of the support personnel. First, the support personnel are constantly exposed to the political clout of the teacher unions. The teacher unions already function in the schools, hence they have a big advantage over the nonteacher unions in representation elections. Furthermore, the teacher unions have a stake in the matter that goes beyond the issue of union dues and resources; the ability of teacher unions to engage in successful strikes depends partly on their support from nonteacher personnel. Significantly, the NEA and AFT have recently amended their constitutions to provide representation and

142

governance rights within the union to support personnel. In some states, the independent state associations of support personnel may eventually affiliate with the AFL-CIO whether or not they merge with NEA/AFT.

Over time, however, merger will exacerbate the bargaining problems facing school boards. The NEA/AFT is likely to be even more successful than its two predecessors in enacting legislative changes favorable to teacher unions. Legalizing the right to strike, or expanding the scope of bargaining are likely to be legislative objectives of the merged union at the state level. As such legislative changes are enacted and affect bargaining at the district level, school boards will find it even more difficult than they do now to negotiate effectively or to manage their districts. Funds and resources devoted to organizational rivalry will be devoted to squeezing more from school boards and legislative bodies at all levels.

It is also likely that merger will exacerbate union militancy on certain issues. At all levels (local, state and federal), we can expect an intensive union drive to require or at least to authorize agency shop fees. In some situations, the minority union has objected to them, citing much the same arguments that are made by non-union or even anti-union forces. Legislators and school board members have sometimes cited these objections as a reason to oppose agency shop fees.

With merger impending or consummated, there is much less likelihood that the minority union will object to the fees; it will soon be part of the union that benefits from forcing every teacher and support employee to pay them. There is no point to objecting to agency shop fees if your union is going out of business, and your only objection to the fees was that a rival union would be the beneficiary of them.

Both the NEA and AFT are strong proponents of government subsidized health care. It is naive to assume their interest in it is primarily idealistic. Health insurance for school district employees requires a growing proportion of school budgets. To the extent that the costs of health care can be shifted to the federal government, more state and local funds will be available for teacher salaries. NEA and AFT support for a federal takeover of the costs of health care is based on their interest in promoting the welfare of persons who already have health care, not the interests of those who do not have it.

The teacher unions will adopt the position that the funds being spent for health insurance are essentially for teacher welfare; inasmuch as the general government is absorbing these costs, or to the extent that it does, the state and local funds no longer required for this purpose should be reallocated to teacher salaries. This negotiating objective will undoubtedly materialize even in the absence of merger, but the reallocation will be a major union objective in both the public and private sectors if and when comprehensive federal health care is enacted.

NEA/AFT AND HIGHER EDUCATION

In 1992-93, the NEA and AFT each enrolled about 80,000 faculty in higher education. An NEA/AFT merger will have conflicting tendencies with respect to the union's role in higher education. Some aspects of merger will be conducive to increased membership and influence; merger will also create the potential for sizable defections from the NEA/AFT.

Let us consider first the tendency for merger to expand NEA/AFT membership in higher education. This tendency will result from the dynamics of union rivalry. Suppose that the faculty at university X are voting on whether to be represented by a faculty union. Suppose further that the faculty is divided on the issue as follows:

Percent
- 27   Favor representation by the NEA affiliate.
- 26   Favor no exclusive representative.
- 25   Favor the AFT affiliate.
- 22   Favor the AAUP affiliate.

In this situation, there would be a runoff election between the two highest options, representation by the NEA affiliate or no exclusive representative. The likelihood is that the "no exclusive representative" option would prevail in the runoff. The reason is that most of the faculty who support the AFT or AAUP affiliates would vote against representation by the NEA affiliate. If the vote for representation by the NEA affiliate wins, the AFT and AAUP affiliates will dwindle or even disappear as a player in faculty affairs. If the vote for representation by the NEA affiliate loses, the AFT and AAUP affiliates would still have a role to play in campus affairs. In addition they would also retain the opportunity to become the exclusive representative.

Merger would change the arithmetic and dynamics of this situation. For the sake of discussion, assume that the NEA and AFT affiliates maintained their level of support. In that case, NEA/AFT would carry 52 percent of the vote, enough to eliminate the "no exclusive representative" option. The point is that in some instances, academics favor exclusive representation if and only if their preferred union is the bargaining agent. An NEA/AFT merger would reduce the likelihood that this dog in the manger attitude would prevail. Needless to say, this is not the only reason merger would

144

strengthen the NEA/AFT option in higher education, but it could be decisive in some states.

Notwithstanding the preceding paragraph, merger would also create the potential for some large-scale defections, especially in states where affiliation with the AFL-CIO is newly mandated. The defectors would be most likely to switch to the American Association of University Professors (AAUP), that is, if the AAUP is still in existence at the time.

The AAUP has suffered from inept leadership for at least the past 30 years. In the 1960s, it could easily have enrolled most of the professoriate, or most of it inclined to support collective bargaining. Instead, the AAUP was the Hamlet of public sector bargaining; by the time it made a belated effort to accommodate bargaining, the NEA and AFT had achieved representation rights in several large state systems of higher education. Needless to say, their membership rolls increased substantially as a result.

Currently, the AAUP is in a precarious, perhaps even desperate situation. Its membership has declined from almost 100,000 to 33,000, of whom about 18,000 are in bargaining units on the East Coast and Mid-West. Nevertheless, a sizable minority of AAUP members are still opposed to bargaining. To retain its members, the AAUP adjusts its position on bargaining to whatever will fly at the institutional level. As the NEA Board of Directors Special Committee report states, "AAUP will organize a chapter around anti-collective bargaining issues as readily as around collective bargaining." What hurt the AAUP was not its adjustment to institutional preferences; it was its failure to embrace bargaining where bargaining was clearly the preference or was potentially the preference at the institutional level. Thus, while the AAUP dithered and declined, the NEA and AFT gained a much larger share of the market for unionization among professors.

A merger of the NEA and AFT could provide the AAUP with an opportunity to rise from its cemetery plot. The association has never successfully exploited the fact that higher education interests are inherently subordinate to K-12 interests in the NEA and AFT. The two unions assert that professors will gain additional clout by joining their organizations, and this is no doubt true in some situations. Nevertheless, there are conflicting as well as common interests among professors and K-12 personnel, but the AAUP has failed to take advantage of them.

Also, status is the coin of the realm in higher education. It surely must rankle professors to realize that their national convention is dominated by K-12 personalities. No doubt one reason is that professors tend to think of their national organizations as the subject matter organizations; this tendency has played into the hands of the NEA and AFT. At any rate, the status concerns of professors will be greatly exacerbated if merger requires affiliation with the AFL-CIO in institutions where the faculty as a whole does not want it. Quite possibly, the AAUP is too moribund to take advantage of such opportunities; the possibility should not be discounted.

AN ALTERNATIVE TO NEA/AFT

Merger of the NEA and AFT will create both the need and the opportunity to establish a new teacher organization. For purposes of discussion, we shall refer to it as the National Teachers Association (NTA). The NTA would enroll teachers from the existing independent teachers associations, from private schools, and from the ranks of NEA and AFT members who are dissatisfied with NEA/AFT. Let us comment briefly on these potential sources of membership.

1. *Independent teacher associations not affiliated with either the NEA or AFT.* The NEA estimates that about 160,000 teachers, mainly in states without bargaining laws, are members of the independent teacher associations. These associations have low dues (about $60-100 annually) but some also provide low cost insurance benefits for members. The report of the NEA's Special Committee that proposed merger talks also included several recommendations intended to weaken these independent teacher associations.
2. *Private school teachers.* Private school teachers would constitute an important NTA constituency. In 1991-92, there were about 355,000 private school teachers in the United States. Many were members of denominational or other specialized private school teacher associations.
3. *Defections from NEA/AFT.* An NEA/AFT merger will create the potential for substantial defections from the merged organization. The extent to which defections materialize depends on several complex factors, which are not clear at this time. In our view, individual defections will not play a major role in weakening NEA/AFT. Some individuals here and there will refuse, perhaps at great personal expense, to observe union solidarity or discipline, but reliance on large numbers of teachers to do so individually will be a losing strategy. The crucial issue will be how many teacher leaders at the state and local level will lead large numbers of their fellow teachers into a new organization with a non-union orientation.

It is impractical here to examine all the issues raised by the prospect of an alternative organization, but two major factors deserve brief mention. One is the fact that school management will often welcome a different mode of teacher representation. School management is partly responsible for the growth and influence of the NEA and AFT; it must now play a role in the difficult task of putting the genie back in the bottle. There are many ways to help; the question is whether school boards are willing to absorb immediate political hits to reduce NEA/AFT dominance.

The major negative to public school management will be NTA's acceptance of private schools. An alternative to NEA/AFT that is also supportive of private school options will pose a real dilemma for school boards and school administrators. Actually, if their underlying objective is education instead of public education as an institution, encouragement of NTA would not be such a problem; private school options should be available in order to pressure NEA/AFT locals to drop demands that impair the effectiveness of public schools.

In order to be a viable alternative to NEA/AFT, a teacher organization must have a membership base large enough to provide member benefits comparable to those offered by NEA/AFT. This objective can be reached if most private school teachers join an organization that also enrolls most of the teachers in the independent public school teacher associations. If such a merger could be arranged, NTA would have the critical mass required to provide the comparable benefits.

NEA/AFT will be oriented overwhelmingly to public education. It will do everything it can to weaken private schools. Thus, there is solid policy basis for private school teachers to unite in opposition to NEA/AFT, in addition to the other reasons for doing so.

One problem facing NTA would be how to reconcile the interests of public and private school teachers in the same organization, while remaining sufficiently attractive to both groups. The problem should be resolved on the basis that NTA supports good education, not just public or private education. In other words, NTA would not take sides on public/private school controversies except to argue that both sectors have legitimate interests that should be reflected in legislation and public policy. The analogue here would be to the American Medical Association, which does not get involved in disputes between public and private hospitals. Instead, it considers the interests of doctors in both. Private school management might be reluctant to encourage teachers to join NTA out of fear that its local affiliates would become quasi-unions, but this would be much less of a risk than their growing inability to oppose an organization which is determined to weaken them in every possible way.

Another problem facing NTA would be whether to challenge NEA/AFT locals in representation elections. As the NEA learned to its sorrow in the 1960s, it is extremely difficult to win such elections while being opposed to bargaining per se. The basic issue is whether it would be possible for NTA to avoid both the danger of appearing to be a management-dominated bargaining agent and the negatives associated with teacher bargaining. The issue requires careful study, but our tentative view is that NTA affiliates could avoid both horns of this dilemma. If so, they should challenge NEA/AFT affiliates where the former have a good chance to win.

The extent of defections from NEA/AFT will depend partly on the structure and policies adopted by it. However, AFT affiliates opposed to merger for any reason are not likely to join a non-union organization. Their reasons for opposition to merger are also likely to preclude their joining NTA, hence we doubt whether NTA would be able to enroll many AFT members unhappy about the merger for any reason.

The foregoing is not necessarily true of NEA members and affiliates. In fact, when the NEA adopted a unified dues structure in 1972, requiring members to join the national and state associations simultaneously, the Missouri State Teachers Association (MSTA) refused and withdrew from the NEA. In 1994, it continued to be the largest teacher organization in Missouri. Granted, its survival was due partly to some unique factors that would not be present in most situations elsewhere; for example, MSTA was a well-established organization with substantial resources, fighting against outsiders trying to dictate what it should do. Still, a substantial number of NEA members will be unhappy about NEA/AFT. If a viable alternative were available at the time when the negative features of NEA/AFT emerge, there should be frequent opportunities to persuade disaffected teachers to join the NTA. It will be crucially important whether NTA is functioning when the merger takes place; attempts to organize NTA afterwards will not be as successful. Of course, the very existence of an alternative would force the merger forces to try to accommodate potential defectors, but that is a risk that must be taken. Finally, because we lack data on the number of public school teachers who are not members of either NEA, AFT or an independent teacher association, we hesitate to draw any conclusions about their membership potential for NTA, except that the number is likely to be rather small and should not figure prominently in plans for NTA.

An alternative to NEA/AFT would face a host of other problems, but it would also have some things going for it. One is that as the only other comprehensive national organization, it would have convenient access to media and political forums. If there is a multitude of small teacher organizations it is easy to ignore all of them; none speaks for more than a remnant of the teachers outside of the NEA/AFT. An organization that represented 250,000 or more teachers could not be dismissed so easily. Furthermore, school boards repelled by teacher unionism would have reason to encourage a teacher organization that followed a more constructive approach to educational and employment issues. To be successful, NTA would probably have to enroll 50 percent of the private school teachers and at least 10 percent of those in public schools. Surprising as it may seem, the problem of unifying the private school teachers is probably the more difficult, but the effort has to be made to find out.

MERGER AS A WAKE-UP CALL

The notion that three million or more teachers and another million support employees can be organized as a monolithic political and educational force is true in one sense, not in another. The NEA/AFT will include several hundred independent power bases that are not controlled by the national officers and staff. State and local affiliates will have their own personnel, structure, budgets, objectives, sources of revenue, and access to media. The overwhelming majority will share the common interest of preventing competition in the field of education, so the merged organization will be monolithic on this issue. However, it will be monolithic because of a common perception of member interests, not because of coercion from the top. Similarly, we can anticipate overwhelming support throughout NEA/AFT on noneducational issues that have important ramifications for the interests of NEA/AFT members; for example, the merged organizations will oppose limits on government expenditures or supermajorities to enact higher taxes.

As we move beyond these issues, however, unanimity is less likely. A teacher union in a district where hunting is popular will be likely to oppose gun control; a union in an urban district will support it. In addition, unanimity on cultural issues seems highly unlikely. Even on some educational issues, like tracking and testing, there will be differences, often based on interests. The disadvantaged minorities will oppose standardized tests; others will support them. The unions will often split on proposals regarding school finance; affiliates in districts that are treated favorably under a proposal will support it whereas the affiliates that see themselves as treated inequitably will oppose it. Controversies over "mainstreaming" or "inclusion" of special education students already divide teachers and will do so for many years to come.

The fact, if it turns out to be a fact, that the merged organization will not be monolithic on all issues does not eliminate the problems of monopoly. NEA/AFT will be overwhelmingly supportive of high taxes, high spending, and of government intervention in the economy and in people's lives for all sorts of allegedly idealistic reasons. Generally speaking, NEA/AFT

149

will be oriented to the liberal wing of the Democratic Party. Both unions are now, the NEA more so than the AFT.

TEACHER UNIONS AND THE CONSERVATIVES

Perhaps the most important question about the merger is what will conservatives do about it. We use the term "conservative" to refer to a wide range of leaders, organizations, and political forces that emphasize free markets, minimal government, low taxes, limits on government expenditures, and other objectives commonly associated with a conservative outlook. Although libertarians usually object to being classified as conservatives, we include them in the definition for editorial simplicity.

While far from complete, the evidence we have presented should alert conservatives that they face an uphill battle in legislative arenas at all levels of government. Despite NEA/AFT support for a minuscule number of candidates who are not in the Democratic party, the teacher unions typically constitute a major handicap for conservative candidates that is not easily overcome. Of course conservatives often have their own core of automatic support, but it is minuscule compared to the teacher unions.

Needless to say, what conservatives do about the teacher unions, if anything, will be affected by several factors, but merger is likely to trigger a more intensive conservative interest in, and response to, teacher unions. Inexorably, teacher union political activities and financial operations will come under greater scrutiny than in the past. This is certain to increase public awareness of the conflicts between teacher union interests and the public interest.

In making this prediction, we do not overlook the fact that the teacher unions are geared to political action. Teachers improve their situation by political action, not by increased efficiency or greater productivity. Thus a large share of teacher resources supports an infrastructure that is focused directly on media and politics. The unions have legislative staff, media relations, research departments, and other agencies whose raison d'être is to influence media and politicians. When controversies over educational policy arise, these structures are in place, whereas the resources for opposing union positions must often be raised on an ad hoc basis.

Whatever merger adds to union power may be less important than its consciousness-raising effects, especially if affiliation with the AFL-CIO, if only on an optional or state-by-state basis, is part of the merger agreement. Thus, the fact that union membership will be over 50 percent from the public sector may be less important than public awareness of the fundamental change in the labor movement. The additional political clout resulting from merger may be overshadowed by wider recognition of teacher union political influence. In our view, therefore, the importance of merger lies outside the parameters of organizations, members, revenues, and resources. These may not change very much in toto, but public awareness of them may expand sharply. Thus the outcome of merger may be beneficial, even for those who are concerned, as we are, about the role of teacher unions in education and in American politics generally.

EPILOGUE

Essentially, teacher unions raise two fundamental issues which characterize public sector unionism generally. One issue emerges from the fact that school district labor contracts are public policies. They are personnel policies, but the critical point is their public nature. In terms of our political system, public sector labor contracts are like speed limits, tax rates, eligibility to vote in elections, compulsory education, and the myriad of other matters addressed by legislation. The fact that school district labor agreements are public policies is a point that the teacher unions themselves emphasize.

In this context, the basic issue is whether the formulation and adoption of public policies by means of negotiations with one special interest group is consistent with democratic representative government. After all, school district labor contracts affect pupils, parents, taxpayers, employers, and a host of other interest groups and constituencies whose rights to influence public policy are diminished by teacher bargaining. The political inequality that results is especially evident in the debate over teacher strikes. From a government perspective, a teacher strike is a suspension of a public service. It is a suspension of a public service until one special interest, the teacher union, achieves public policies that are acceptable to it. No other special interest has this right or even claims that it should have it, at least on an ongoing basis.

Clearly, acceptance or even toleration of teacher strikes reflects a political inequality of considerable importance; one special interest group can suspend public services to achieve the public policies they seek, the rest of us cannot do so. The fact that personnel policies are involved ("terms and conditions of employment" in bargaining terminology) does not mitigate this basic inequality or its inconsistency with our political system generally. True, most states have not legalized teacher strikes, but this fact does not vitiate the point that is being made. Even in the states where teacher strikes are not legal, the legislative debates over whether to legalize them do not address the political inequality inherent in legalizing strikes by public school teachers. Obviously, the underlying issues apply to public employment generally and must be addressed in this larger context; it is unlikely that they can or will be resolved only in public education and teacher bargaining.

The second major issue emerges in the private as well as the public sector. While collective bargaining has flourished in the public sector, it has declined in the private sector. Less than 12 percent of the private sector labor force was unionized in 1993, compared to 36 percent in 1953. During this time, private sector employees have increasingly resorted to other techniques and procedures, especially litigation, to protect their interests.

Understandably, the private sector unions allege that the decline in private sector unionization is a deplorable fact to be remedied by strengthening the legal privileges and powers of private sector unions. This position, however, is not likely to prevail, at least in the industries subject to competition from abroad. The irony is that teachers embraced or accepted collective bargaining just when it began an irreversible decline in the private sector.

The fundamental problem here is not the decline of the unions. It is that the framework of labor relations embodied in the National Labor Relations Act is seriously flawed and must be replaced by one that is more responsive to the needs and interests of employees, employers, and the public at large. To be sure, some of the reasons for the decline of unions in the private sector, such as competition from foreign producers, do not apply to public education, which is a government monopoly relatively immune from market competition. Nevertheless, other reasons for the decline are applicable to the public as well as the private sector. For this reason, it is essential to develop and adopt a new framework for public as well as private sector labor relations. Such a new framework is essential to avoid both the negative consequences of teacher bargaining and the unacceptable features of the pre-bargaining era. As long as the NLRA model continues to dominate school district employment relations, however, we can expect the negative consequences of teacher bargaining; any changes for the better are likely to be marginal and succeed only over strong union opposition. It is doubtful whether proposed basic changes in the framework of school district employment relations would result in even greater union opposition.

This point is especially relevant to the possibility of an organizational alternative to the NEA/AFT. If such an alternative is a union committed to the collective bargaining model, the teacher reaction is likely to be "Why bother to change?" On the other hand, if the organizational alternative merely opposes the collective bargaining framework, the implication is that it supports a return to the framework of employment relations in the pre-bargaining era. This is not likely to be persuasive, even among the teachers who were not around at that time. Consequently, a new framework of employment relations is essential. To be viable, an alternative to the NEA and AFT must propose such a framework. Thus the task that lies ahead is not simply to criticize the teacher unions, but to create a system of educational employment relations that avoids the deficiencies of the pre-bargaining era as well as those inherent in public sector bargaining. Unfortunately, relatively little attention is being paid to this task.

New Business Item 1993-A
Adopted as Amended, NEA Convention
July 2-5, 1993, San Francisco, California

The circumstances which led the 1976 Representative Assembly to adopt a prohibition against any type of AFL-CIO affiliation by NEA and its affiliates have changed.
Because of this change, and because the 1976 prohibition affects NEA's ability to
achieve its long-standing goal of uniting all education employees in a single national
organization, NEA should have some flexibility in regard to the question of AFL-CIO
affiliation. Accordingly, the Representative Assembly directs the President to invite
AFT and/or other labor organizations to enter into discussions with NEA regarding the
possible establishment of a unified organization. Any organization that is proposed
shall:
  a. Guarantee minority group participation in the governance and operation of said
     organization;
  b. Have democratic decision making procedures, including the use of the secret
     ballot to elect the officers and change the governing documents of said organiza-
     tion;
  c. Be free to take positions and pursue objectives that are in the best interests of its
     members; and
  d. Not require any current affiliate of NEA to affiliate with or make per capita pay-
     ments to AFL-CIO.
Consistent with the prohibition in paragraph (d) above, the NEA representatives
shall have the flexibility in the discussions to explore whether some type of affiliation
relationship with AFL-CIO is compatible with the goals and objectives of NEA and its
affiliates.
  The President shall report the status of the discussions to the Board of Directors on
a regular basis, and shall submit to the Board on or before April 1, 1994, a written
report, which shall include specific recommendations regarding the possible establishment of a single national organization of education employees. The NEA Board of
Directors shall implement a systemic process by which every state affiliate shall be
kept fully informed throughout the course of the exploratory discussions between
the NEA and the AFT—and other organizations—regarding the issue of merger/affilia-
tion. In addition, the report that the President will submit to the board of directors on
April 1, 1994, along with a full account of board action, shall be made available to all
state affiliates well in advance of the 1994 NEA Representative Assembly. The Board
of Directors shall act on the written report at its May 1994 meeting. The action taken by
the Board of Directors, together with the written report, shall be submitted to the 1994
Representative Assembly. No final commitments shall be made and no final actions
shall be taken by NEA with regard to the merger and/or AFL-CIO affiliation without the
approval of the 1994 Representative Assembly.

Any proposal(s) for merger and/or affiliation shall be voted by the RA after full debate at a regular session of the RA. The RA vote shall be by secret ballot.

Except as expressly modified by this New Business Item, New Business Items 1976-A and 1976-B shall remain in effect pending action by the 1994 Representative Assembly, and the Executive Committee shall continue in the interim to apply the concepts embodied in those New Business Items.

New Business Item 1993-B
If NEA enters into national level unification discussions with AFT and/or other labor organizations pursuant to New Business Item 1993-A, NEA shall at the outset of such discussions propose that the parties agree to the following two "moratoriums" at the state and local levels while the national level unification discussions are in progress: (a) a moratorium on unification discussions between NEA affiliates and affiliates of AFT and/or other labor organizations involved in the national discussions and (b) a moratorium on representational challenges between NEA affiliates and affiliates of AFT and/or other labor organizations involved in the national discussions.

Rationale
If New Business Item 1993-A is adopted by the Representative Assembly and the NEA enters into a national level unification discussions with AFT and/or other labor organizations, the Board believes that the two moratoriums should be proposed at state and local levels, while unification discussions are in progress. See pp. 4 and 5 of the Report of the Special Committee on Relationships with Other Organizations for further rationale.

The first moratorium would prohibit unification discussions at state and local levels. The second would rule out representional challenges at state and local levels.

New Business Item 1993-B will be voted on only if the 1993 Representative Assembly first adopts 1993-A. If the Representative Assembly rejects New Business Item 1993-A, the Board will withdraw 1993-B.

Cost Implication
No additional cost to implement 1993-B if 1993-A is adopted.

THE CHARTER OF THE
NATIONAL EDUCATION ASSOCIATION

1857-70
THE NATIONAL TEACHERS' ASSOCIATION
Organized August 26, 1857, at Philadelphia, Pennsylvania.

PURPOSE *To elevate the character and advance the interests of the profession of teaching and to promote the cause of popular education in the United States.* [The word "popular" was dropped in the 1907 Act of Incorporation.]

The name of the Association was changed at Cleveland, Ohio, on August 15, 1870, to the "National Educational Association."

1870-1907
NATIONAL EDUCATIONAL ASSOCIATION
Incorporated under the laws of the district of Columbia, February 24, 1886, under the name "National Education Association," which was changed to "National Educational Association," by certificate filed November 6, 1886.

1907-
NATIONAL EDUCATION ASSOCIATION OF THE UNITED STATES
Incorporated under a special act of Congress, approved June 30, 1906, to succeed the "National Educational Association." The Charter was accepted and Bylaws were adopted at the Fiftieth Anniversary Convention held July 10, 1907, at Los Angeles, California.

Act of Incorporation
An Act to Incorporate the National Education
Association of the United States

Be it enacted by the Senate and House of Representatives of the United States of America in Congress assembled:

List of Incorporators
Section 1. That the following-named persons, who are not officers and directors and trustees of the National Educational Association, a corporation organized in the year eighteen hundred and eighty-six, under the Act of General Incorporation of the Revised Statutes of the District of Columbia viz.: Nathan C. Schaeffer, Eliphalet Oram Lyte, John W. Lansinger, of Pennsylvania; Isaac W. Hill, of Alabama; Arthur J. Matthews,

of Arizona; John H. Hinemon, George B. Cook, of Arkansas; Joseph O'Connor, Josiah L. Pickard, Arthur H. Chamberlain, of California; Aaron Gove, Ezekiel H. Cook, Lewis C. Greenlee, of Colorado; Charles H. Keyes, of Connecticut; George W. Twitmyer, of Delaware; J. Ormond Wilson, William T. Harris, Alexander T. Stuart, of the District of Columbia; Clem Hampton, of Florida; William M. Slaton, of Georgia; Frances Mann, of Idaho; J. Stanley Brown, Albert G. Lane, Charles I. Parker, John W. Cook, Joshua Pike, Albert R. Taylor, Joseph A Mercer, of Illinois; Nebraska Cropsey, Thomas A. Mott, of Indiana; John D. Benedict, of Indian Territory; John F. Riggs, Ashley V. Storm, of Iowa; John W. Spindler, Jasper N. Wilkinson, A. V. Jewett, Luther D. Whittemore, of Kansas; William Henry Bartholomew, of Kentucky; Warren Easton, of Louisiana; John S. Locke, of Maine; M. Bates Stephens, of Maryland; Charles W. Eliot, Mary H. Hunt, Henry T. Bailey, of Massachusetts; Hugh A. Graham, Charles G. White, William H. Elson, of Michigan; William F. Phelps, Irwin Shepard, John A. Cranston, of Minnesota; Robert B. Fulton, of Mississippi; F. Louis Soldan, James M. Greenwood, William J. Hawkins, of Missouri; Oscar J. Craig, of Montana; George L. Towne, of Nebraska; Joseph E. Stubbs, of Nevada; James E. Klock, of New Hampshire; James M. Green, John Enright, of New Jersey; Charles M. Light, of New Mexico; James H. Canfield, Nicholas Murray Butler, William H. Maxwell, Charles R. Skinner, Albert P. Marble, James C. Byrnes, of New York; James Y. Joyner, Julius Isaac Fust, of North Carolina; Pitt Gordon Knowlton, of North Dakota; Oscar T. Corson, Jacob A. Shawan, Wills L. Griswold, of Ohio; Edgar S. Vaught, Andrew R. Hickham, of Oklahoma; Charles Carroll Stratton, Edwin D. Ressler, of Oregon; Thomas W. Bicknell, Walter Ballou Jacobs, of Rhode Island; David B. Johnson, Robert P. Pell, of South Carolina; Moritz Adelbert Langer, of South Dakota; Eugene F. Turner, of Tennessee; Lloyd E. Wolt, of Texas; David H. Christensen, of Utah; Henry O. Wheeler, Isaac Thomas, of Vermont; Joseph L. Jarmon, of Virginia; Edward T. Mathes, of Washington; T. Marcellus Marshall, Lucy Robinson, of West Virginia; Lorenzo D. Harvey, of Wisconsin; Thomas T. Tynan, of Wyoming; Cassia Patton, of Alaska; Frank H. Ball of Puerto Rico; Arthur F. Griffiths, of Hawaii; G. H. Maxson, of the Philippine Islands; and such other persons as now are or may hereafter be associated with them as officers or members of said Association, are hereby incorporated and declared to be a body corporate of the District of Columbia by the name of the "National Education Association of the United States," and by that name shall be known and have a perpetual succession with the powers, limitations, and restrictions herein contained.

Purpose and Departments
Section 2. That the propose and objects of the said corporation shall be to elevate the character and advance the interests of the profession of teaching and to promote the cause of education in the United States. This corporation shall include the National Council of Education and the following departments, and such others as may hereafter be created by organization or consolidation, to wit: The Departments, first, of Superintendence; second, of Normal Schools; third, of Elementary Education; fourth, of Higher Education; fifth, of Manual Training; sixth, of Art Education; seventh, of Kindergarten Education; eighth, of Music Education; ninth, of Secondary Education; tenth, of Business Education; eleventh, of Child Study; twelfth, of Physical Education; thirteenth, of Natural Science Instruction; fourteenth, of School Administration; fifteenth, of the Library; sixteenth, of Special Education; seventeenth, of Indian Education; the powers and duties and the numbers and names of these departments and of the National Council of Education may be changed or abolished at the pleasure of the corporation, as provided in its Bylaws.

Powers of Corporation
Section 3. That the said corporation shall further have power to have and to use a common seal, and to alter and change the same at its pleasure; to sue or to be sued in any court of the United States, or other court of competent jurisdiction; to make bylaws not inconsistent with the provisions of this Act of the Constitution of the United States; to take or receive, whether by gift, grant, devise, bequest, or purchase, any real or personal estate, and to hold, grant, transfer, sell, convey, hire, or lease the same for the purpose of its incorporation; to accept and administer any trust of real or personal estate for any educational purpose within the objects of the corporation; and to borrow money for its corporate purposes, issue bonds therefor, and secure the same by mortgage, deed of trust, pledge, or otherwise.

Property to be Tax-Exempt
Section 4. That all real property of the Corporation within the District of Columbia which shall be used by the corporation for the educational or other purposes of the corporation as aforesaid other than the purposes of producing income and all personal property and funds of the corporation held, used, or invested for educational purposes aforesaid, or to produce income to be used for such purposes, shall be exempt from taxation: *provided, however,* that this exemption shall not apply to any property of the corporation which shall not be used for, or the income of which shall not be applied to, the educational purposes of the corporation; and, *provided further,* that the corporation shall annually file, with the Commissioner of Education of the United States, a report in writing, stating in detail the property, real and personal, held by the corporation, and the expenditure or other use or disposition of the same or the income thereof, during the preceding year.

Members
Section 5. The qualification, classifications, rights, and obligations of members of said corporation shall be prescribed in the Bylaws of the corporation.

Officers
Section 6. (a) The officers of the corporation shall be a president, one or more vice-presidents, a secretary, a treasurer, a Board of Directors, an Executive Committee, and such boards, councils, committees, and other officers as shall be prescribed in the Bylaws.

Additional Boards, Councils, Committees, and Officers
(b) Except as limited by this Act, as amended, the Bylaws of the corporation shall prescribe the powers, duties, terms of office, and the manner of election or appointment of the said officers, boards, councils, and committees; and the said corporation may by its Bylaws make other and different provisions as to the numbers and names of the officers, boards, councils, and committees.

[Section 7 has been deleted.]

Section 8. That the principal office of the said corporation shall be in the city of Washington, D.C.; *provided,* that the meetings of the corporation, its officers, committees, and departments, may be held, and that its business may be transacted, and an office of offices may be maintained elsewhere within the United States, as may be determined in accordance with the Bylaws.

Acceptance of This Charter

Section 9. That the charter, constitution, and bylaws of the National Educational Association shall continue in full force and effect until the charter granted by this Act shall be accepted by such Association at the next annual meeting of the Association, and until new Bylaws shall be adopted; and that the present officers, directors, and trustees of said Association shall continue to hold office and perform their respective duties as such until the expiration of terms for which they were severally elected or appointed, and until their successors are elected. That at such annual meeting the active members of the National Educational Association, then present, may organize and proceed to accept the charter granted by this Act and adopt bylaws, to elect officers to succeed those whose terms have expired or are about to expire, and generally to organize the "National Education Association of the United States"; and that the Board of Trustees of the corporation hereby incorporated shall thereupon, if the charter granted by this Act be accepted, receive, take over, and enter into possession, custody; and management of all property, real and personal, of the corporation heretofore known as the National Educational Association incorporated as aforesaid, under the Revised Statutes of the District of Columbia, and all its rights, contracts, claims, and property of every kind and nature whatsoever, and the several officers, directors, and trustees of such last-named Association, or any other person having charge of any of the securities, funds, books, or property thereof, real or personal, shall on demand deliver the same to the proper officers, directors, or trustees of the corporation hereby created. *Provided*, that a verified certificate executed by the president officer and secretary of such annual meeting, showing the acceptance of the charter granted by this Act by the national educational Association, shall be legal evidence of the fact, when filed with the Recorder of Deeds of the District of Columbia; and *provided further*, that in the event of the failure of the Association to accept the charter granted by this Act at said annual meeting, then the charter of the National Educational Association and its incorporate existence shall be and are hereby extended until the thirty-first day of July, nineteen hundred and eight, and at any time before said date its charter may be extended in the manner and form provided by the general corporation of the District of Columbia.

Rights of Creditors

Section 10. That the rights of creditors of the said existing corporation, known as the National Educational Association, shall not in any manner be impaired by the passage of this Act, or the transfer of the property heretofore mentioned, nor shall any liability or obligation, or payment of any sum due or to become due, or any claim or demand, in any manner, or for any cause existing against the said existing corporation, be released or impaired; and the corporation hereby incorporated is declared to succeed to the obligations and liabilities, and to be held liable to pay and discharge all of its debts, liabilities, and contracts of the said corporation so existing, to the same effect as if such new corporation had itself incurred the obligation or liability to pay such debts or damages, and no action or proceeding before any court or tribunal shall be deemed to have abated or been discontinued by reason of this Act.

Amendments to Charter

Section 11. That Congress may from time to time, alter, repeal, or modify this Act of Incorporation, but no contract or individual right made or acquired shall thereby be divested or impaired.

160

Creation of Representative Assembly

Section 12. That said corporation may provide, by amendment to its Bylaws, that the powers of the active members exercised at the annual meeting in the election of officers and the transaction of business shall be vested in and exercised by a representative assembly composed of delegates apportioned, elected, and governed in accordance with the provisions of the Bylaws adopted by said corporation.

Sections 1-11 were passed by Congress and approved by the President, June 30, 1906. They were accepted and adopted as the Constitution of the National Education Association of the United States by the active members of the National Educational Association in annual session at Los Angeles, California, July 10, 1907.

Section 12 was passed by Congress and approved by the President of the United States, May 13, 1920, as an amendment to the original Act of Incorporation. It was accepted and adopted as an amendment to the Constitution of the National Education Association of the United States by the active members thereof in an annual session at Salt Lake City, Utah, July 9, 1920.

Sections 5-8 were amended by Congress and approved by the President of the United States, June 14, 1937. These amendments were accepted as amendments to the Charter and adopted as amendments to the Constitution by the Representative Assembly of the National Education Association of the United States at Detroit, Michigan, June 29, 1937.

Sections 3, 6 and 7 were amended by Congress and approved by the President of the United States in June 1969. In addition, Congress gave to the NEA Representative Assembly the power to make Section 7 of no further force and effect by permitting the Representative Assembly to make bylaw amendments affecting the administration of the property of the Corporation (see Article XI, NEA Bylaws[1]) and the selection of the secretary of the Association (see Article V, Section 3[i], NEA Bylaws.[2])

---

[1]This is a reference to the Bylaws that were in effect in June 1969. In the current Bylaws the comparable provision is Bylaw 11.

[2]This is a reference to the Bylaws that were in effect in June 1969. In the current Bylaws the comparable provision is Bylaw 10-1.

CONSTITUTION OF THE NATIONAL EDUCATION ASSOCIATION OF THE UNITED STATES

Preamble

We, the members of the National Education Association of the United States, in order that the Association may serve as the national voice for education, advance the cause of education for all individuals, promote the health and welfare of children and/ or students, promote professional excellence among educators, gain recognition of the basic importance of the teacher in the learning process and other employees in the educational effort, protect the rights of educational employees and advance their interests and welfare, secure professional autonomy, unite educational employees for effective citizenship, promote and protect human and civil rights, and obtain for its members the benefits of an independent, united education profession, do hereby adopt this Constitution.

ARTICLE I. NAME, GOALS, OBJECTIVES, AND AUTHORITIES FOR GOVERNANCE

Section 1. Name.

The name of this organization shall be the National Education Association of the United States.

Section 2. Goals and Objectives.

The goals of the Association shall be as stated in the Preamble. The Association shall have all power necessary and proper to take action for the attainment of these goals. Nothing in this Constitution or in the Bylaws shall be construed to prevent the Association from pursuing objectives which are consistent with the stated goals of the Association.

Section 3. Governance.

The Association shall be governed by its Charter, this Constitution, the Bylaws, the Standing Rules, and such other actions as the Representative Assembly, the Board of Directors, and the Executive Committee may take consistent therewith.

ARTICLE II. MEMBERSHIP

Section 1. Categories of Membership.

Membership in the Association shall comprise a category of Active members and such other categories as may be provided in the Bylaws.

Section 2. Membership Eligibility: Provisions and Limitations.

a. Membership, as provided in the Bylaws, shall be open to all persons actively engaged in the profession of teaching or in other educational work or to persons interested in advancing the cause of public education who shall agree to subscribe to the goals and objectives of the Association and to abide by its Constitution and Bylaws.

b. Members engaged in teaching or in other educational work shall adhere to the *Code of Ethics of the Education Profession.*

c. An application for membership shall be subject to review as provided in the Bylaws.

d. The Association shall not deny membership to individuals on the basis of race, color, national origin, creed, gender, sexual orientation, age, handicap, marital status, or economic status, nor shall any organization which so denies membership be affiliated with the Association.

Section 3. Property Interest of Members.

All right, title, and interest, both legal and equitable, of a member in and to the property of the Association shall end upon the termination of such membership.

ARTICLE III. REPRESENTATIVE ASSEMBLY
Section 1. Accountability.

The Representative Assembly, comprising members of the Association, derives its powers from and shall be responsible to the membership.

Section 2. Allocation of Delegates.

a. Allocation of delegate credentials to state affiliates shall be based on the ratio of 1:1,000 Active members of the Association within the state. No state shall receive fewer than fifteen (15) delegate credentials. Other delegate credentials shall be allocated as provided in the Bylaws.

b. Allocation of delegate credentials to local affiliates shall be based on the ratio of 1:150 Active members of the Association or major fraction thereof. Local affiliates within a state may similarly join together to form membership units for the purpose of representation. Allocation of delegate credentials for such clustered local affiliates shall be based on the ratio of 1:150 Active members of the Association or major fraction thereof.

c. The Bylaws shall define the term *ethnic minority* and shall seek to achieve ethnic-minority representation in the Representative Assembly.

Section 3. Election of Delegates.

a. Members of the Representative Assembly shall be elected in accordance with the one-person one-vote principle. Specific exceptions to the application of this principle may be set forth in this Constitution and/or the Bylaws.

b. Election to the Board of Directors by the Active NEA members within the state shall constitute election to the Representative Assembly for all purposes.

Election to the Board of Directors by the Active NEA members elected to serve as delegates to the state representative body shall constitute election to the Representative Assembly for all purposes except voting in elections for Association officers.

Election to the Board of Directors as a retired or student director shall constitute election to the Representative Assembly for all purposes except voting in elections for Association officers.

Election to executive office or to the Executive Committee shall constitute election to the Representative Assembly for all purposes except voting in elections for Association officers.

Election to the presidency of a state affiliate by vote of members in the state who are eligible to vote in such election shall constitute election to the Representative Assembly for all purposes.

Election to the presidency of a state affiliate by the state representative body shall constitute election to the Representative Assembly for all purposes except voting in elections for Association officers.

c. Election of delegates to the Representative Assembly shall be by secret ballot for each individual position. The NEA members within each membership group entitled to delegate allocations as set forth in the Constitution and the Bylaws shall be eligible to vote.

d. If the number of candidates for delegate positions is equal to or less than the number of positions to be filled, elections may be waived, and the candidates declared elected to the delegate positions in question.

Section 4. Seating of Delegates.

The Representative Assembly shall have jurisdiction over the seating of its delegates.

Section 5. Meetings.

The Representative Assembly shall meet at least annually. This stipulation shall apply except in cases of emergency.

Section 6. Committees.

All appointive bodies of the Association except the Review Board shall be designated by the term *committee*. A Committee on Constitution, Bylaws, and Rules shall be established by the Representative Assembly. All other committees shall be established or discontinued as provided in the Bylaws. All committees except the Standing Committee on Educational Support Personnel and the Advisory Committee of Student Members shall comprise at least seventy-five (75) percent classroom teachers. There shall be a minimum of twenty (20) percent ethnic-minority representation on each committee.

Section 7. Functions.

The Representative Assembly shall

a. Establish Association policies and objectives;

b. Elect the President, the Vice-President, the Secretary-Treasurer, the at-large members of the Board of Directors, and the members of the Executive Committee as provided in this Constitution and/or the bylaws;

c. Adopt the annual budget;

d. Establish dues;

e. Approve or ratify the establishment of subsidiary corporate structures;

f. Exercise final authority in all matters of the Association;

g. Amend this Constitution and the Bylaws in accordance with Article IX hereof;

h. Adopt the rules and agenda governing its meetings; and

i. Enact such other measures as may be necessary to achieve the goals and objectives of the Association which are not in conflict with the Charter, this Constitution, or the Bylaws.

Section 8. Objectives.

The Representative Assembly may periodically establish specific objectives in the pursuance of the stated goals of the Association.

Section 9. Postponement of Annual Meeting.

In the event of an emergency, the Board may postpone the Annual Meeting as provided by the Bylaws. In the event of such postponement, all officers and members of boards and committees authorized by this Constitution and by the Bylaws shall remain in office until the Representative Assembly convenes. It shall then provide for their successors.

ARTICLE IV. EXECUTIVE OFFICERS

Section 1. Executive Officers.

The executive officers of the Association shall be the President, the Vice-President, and the Secretary-Treasurer.

164

Section 2. Qualifications for Executive Officers.
All candidates for the office of President, Vice-President, and Secretary-Treasurer shall have been Active members of the Association for at least two (2) years immediately preceding the election. All executive officers shall maintain Active membership in the Association.

Section 3. Elections, Terms, and Salaries.
   a. Beginning in 1993 and each third year thereafter, the President and the Vice-President shall be nominated at and elected by the Representative Assembly at the Annual Meeting in accordance with this Constitution, the Bylaws, and the Standing Rules.

   b. Beginning in 1994 and each third year thereafter, the Secretary-Treasurer shall be nominated at and elected by the Representative Assembly at the Annual Meeting in accordance with this Constitution, the Bylaws, and the Standing Rules.

   c. In an election for President, Vice-President, or Secretary-Treasurer, if there is only one (1) candidate for the position, the chair shall declare such candidate elected.

   d. The terms of the President, of the Vice-President, and of the Secretary-Treasurer shall be three (3) years beginning September 1 following their election.[1] Each executive officer shall remain in office through August 31 of the year in which a successor is elected, unless otherwise provided in this Constitution. An executive officer shall serve no more than two (2) terms in the office to which elected.

   e. The executive officers shall serve full time; their salaries shall be established by the Board of Directors.

Section 4. Affirmative Action Procedure.
By December 1 of each membership year immediately preceding the next membership year in which a presidential election is to be held (i.e., approximately 18 months prior to the date of the election), appropriate information about the office of President and the electoral process, including all relevant timelines, shall be sent to each of the ethnic-minority special interest groups identified in Bylaw 12; and

During the membership year in which the aforesaid presidential election is to be held, a copy of this section of the Constitution, with an appropriate explanation as to its background and intent, shall be included in (a) an Association publication sent to all members by December 1 and (b) the material that is sent to the delegates to that year's Representative Assembly.

If after any period of eleven (11) consecutive membership years a member of an ethnic-minority group has not served as President, the Association shall take such steps as may be legally permissible to elect a member of an ethnic-minority group.

Section 5. Succession and Vacancies.
Vacancies occurring by reason of death, resignation, incapacity, judgment of impeachment, or other disqualification shall be filled as follows:

   a. A vacancy in the office of President shall be filled by the Vice-President.

   b. If during the first or second year of a term a vacancy in either the office of Vice-President or the office of Secretary-Treasurer occurs, such vacancy shall be filled by the Board of Directors, which shall elect a successor to serve until the next meeting of the Representative Assembly. The Representative Assembly shall then elect a successor for the remainder of the term. In the event a vacancy occurs during the third year of a term, the Board of Directors shall elect a successor for the remainder of the term.

Section 6. Impeachment.
Executive officers of the Association may be impeached for violation of the *Code of*

---

[1]The three-year terms shall be effective pursuant to the dates set forth in Section 3(a) and (b) above.

Ethics of the Education Profession, for misfeasance, for malfeasance, or for nonfeasance in office.

a. Impeachment proceedings against an executive officer shall be initiated by written petition submitted to the Review Board by at least fifteen (15) percent of the certified delegates to the Representative Assembly.

b. If, after a due process hearing, a two-thirds (2/3) vote of the Review Board shall sustain the charge, the office shall become vacant.

c. The officer may appeal the decision to the Board of Directors.

ARTICLE V. BOARD OF DIRECTORS
Section 1. Composition.
The board shall consist of (a) at least one (1) director from each association affiliated with the Association as a state affiliate, (b) six (6) directors for the Retired members of the Association, and (c) three (3) directors for the Student members of the Association.

Each state unit shall be entitled to an additional director for each 20,000 Active members of the Association, provided that if the number of state directors reaches one hundred fifty (150), the number of directors to which the state units are entitled shall be adjusted to prevent the total from exceeding one hundred fifty (150). The Board of Directors shall adopt rules for implementing this provision.

The executive officers and other members of the Executive Committee shall be members of the Board of Directors ex officio.

a. At least one (1) director elected within each state shall be a nonsupervisor, and if a state is entitled to more than one (1) director, at least one (1) shall be a classroom teacher. The total number of additional directors representing the members in each state affiliate after the first shall be on the basis of proportional representation by educational position of NEA members.

b. In the event that the first three (3) directors from a state or the first three (3) retired directors or the first three (3) student directors do not include at least one (1) ethnic-minority person, the state affiliate or the retired or student delegates to the Representative Assembly, as the case may be, shall take all legally permissible steps to elect a fourth director who is from an ethnic-minority group.

c. Members from ethnic minorities shall comprise at least twenty (20) percent of the Board. The Representative Assembly shall elect additional directors as appropriate to assure such ethnic-minority representation. If between meetings of the Representative Assembly ethnic-minority representation on the Board falls below twenty (20) percent, the Board shall elect additional directors as appropriate to assure the necessary ethnic-minority representation, provided that such an election can be held at a Board meeting prior to the meeting that takes place in connection with the Annual Meeting. Candidates for these positions shall be nominated by members of the Board and ethnic-minority caucus chairpersons, and any ethnic-minority person who otherwise is eligible to serve on the Board may be a candidate. The person(s) elected shall serve until an election can be held by the next Representative Assembly in accordance with this section.

d. Administrators shall be represented on the Board in proportion to their membership in the Association. If the percentage of administrators elected to the Board of Directors fails to achieve proportional representation, the Representative Assembly shall elect at large the number required to assure such representation. Candidates for these positions shall be nominated by the delegates at the Representative Assembly who are administrators.

e. Classroom teachers in higher education shall be represented on the Board at least in proportion to their membership in the Association. If the percentage of classroom teachers in higher education elected to the Board of Directors fails to achieve such proportional representation, the Representative Assembly shall elect at large the number required to assure such representation. Candidates for these positions shall be nominated by the delegates at the Representative Assembly who are classroom teachers in higher education.

f. Active members employed in educational support positions shall be represented on the Board at least in proportion to their membership in the Association. If the percentage of such members elected to the Board fails to achieve such proportional representation, the Representative Assembly shall elect at large the number required to assure such representation. Candidates for these positions shall be nominated by the delegates at the Representative Assembly who are Active members employed in educational support positions.

g. In elections for at-large positions on the Board of Directors at the Representative Assembly, if the number of candidates nominated equals the number of positions to be filled, the chair shall declare such candidates elected.

h. Student and retired representation on the Board of Directors shall not be computed in determining the representation entitlements of administrators, classroom teachers in higher education, or Active members employed in educational support positions.

Section 2. Terms of Office.

a. The term of office of NEA state, at-large, and retired directors shall be three (3) years.

b. NEA state and at-large directors shall serve no more than two (2) terms. Prior service as a student director shall not be counted toward the two (2) term limit for state and at-large directors.

c. Retired directors shall serve no more than two (2) terms. Prior service on the Board of Directors in a position other than a retired director position shall not be counted toward the two (2) term limit for a retired director.

d. All candidates for NEA state director shall have been Active members of the Association for at least two (2) years immediately preceding the election. All state directors shall maintain throughout their terms of office Active membership in the Association.

e. Retired directors shall maintain Retired membership throughout their terms of office.

f. Student directors shall serve terms of one (1) year and may not serve more than two (2) terms. The directors shall be Student members of the Association.

Section 3. Functions.

Consistent with the goals and objectives and the existing policies of the Association, the Board of Directors shall act for the Association between meetings of the Representative Assembly and in addition shall have the sole responsibility for any matter expressly delegated to it by the Representative Assembly.

ARTICLE VI. EXECUTIVE COMMITTEE
Section 1. Composition.

The Executive Committee shall consist of three (3) executive officers and six (6) members who shall be officers of the Association.

a. The executive officers and the six (6) members of the Executive Committee shall be nominated and elected at large by the Representative Assembly by majority vote and by secret ballot for each individual office.

167

b. If the number of candidates for the Executive Committee equals the number of positions to be filled, the chair shall declare such candidates elected.

c. Members from ethnic minorities shall comprise at least twenty (20) percent of the Executive Committee members as appropriate to assure such ethnic-minority representation.

Section 2. Qualifications and Terms of Office.

a. Terms of the Executive Committee members shall be three (3) years beginning September 1 following the election.[2] Such members of the Executive Committee shall not serve more than two (2) terms.

b. All candidates shall have been Active members of the Association for at least two (2) years immediately preceding the election. All Executive Committee members shall maintain throughout their terms of office Active membership in the Association.

Section 3. Functions.

Consistent with the goals and objectives and the existing policies of the Association, the Executive Committee shall act for the Association between meetings of the Board of Directors and in addition shall have the sole responsibility for any matter expressly delegated to it by the Representative Assembly and/or the Board of Directors.

Section 4. Impeachment.

Officers of the Association may be impeached for violation of the *Code of Ethics of the Education Profession*, for misfeasance, for malfeasance, or for nonfeasance in office.

a. Impeachment proceedings against an officer may be initiated by written petition submitted to the Review Board by at least fifteen (15) percent of the certified delegates to the Representative Assembly.

b. If, after a due process hearing, a two-thirds (2/3) vote of the Review Board shall sustain the charge, the office shall become vacant.

c. The officer may appeal the decision to the Board of Directors.

ARTICLE VII. REVIEW BOARD
Section 1.

The judicial powers of the Association as described in this Article shall be vested in the Review Board.

Section 2. Powers.

The jurisdiction of the Review Board shall extend to cases as herein defined:

a. The Review Board shall have original jurisdiction in the following cases:

1. Impeachment of an officer who is a member of the Executive Committee;

2. Alleged violations of the *Code of Ethics of the Education Profession*;

3. The censure, suspension, or expulsion of a member;

4. Review, upon request, of an action of the Executive Committee, Board of Directors, or Representative Assembly regarding consistent application of the Constitution or Bylaws of the Association.

b. The Review Board shall have the following powers subject to the conditions as herein outlined:

1. To impeach an officer. The officer shall have the right to appeal to the Board of Directors;

2. To censure, suspend, or expel a member for violation of the *Code of Ethics of the Education Profession* or other sufficient cause. The member shall have the right to appeal to the Executive Committee on procedural grounds only;

[2]The executive officers shall serve three-year terms effective with dates set forth in Article IV, Section 3(a) and (b).

168

3. To vacate censure, life suspension, or reinstate a member;

4. To review an action of the Executive Committee, Board of Directors, or Representative Assembly for consistency with the Constitution and Bylaws and to recommend to the appropriate governing body remedial action if necessary. Requests for review may be made only by the Executive Committee, Board of Directors, Representative Assembly, a local or state affiliate (by official action), or upon petition of ten (10) percent of the certified delegates of the Representative Assembly.

Section 3. Review Board Appointment.

The Review Board shall be appointed by the President with the advice and consent of the Board of Directors.

Section 4. Review Board Prerogatives.

The Review Board shall establish its rules of procedure with the approval of the Board of Directors. Due process must be guaranteed in all its proceedings.

Section 5. Impeachment.

a. Members of the Review Board may be impeached for violation of the *Code of Ethics of the Education Profession*, for misfeasance, for malfeasance, or for nonfeasance in office.

b. The process for impeachment of Review Board members shall be as follows:

1. Proceedings against a member of the Review Board shall be initiated by action of the Representative Assembly, or by official action of a local or state affiliate or upon petition of ten (10) percent of the certified delegates of the Representative Assembly under rules determined by the Board of Directors.

2. An affirmative vote of the Executive Committee shall be required to order an impeachment hearing on specified charges.

3. An affirmative vote of at least two-thirds (2/3) of the members of the Executive Committee shall be required to sustain a charge following a due process hearing before the Committee and the position shall become vacant.

4. The member has the right to appeal the Executive Committee decision to the Board of Directors. No member of the Executive Committee shall be a party to the appellate procedure.

ARTICLE VIII. AFFILIATES AND SPECIAL INTEREST GROUPS

Section 1. Affiliation.

Affiliation shall mean a relationship based on a reciprocal contractual agreement between the Association and an organization involved with or interested in education and shall continue until the affiliate withdraws or becomes disaffiliated.

Section 2. Ethnic-Minority Representation.

Affiliates of the Association shall take all reasonable and legally permissible steps to achieve on their elective and appointive bodies ethnic-minority representation that is at least proportionate to the ethnic-minority membership of the affiliate.

Section 3. Classes.

The classes of affiliates shall be governance, nongovernance, and such other affiliates as may be provided in the Bylaws.

a. The governance class shall comprise local and state affiliates exclusively.

b. The nongovernance class shall comprise all other affiliated professional and nonprofessional organizations.

Section 4. Rights of Active Members in Governance Affiliates.

Each governance affiliate shall guarantee its active members an open nomination procedure and a secret ballot except as otherwise provided in this Constitution or in the Bylaws. No governance affiliate shall discriminate against its active members in their right to vote, seek office, or otherwise participate in the affairs of the affiliate, of other governance affiliates, or of the Association.

Section 5. Standards and Procedures for Affiliation.

Affiliates which fail to comply with standards and procedures set forth in the Bylaws shall be subject to censure, suspension, or disaffiliation as prescribed in this Constitution.

Section 6. Special Interest Groups.

Any organized group of Association members having a common interest or purpose may be recognized as a Special Interest Group, provided such group is not eligible for any class of affiliation.

ARTICLE IX. AMENDMENT OF CONSTITUTION AND BYLAWS

Section 1. Proposal of Amendments.

Amendments to the Constitution or the Bylaws may be proposed to the Representative Assembly by one or more of the following methods:

a. By petition signed by at least one hundred (100) Active members from two (2) or more states and submitted to the Committee on Constitution, Bylaws, and Rules for presentation to the Representative Assembly;

b. By petition signed by at least fifty (50) certified delegates and submitted to the Committee on Constitution, Bylaws, and Rules for presentation to the Representative Assembly;

c. By at least two (2) state delegations in the Representative Assembly whose concurrence in the proposed amendment is evidenced either by a majority vote of those delegates present and voting in each delegation at a regularly called meeting of the delegation held in connection with the Annual Meeting or by petition signed by a majority of the members of each delegation. Proposals shall then be submitted to the Committee on Constitution, Bylaws, and Rules for presentation to the Representative Assembly.

d. By majority vote of the NEA Board of Directors and submitted to the Committee on Constitution, Bylaws, and Rules for presentation to the Representative Assembly; or

e. By a majority vote of the Committee on Constitution, Bylaws, and Rules.

Section 2. Amendment of the Constitution.

a. A proposed amendment to the Constitution shall be presented in writing to the Committee on Constitution, Bylaws, and Rules and read by title to the Annual Meeting immediately prior to its proposed adoption. Documentation of timely submission of an amendment shall be the responsibility of the contact person for the amendment.

b. The text of the proposed amendment shall be printed in an official publication sent to all members at least sixty (60) days prior to its consideration.

c. This Constitution may then be amended at the Annual Meeting by a two-thirds (2/3) vote of delegates present and voting.

Section 3. Amendment of the Bylaws.

a. A proposed amendment to the Bylaws shall be presented in writing to the Committee on Constitution, Bylaws, and Rules, postmarked no later than one hundred twenty (120) days preceding the Annual Meeting. Documentation of timely submission of an amendment shall be the responsibility of the contact person for the amendment.

b. The text of the proposed amendment shall be printed in an official publication sent to all members at least sixty (60) days prior to its consideration.

c. The Bylaws may then be amended at the Annual Meeting by a majority vote of the delegates present and voting.

Section 4. Voting on Amendments.

a. Voting on proposed amendments to this Constitution or to the Bylaws shall be by secret ballot.

b. Unless otherwise provided, all amendments shall take effect at the beginning of the fiscal year following their adoption.

Section 5. Withdrawal of Proposed Amendments.

Requests for withdrawal of proposed amendments shall be submitted in writing to the Committee on Constitution, Bylaws, and Rules. Such withdrawal shall be effective when approved by the Representative Assembly. Requests for withdrawal of proposed amendments to this Constitution or to the Bylaws may be granted by action of the Representative Assembly based on requests made in the following manner:

a. If originally proposed by petition of one hundred (100) or more members from two (2) states or fifty (50) or more delegates, the request shall be signed by at least two-thirds (2/3) of such members or delegates;

b. If originally proposed by two (2) state delegations, the request shall be signed by at least two-thirds (2/3) of the delegates from each state;

c. If originally proposed by the NEA Board of Directors, the request shall be made by a majority of the Board;

d. If originally proposed by the Committee on Constitution, Bylaws, and Rules, the request shall be made by a majority committee.

Constitution of the
American Federation of Teachers, AFL-CIO

Correct as of August, 1992

NOTE: *Underlined words indicate new language adopted at the 1992 convention.*

ARTICLE I
NAME

This organization shall be known as the American Federation of Teachers, with divisions known as Public and Private School Teachers, Paraprofessionals and School-Related Personnel, the Federation of Nurses and Health Professionals, the Federation of Higher Education Faculty and Professionals and the Federation of Public Employees.

ARTICLE II
OBJECTS

Section 1. To obtain exclusive bargaining rights, including the right to strike, for teachers, paraprofessionals and school-related personnel, higher education faculty and professionals, state and local public employees, health care employees and other workers.

Section 2. To bring local and state federations of teachers and other workers into relations of mutual assistance and cooperation.

Section 3. To obtain for teachers and other workers all of the rights to which they are entitled in a free society.

Section 4. To improve standards for teachers, paraprofessionals and school-related personnel, higher education faculty and professionals, state and local public employees, health care employees and other workers, by promoting better preparation, encouraging relevant in-service training and securing the working conditions essential to the best performance of professional service.

Section 5. To improve the standards for registered nurses, allied health professionals and other health care employees by advancing economic status, promoting better preparation in basic education programs, encouraging and promoting continuing education, securing working conditions essential to the best performance of services and the most effective delivery of health care.

Section 6. To improve standards for public employees by working for the passage and strengthening of collective bargaining and civil service legislation in the states, promoting continuing education for state employees and securing working conditions conducive to the best performance and delivery of public service.

Section 7. To encourage the hiring and retention of competent teachers, paraprofessionals and school-related personnel, the maintenance of modern, well-equipped schools and the promotion of such educational programs and conditions in American schools as will enable their students to equip themselves better to take their places in the economic, social and political life of the community.

Section 8. To promote the welfare of children by providing progressively better educational opportunities for all, regardless of race, creed, sex and social, political or economic status.

Section 9. To promote the welfare of the health care consumer by promoting progressively better access to and utilization of health care resources in this country.

Section 10. To fight all forms of bias due to race, creed, sex, social, political or economic status or national origin.

Section 11. To support and promote the ideals of democracy as envisioned in the Constitution of the United States of America, its Bill of Rights and other Amendments, to work for passage and retention of just laws that will improve the educational climate for students, teachers and other workers in education and to encourage them to exercise their proper rights and responsibilities under these laws.

Section 12. To encourage state federations and locals to organize retired members.

ARTICLE III
MEMBERSHIP

Section 1. This organization shall consist of <u>divisions</u> of public and private school teachers, paraprofessionals and school-related personnel, higher education faculty and professionals, nurses, allied health professionals and other health care employees, state and local public employees and other workers organized in conformity with the provisions of this constitution. Other employees may be members of any local whose constitution so permits.

Section 2. <u>A program and policy council shall be created to represent each division of membership. Members of program and policy councils and their chairpersons shall be appointed by the AFT executive council, upon recommendation by the AFT president. Recommendations from the program and policy councils will be presented to the AFT executive council for its consideration.</u>

Section 3. Classroom teachers with supervisory authority may be admitted to membership by any local whose constitution so permits.

Section 4. Any teacher residing outside of the jurisdiction of an established local may be accepted as a member of the nearest local or as a member at large of the state federation. The state federation shall have full jurisdiction in the determination of a procedure for participation by these at-large members in all activities of the state federation.

Section 5. The executive council may exercise its discretion in the chartering of groups of teachers, paraprofessionals and school-related personnel, higher education faculty and professionals, nurses, allied health professionals, other health care employees, state and local public employees or other workers.

Section 6. Locals may establish the following special classes of membership:

    (a) Employees who are eligible for membership whose salary is less than the beginning teacher's salary or employees whose salary is less than $15,000, whichever salary is higher. Such locals pay per-capita tax for such members at one-half the regular rate.

    (b) Employees earning under $10,000. Such locals pay per-capita tax for such members at one-quarter the regular rate.

    (c) Laid-off employees, or employees on unpaid leave. Such locals shall pay per-capita tax for such members at the rate of $1.00 per month.

    Such members shall be entitled to receive full benefits of membership.

Section 7. Where a local of the American Federation of Teachers exists in or near a

173

college or university having a department of education, that local may accept prospective teachers as student members. Annual dues of $5.00 per year shall be paid directly to the national office by the local for each student member. Student members shall have only visitors' privileges at the convention. A student teacher may also be accepted as a member at large of the state federation.

Section 8. In jurisdictions where there are no college or university locals of the American Federation of Teachers, membership may be granted to individual college and university teachers by a local in that vicinity. Such membership may be maintained until there is chartered a college or university local in which such a member would be eligible for membership.

Section 9. In jurisdictions where there is no local, employees may be admitted as associate AFT members without AFT voting rights but with rights to participate in benefit programs such as insurance, travel and discount buying programs. The dues for associate AFT members shall be determined by the AFT executive council.

Former active members who are not eligible to continue their active membership may be admitted as associate members without voting rights but with the right to participate in benefit programs such as insurance, travel and discount buying services. The dues for this category of associate member shall be determined by the AFT executive council.

The AFT executive council is authorized to establish an organization(s) of associate AFT members without AFT voting rights. Associate AFT members in such organization(s) shall elect their chief executive officer.

Section 10. Effective September 1, 1990, an active member who retires from his/her present position shall be admitted as an AFT retiree member whose sole AFT voting rights are provided in Article VIII, Section 6, (new) and with the right to participate in benefit programs such as insurance, travel and discount buying services.

Section 11. No discrimination shall ever be shown toward individual members or applicants for membership because of race, creed, sex, sexual orientation, social, political or economic status or national origin. Locals may establish procedures for admission of new members except that no discrimination shall ever be shown toward individual members or applicants for membership because of race, creed, sex, sexual orientation, social, political or economic status or national origin.

Section 12. Nothing contained in this article shall permit this organization to admit into membership any organization of nonteaching persons who hold the position of principal or any higher position. This provision shall not be applicable to locals chartered prior to its adoption.

Nothing contained in this article shall permit locals to admit into or retain in membership any nonteaching person who holds the position of principal or any higher position. This provision shall not be applicable to holders of such positions who held membership in any local prior to the adoption of this article.

The executive council may permit locals to admit such persons into membership only where the exclusion of such persons from membership would legally bar a local from achieving exclusive representation for classroom teachers.

ARTICLE IV
CHARTERS

Section 1. Ten or more teachers and/or workers, upon application to the executive council and the payment of $25.00, may be granted a charter, and such locals shall establish and maintain at least a minimum dues of $50.00 per year unless, in the opinion of the executive council, special circumstances exist.

Section 2. Upon application to the executive council and the payment of a fee of $25.00, a charter may be issued to ten or more teachers in educational institutions not supported by public funds.
Section 3. Charters may be granted by the executive council to state federations upon the payment of a charter fee of $10.00. A state federation shall consist of no fewer than three locals of the American Federation of Teachers, except when fewer than three locals represent jurisdictions embracing 50 percent of the teacher strength in the state. No dues shall be assessed on the state federations by the national organization except for the members at large as provided in the constitution.
Section 4. Charters may be granted by the AFT executive council to organizations of retired members upon payment of a charter fee of $5.00. Applications for such charters shall be made only by established local unions, state federations or regional councils.

The AFT executive council shall make such rules and regulations as are necessary for the administration of this section such as, but not limited to, the number of retirees required for issuing a charter and a definition of retiree.

The voting status of such organizations shall be as defined in Article VIII, Section 6.
Section 5. All locals and state federations shall submit three copies of their constitution and bylaws to the national organization within three months of receiving their charter or <u>as</u> of September 1, 1955, whichever is the later date, and they shall similarly submit all subsequent amendments to their constitution and bylaws. No such constitution or bylaws shall be in conflict with the constitution of the American Federation of Teachers. <u>Effective September 1, 1994, and thereafter, the constitution and bylaws of each affiliated local and state federation shall provide for regular meetings of an executive body and regular meetings of the general membership or a representative body of the general membership. The conduct of elections shall be consistent with the standards for such elections developed under Title IV of the Labor-Management Reporting and Disclosure Act (LMRDA). Terms of office for officers shall not exceed four years, or fewer if required by applicable state or federal laws.</u>
Section 6. Effective September 1, 1985, and thereafter, each affiliated local shall increase the local dues to equal any increase in per-capita payments that are required to be made to the American Federation of Teachers and any increase to either the state federation or the regional council with which the local is affiliated. <u>Effective September 1, 1993, and at least every two years thereafter, each affiliated local and state federation shall convene a committee of at least three members to conduct an internal financial review according to a format to be determined by the AFT executive council, or the local or state federation shall contract for an outside audit that meets the standards of generally accepted accounting principles. Either of these reviews must be made available to its membership and provided to the national office by January 1, 1994, and at least every two years thereafter.</u>
Section 7. The charter granted to any local shall not be revoked or suspended because it has a membership of less than ten but not less than seven.
Section 8. A charter issued to any local or state federation may be suspended or revoked by the executive council when the existence of such local or state federation is detrimental to the development of democracy in education. However, except for the nonpayment of dues to this organization, no local or state federation shall have its charter suspended or revoked until the executive council has (a) served the local or state federation with written specific charges, (b) provided the local or state federation a reasonable time to prepare its defense and (c) afforded a full and fair hearing within the jurisdictions of the local or state federation.

Except for nonpayment of dues, such suspension or revocation may be appealed to the next national convention. The appeal shall be the first order of convention business. The local may present its own case without the right to vote. A two-thirds vote of the convention shall be required to sustain such suspension or revocation.

Section 9. In the event a local or state federation disbands, the balance in the treasury shall be forwarded to the Defense Fund of the American Federation of Teachers.[1]

Section 10. No charter of the American Federation of Teachers that defines or recognizes jurisdiction on a basis of race, creed, sex, sexual orientation, social, political or economic status or national origin or permits the practice of such jurisdiction shall be recognized as valid, and the practice of any local in limiting its membership on account of race, creed, sex, sexual orientation, social, political or economic status or national origin shall render its charter void.

Section 11. A student federation of teachers may be chartered in any college or university. There must be a minimum of ten members. Per capita for each member to the national organization shall be $5.00, payable annually.

A student federation of teachers may be chartered in any high school upon an application of the sponsoring local and payment of not less than $10.00 per year for such organization of at least ten members. Locals may establish reasonable dues for members of the student federation.

The executive council shall make such rules and regulations as are necessary for the administration of this section.

Such student-teacher members shall have no voting status in either the national or state federations.

Section 12.

A. Jurisdiction of Locals

The executive council shall have power to allocate and define and, from time to time, redefine and reallocate the jurisdictions within which locals may exercise their jurisdictions. In doing so, the executive council shall be guided by the primary purpose of the American Federation of Teachers, which is to organize teachers and other workers into strong, effective unions for the purpose of achieving and engaging in collective bargaining.

B. Rules for Defining and Allocating Jurisdiction

(1) In the exercise of this power, the executive council shall give preference to a local operating within a specific geographic area whose members shall constitute a bargaining unit of employees of a single employer or employees of two or more employers within a geographic area. Where a statute, regulation or decision by a court or other regulatory agency defines a bargaining unit on some other basis, exceptions may be made to conform thereto.

(2) It will not be considered an infraction of this principle if there are several employers of teachers and other workers within the same general geographic area and the employees of each such employer are organized separately.

(3) No teacher or other worker who is a member of the bargaining unit of a local in a defined jurisdictional area may be a member-at-large of a state federation or be a member of a local having a general jurisdiction.

(4) A teacher or other worker who is a member-at-large of a state federation or a local having a general jurisdiction and is employed within the jurisdiction of another local now or hereafter chartered shall terminate such membership within 30 days.

---

[1]IRS regulations prohibit the assets of defunct, nonprofit organizations from accruing to the personal benefit of former officers or members of the organization.

(5) No local shall have or maintain jurisdiction in an area that crosses state lines or has jurisdiction in more than one state without the specific approval of the executive council.

(6) Nothing in this section shall prohibit a local from representing educational workers employed by labor organizations (other than AFT) in worker education or by other private employers or government agencies or in places where no AFT local is chartered, but any person so employed shall cease to be a member of the first-mentioned local within 30 days after the chartering of a local that has jurisdiction of the employees of the employer of any such person.

(7) Nothing in this section shall prohibit the existence or chartering of locals of educational workers other than teachers (such as clerks, truant officers, nurses, librarians and the like) where such local is otherwise in conformity with this section; nor shall anything in this section prohibit locals of non-public teachers and other educational workers in the same or overlapping geographic area as another local.

(8) The executive council may make rules to carry out any of the provisions of this section and shall determine all questions arising hereunder.

(9) All decisions of the executive council that the executive council makes in the exercise of the powers defined in Section 11, Article IV, may be appealed to the next national convention.

ARTICLE V
OFFICERS

Section 1. The elected officers of the AFT shall be a president, secretary-treasurer and thirty-eight vice presidents. <u>All divisions must be represented among the thirty-eight vice presidents</u>. These forty shall constitute the executive council. They shall be elected in the even years by the convention for the term of two years. Vacancies shall be filled as provided in Article VI.

Section 2. The president shall be the chief executive officer of the federation and administer all of the affairs of the federation and execute policies of the federation as determined by the convention and the executive council.

Section 3. The secretary-treasurer shall be the financial officer of the federation. His or her duties shall include:

(a) the collection of all monies, properties, files and effects of the federation.

(b) the payment of all monies properly authorized by the council or the president through the adopted budget of the federation.

(c) to arrange from time to time but no less than annually for the audit of all books, accounts, records and financial transactions of the federation by an independent auditing firm. Such audit to be provided to the officers of the federation.

(d) to issue the Call for the convention and cause the proceedings of the convention to be recorded.

(e) to work under the direction of the president in the performance of all other responsibilities as may be given him or her by the president or the executive council.

Section 4. No one shall be elected an officer of the federation unless he/she is a member of an affiliated local or a state federation.

Section 5. No vice president shall be a full-time salaried employee of the American Federation of Teachers.

Section 6. The delegates to the convention of the American Federation of Labor and Congress of Industrial Organizations shall be the president and other delegates elected by the biennial convention.

ARTICLE VI
EXECUTIVE COUNCIL

Section 1. It shall be the duty of the executive council to obey the instructions of national conventions, except that any action by the convention involving expenditure of funds shall be referred to the executive council with power to revise in conformity with the budget.

Section 2. Upon the recommendation of the president the executive council may employ such employees as it shall deem necessary. Administrative employees shall be employed by individual or union contract with provision for orderly dismissal with the right of hearing and counsel available to the employee.

Other employees may be employed by union contract and procedure shall be established in all such contracts for orderly dismissal with the right of hearing and counsel unless otherwise provided in a union contract. The provisions of this section shall not apply to officers of the federation.

Section 3. The executive council shall have the power to designate one of the officers of the federation to act in place of the president in event of temporary or permanent vacancy of the office during his/her term.

Section 4. The executive council, upon recommendation of the president, shall fill a temporary or permanent vacancy in the office of the secretary-treasurer.

Section 5. The executive council shall set the salary of the president. Such salary shall not be diminished during the president's term in office.

Section 6. The executive council shall have the power to fill vacancies in its membership until the next regular convention.

Section 7. The executive council shall have the authority to assign duties and areas of responsibility for each vice president.

Section 8. The executive council shall have the power to interpret and enforce this constitution and to make rules not in conflict with this constitution and shall report such rules to the succeeding convention for approval or rejection. Any interpretation of the constitution by the executive council may be appealed at any subsequent convention.

Section 9. The executive council shall appoint such committees as it deems necessary, not inconsistent with the constitution.

Section 10. The executive council shall meet at its discretion during the period between conventions. The expenses of executive council meetings shall be paid by the American Federation of Teachers, each member of the executive council submitting an expense account to the national office.

Section 11. The executive council shall have authority to deal with all of the affairs of the federation in the period between the conventions.

Section 12. (a) The executive council may authorize the president to appoint a committee of the executive council to conduct an investigation of a local:

(i) upon the appeal of the officers or of the executive board or 30 percent or more of the membership of that local,

(ii) upon the appeal by a two-thirds vote of the officers and executive board of a state federation or by state convention action or by 30 percent of the locals affiliated with a state federation, or

(iii) upon the appeal of locals representing 30 percent of the membership of the American Federation of Teachers within the state.

The executive council may authorize a similar investigation of a state federation or of disputes between a local or locals and a state federation upon the appeal of one or more locals of that state.

In any of these situations, the committee shall conduct an investigation and make a full report with recommendations to the executive council, which shall have full power to take appropriate action to resolve the matter. One-third of the cost of the investigation shall be borne by the national office. The executive council shall require the initiating party to advance $250.00 before proceeding, but may, in its final decision, assess up to two-thirds of the cost against the parties in such manner as it deems just. At its discretion, the executive council may return the $250.00, or any portion of it, advanced by the initiating party.

Section 12. (b) The executive council may, by a two-thirds vote, authorize the president to appoint a committee to investigate a local or state federation where an election appears to have been conducted in violation of the local or state federation constitution, the AFT constitution or applicable federal law or a local whose conduct is not in harmony with the principles of the AFT and tends to bring the AFT into disrepute or a local that fails to maintain affiliation mandated in Sections 2 and 3 of Article XI. The local or state federation shall be given an opportunity to present its position to the committee. The committee shall submit its findings and recommendations to the council, which shall have the power to take action to resolve the matter, including the imposition of the penalty contained in Article XI, Section 3 and/or other appropriate penalties. The action of the council in such cases shall be final. The cost of such an investigation shall be borne by the national office.

Section 12. (c) The executive council may authorize the president to investigate the alleged failure of local unions and state federations to comply with provisions of the AFT constitution. Such an investigation shall determine whether or not a violation exists, and if so, what steps must be taken by the state federation or local to comply with the AFT constitution as well as what assistance may be offered by the national union to help the state federation or local to address circumstances that may have led or contributed to the violation. If such an investigation, or assistance provided as a result of such an investigation, fails to bring the state federation or local union into compliance with the AFT constitution, then the president shall submit findings and recommendations to the council, which shall have the power to take action to resolve the matter, including but not limited to the following, plus any other measures enforceable through legal action or any other means:

(i) The ordering and enforcement of compliance;

(ii) Communication to the members of the state federation or local that informs them about the violation and how it affects their status as AFT members;

(iii) The withholding of any AFT services or assistance provided to the state federation or local;

(iv) The denial of access to the AFT Militancy Fund and/or the AFT Defense Fund;

(v) The denial of delegate representation to the AFT convention;

(vi) Suspension or revocation of charter as provided for in Article IV, Section 8; and

(vii) In the case of delinquent per capita to the national union or a state federation, interest levied on the amount in arrears and/or suspension as provided for in Article IX, Section 6.

Section 13. The executive council shall have power to accept gifts and devises to the American Federation of Teachers if the conditions or purposes of any such gift or devise are not inconsistent with this constitution. The executive council may establish trusts or other agencies to hold and administer any such gift or devise and provide for appointment of trustees or managers thereof, upon such conditions as it may determine, subject to ratification at the next regular convention.

Section 14. The executive council shall have the power to carry on all the business affairs of the American Federation of Teachers, including, without limitation, the power to do on its behalf any or all of the following:

(a) to sue and be sued, complain and defend on behalf of and for the use of the federation;

(b) to employ attorneys and counselors to advise the convention, executive council and the national officers and employees on all matters pertaining to its business and affairs;

(c) to employ accountants, agents and other persons having skills and knowledge needed in the conduct of the business;

(d) to adopt an official seal, which may be altered at pleasure, and to use the same by causing it or a facsimile thereof to be impressed or affixed or in any manner reproduced;

(e) to purchase, take, receive, lease as lessee, take any gift, devise or bequest or otherwise acquire and to own, hold, use, deal in or with any real or personal property or any interest therein;

(f) to sell, convey, mortgage, pledge, lease as lessor and otherwise dispose of all or any part of its property and assets;

(g) to purchase, take, receive or otherwise acquire, own, hold, vote and use shares or other interests in or obligations of domestic or foreign corporations, associations, partnerships or individuals; and to sell, mortgage, loan, pledge or otherwise dispose of such shares, interests or obligations;

(h) to make contracts and incur liabilities that may be appropriate to enable it to accomplish any or all of its purposes; to borrow money for federation purposes at such rates of interest and terms and conditions as they may determine; to issue notes, bonds, and other obligations; and to secure any of its obligations by mortgage, pledge or deed of trust of all or any of its property and income;

(i) to invest the funds of the federation from time to time in any real or personal property; and to take and hold real and personal property as security for the security of funds so invested or loaned; and

(j) to do anything they deem necessary or appropriate to the exercise of the foregoing power or any other power granted to the executive council in this constitution.

Section 15. (a) The executive council may establish and/or revise regional councils to facilitate organization, professional growth, political and legislative activities and other purposes for the good of the union.

(b) The executive council may provide for the affiliation of locals to a regional council in lieu of the requirement of Article XI, Section 2, and that these locals shall not be comprised of employees of local education agencies, colleges or universities or locals affiliated with existing state federations on July 1, 1981.

(c) The executive council shall establish and the AFT shall collect additional per capita from such locals to provide services to the regional councils with the approval of the executive council.

ARTICLE VII
CONVENTIONS

Section 1. Effective in 1984, conventions of this organization shall be held biennially in even-numbered years at such time and in such place as the previous convention or the executive council may determine.

Section 2. A special convention may be called in odd-numbered years by a two-thirds (2/3) vote of the executive council or upon request from at least 30 locals representing a minimum of 30 percent of the AFT membership then in good standing from at least five (5) states.

Section 3. The members of the executive council who are not delegates from their local or state federation shall be ex-officio delegates at the convention and shall have one vote at the convention.

ARTICLE VIII
REPRESENTATION

Section 1. (a) Delegates and/or alternates to the convention from a local or retiree organization shall be elected by secret ballot. Members of each local must be given suitable opportunity to nominate candidates for the office of delegate and alternate. Notice of the right to make nominations must be sent to each member or given a prominent place in the local publication and on bulletin boards. Notice of the right to make nominations and notice of the election may be combined in one notice. Written notice announcing the time and place of election of delegates must be mailed to each member at least 15 days prior to the election. The results of the election must be published and the ballots kept for one year.

Section 1. (b) Locals with fewer than 100 members each, but in the aggregate fewer than 300 members from a contiguous geographic area, may form councils of locals for the exclusive purpose of electing a common delegate to the convention. Locals that form such a council under this section: (1) shall adopt a common resolution to establish the council in a regular meeting of such local no later than five months prior to the convention; (2) shall nominate at the same meeting of each local a member or members, if any, for the council's delegate to the convention; (3) shall elect at a meeting of each such local or by mail ballot agreed to by all locals in the council and in conformity with federal law no later than three months prior to the convention a delegate and alternate, if any, by a secret ballot common to each local in the council listing all nominees and their local numbers, the nominee receiving the highest number of votes totalled among all locals in the council to be the delegate and the second highest, if any, the alternate; (4) shall forward properly signed credentials from each local in the council for the duly elected delegate and alternate, if any, of the council in time to reach the national office no later than two months prior to the convention; and, (5) the executive council shall approve procedures consistent with the requirements of this section for the election of the council delegate. The secretary-treasurer shall forward such procedures to all locals reporting fewer than 100 members in per-capita and to all state federations seven months prior to the convention. No local participating in the council shall have any other delegates seated in the convention. The voting strength of the council's delegate shall be based on the aggregate of the members in the locals that credential the council's delegate.

This section shall also authorize the executive council to recognize a council of locals organized for the convenience of doing business with one employer common to all of the council's locals for the purpose of electing delegates to the convention. Nomination procedures shall be established by such council to permit all such locals to nominate from their respective memberships at least thirty days in advance of the election, which shall be conducted by mail ballot in conformance with federal law. The election of such council's delegates shall be further subject to the provisions of Article VIII, Section 2, of this constitution, provided that no other delegates shall be seated in the convention from any individual local of the council unless such local has notified the national office three months prior to convention that it is not participating in such council for the purposes of electing delegates to the convention. The voting strength of such council shall be based upon the aggregate membership of all such locals that individually credential all delegates common to the council.

Section 1. (c) Delegates and alternates of state federations shall be elected according to its constitution provided that the delegates to the state convention are themselves elected by secret ballot as herein provided, subject to applicable federal and state laws and rules and regulations promulgated pursuant thereto.

Section 1. (d) Each local, state, federation or retiree organization must send by registered or certified mail to the national office a certified list of all elected delegates and alternates not later than fifteen days prior to the opening date of the convention. Only delegates and alternates on this certified list shall be registered and seated at the convention.

Section 1. (e) In the event of non-delivery to the national office of the certified list of the elected delegates and alternates, the executive council may recommend the seating of the delegates and alternates only upon the submission by the president, secretary or ranking delegate of the local, state federation or retiree organization of a statement certifying the list of elected delegates and alternates accompanied by the duly authorized duplicate credentials and receipts showing that the originals were sent to the national office by registered or certified mail, postmarked no later than fifteen days prior to the opening of the convention.

Section 1. (f) To be entitled to representation at the convention, the full per-capita tax of the local and all other monies due the American Federation of Teachers shall be paid through the two months immediately preceding the convention date, such payment to be made to the national office no later than the last day of second month prior to the opening date of the convention.

Section 2. One delegate to the convention may be elected by each affiliated local having a membership of twenty-five or less. (For each 100 members or major fraction thereof, one additional delegate may be elected.)

Section 3. Effective July 1, 1986, for the purpose of this article, membership shall mean the average number on which the per-capita tax has been paid for the first twenty-four months of the twenty-six-month period immediately preceding the month in which the convention meets, provided:

(a) that no local in arrears for two months at the time of the convention shall be entitled to representation.

(b) that, in the case of locals that have been chartered during the two years preceding the convention, the average shall be computed on the basis of the number of months of affiliation, the minimum for such computation to be two.

Section 4. That, in the case of locals which receive fees from nonmembers for representing them under an agency shop agreement, the average number on which the per-capita tax has been paid shall be increased by including, as if it were per-capita tax, the sum equal to the per-capita tax paid as required by Article VIII, Section 1, of the bylaws.

Section 5. State federations, upon compliance with Article VIII, Section 1, shall have the right to send delegates to the conventions of the American Federation of Teachers. Each state federation may elect one delegate to the convention, regardless of its at-large membership. Additional delegates may be elected by the state federations, according to their at-large membership, by applying the formula established for locals as set forth in Section 2 of this article.

All such delegates shall be either members of the state federation or its affiliated locals, provided such locals are in full compliance with Section 1 of this article. All state delegates shall be members of the convention, with all privileges, and shall be entitled to cast votes for their state federation pursuant to Section 6 of this article.

Section 6. Each chartered organization of retired members may elect one delegate to the AFT convention in the manner prescribed by Sections 1(a) and 1(d) of this Article and shall be entitled to one vote at the convention. Such delegates shall be entitled to all rights and privileges of a delegate except that such delegate shall not be entitled to nominate any candidate for federation office or cast a vote in the election of federation officers unless such delegate has been elected to that position by secret ballot vote.

Section 7. Locals entitled to two (2) delegates may not elect more than one (1) who is a full-time paid, elected official of the local. Locals entitled to more than two (2) delegates may not elect more than one-third who are full-time, paid, elected officials of the local.

Section 8. On all roll calls at the convention, each local represented shall be entitled to a number of votes equal to the average membership as defined in Section 3 of this article.

The votes of a local shall be distributed as evenly as possible among the delegates present at the time of the voting, but votes shall not be fractioned. All additional votes shall be assigned by lot or by an objective formula that has been previously reported to the secretary-treasurer of the American Federation of Teachers with no delegate getting more than one of the additional votes. In the election of officers and delegates to the AFL-CIO convention, all voting shall be by roll-call vote and each local represented shall be entitled to the average membership as defined in Section 3 of this article.

Section 9. When a delegate leaves the convention, his place in the convention may be taken by an alternate, if any has been certified as provided in Section 1, Article VIII, and in the order as listed. No other transfer or substitution of voting rights shall be allowed.

ARTICLE IX
REVENUES

Section 1. Twenty-five cents (25¢) of each member's per capita shall be set aside for an AFT Militancy Fund. The executive council shall establish clear guidelines and procedures that guarantee that the benefits available through the fund shall be distributed on an equitable basis. Benefits shall not be provided unless the strike action is in conformity with the AFT strike policy. An annual financial report of the Militancy Fund shall be made to the AFT executive council and to the convention.

Section 2. Two cents of each member's monthly per-capita tax shall be set aside for the Defense Fund.

Section 3. The payment of the per-capita tax shall entitle each active member to a subscription to the official periodicals of the American Federation of Teachers.

Section 4. State federations shall pay to the national office, for each member at large, the prevailing per-capita tax required for each member of a chartered local.

Section 5. Effective September 1, 1990, the treasurer of each affiliated local shall fill out and forward to the national office, on or before the 15th day of each month, the report of active members in good standing, and retiree members who have retired since the last reporting period. Members in good standing of chartered retiree organizations shall be reported to the national office on or before the 15th day of each month together with mailing addresses, on the first day of that month, together with all taxes and assessments due the American Federation of Teachers. Locals that have once submitted names and addresses of the members shall revise and correct the membership list with each per-capita payment. The report shall be subject to an audit by the secretary-treasurer's office.

Section 6. Any affiliated local not paying its per-capita tax on or before the 15th of each month shall be notified of the fact by the national office. A local that is more than three months in arrears shall pay interest on all monies owed in excess of three months; per capita. The rate of interest shall be at the rate then paid or payable for borrowed funds by the AFT, unless the executive council by a two-thirds vote, shall decide to waive the interest provision where there is substantial justification. The local shall become suspended from membership and can be reinstated only by a majority vote of the executive council upon payment of arrearages in full. A local that the executive council refuses to reinstate shall have the right to appeal to the next convention.

Section 7. The treasurer of each affiliated local shall report monthly to the national office on forms furnished by the latter for that purpose and shall certify that the report is for the full number of members in good standing in the local.

Section 8. The executive council shall have power to employ an auditor to examine the books of any affiliated local or state federation upon the direction of a majority vote of the executive council.

Section 9. Beginning January 1, 1971, each local shall submit a financial statement for the local including a statement of assets and liabilities and a statement of income and expenses to the AFT secretary-treasurer within five months of the end of the fiscal year for the local.

ARTICLE X
AMENDMENTS

Section 1. Proposed amendments to the constitution may be submitted to the convention either by request of the executive council or the convention or executive council of any state federation or by request of a local. All amendments shall bear the signature of at least two elected officers of the federation introducing the amendment. The officers signing the amendment shall certify that the amendment was approved for submission to the convention by the executive board or membership of the local or by the executive board or convention of the state federation or by the executive council of the AFT.

Section 2. Proposed amendments may be submitted to a referendum vote under the procedure set up in Article XII.

Section 3. If a proposed amendment is to be submitted to a national convention, it must reach the national office by March 15 and must be sent by the national office to the local by April 15.

Section 4. The constitution shall be amended at the convention by two-thirds (majority) of the votes cast.

ARTICLE XI
AFFILIATION

Section 1. This organization shall immediately affiliate with the American Federation of Labor and Congress of Industrial Organizations and shall permanently maintain that affiliation.

Section 2. Effective September 1, 1968, each local union of this organization shall maintain affiliation with its state federation, and delegate representation of each local in the state federation shall be no less than the formula delineated in Section 2 of Article VIII of this constitution. Each state federation shall, in its convention, follow all voting procedures as delineated in Section 8 of Article VIII of this constitution.

Section 3. Effective September 1, 1969, each local union of this organization shall maintain affiliation with its AFL-CIO state labor council and its local AFL-CIO labor council(s) if such council(s) exist. Failure of any local union to maintain the affiliations as required in Sections 2 and 3 of this Article shall be grounds for denial of delegate representation at any state or national convention of this organization or other appropriate penalties set by the executive council.

Section 4. The AFT executive council, by majority vote, may require each affiliated local to pay for each member the per-capita tax levied by its respective AFL-CIO state central labor body to the AFT on the regular AFT per-capita forms. The AFT shall submit payment to each state AFL-CIO central labor body in accordance with the AFL-CIO constitution.

ARTICLE XII
REFERENDA

Section 1. Proposed actions, including actions of the convention and amendment to the constitution and the bylaws, shall be submitted to a referendum vote by order of the convention or of the executive council or by request of fifteen (15) or more locals representing not less than fifteen (15) percent of the members then in good standing or by petition signed by not less than ten (10) percent of the members, except that the executive council shall not order a convention action to be submitted to a referendum; provided, however, that in no case shall a referendum be held whose termination date is between June 1 and November 1; and provided that actions taken by the executive council concerning:

(a) actions of the convention involving expenditure of funds;

(b) the employment, reemployment or dismissal of officers, organizers, office employees and other general employees who are appointed and whose salaries or other remuneration are fixed by the executive council;

(c) the power to interpret and enforce the constitution and to make rules and bylaws not in conflict with the constitution subject to report to succeeding convention for approval, rejection or modification;

(d) the power to appoint committees not inconsistent with the constitution;

(e) the time and place for the meetings of the executive council and the expenses involved therein;

(f) the power to fill vacancies on the executive council; and

(g) the power to investigate locals shall not be the subject of referendum; and further provided that action taken by the convention under authority of the bylaws, Article VI, governing nominations and elections procedures, shall not be the subject of referendum.

Section 2. After receipt of order or request for a referendum, it shall be the duty of the AFT president to transmit the question to be voted on to the locals within two weeks of its receipt by him/her. Following this, there shall be a period of six weeks during which the proponents and opponents shall be given opportunity to debate the issue through the regular channels of the union, at the end of which time the president shall send to the individual members of all locals in good standing ballots upon which the members shall cast their votes and shall also send to the members at large of the state federations, ballots upon which the members at large of the state federations shall cast their votes.

Section 3. The president of the AFT shall rent a postal deposit box. The individual members will mail the ballots to this postal box. The closing date of the referendum shall be 30 days from the date ballots are mailed from the national office. At the end of 30 days, the president, or the president's representative, accompanied by at least two representatives of each side of the issue on the ballot, shall remove the ballots and cause them to be counted. Ballots received after the opening of the postal box will not be counted. In the alternative, the president, with the consent of the executive council, may engage an independent agency to conduct the balloting and to count the votes. In such event, the agency shall count only those ballots received during the thirty-day period following the mailing of the ballots to the members.

Section 4. The number of the local shall appear on the ballot and only those ballots of members of locals or of state federations in good standing shall be counted. These votes shall not exceed in number the number of members and members at large for which per capita was last paid prior to the date on which ballots were sent from the national office. Should the number of ballots cast by any local or state federation exceed the number to which that local or state federation is entitled, the "ayes" and "nays" shall be reduced proportionately to come within the required number.

Section 5. The president shall notify the locals of the results of the referendum as soon as possible but no later than two weeks following receipt of the count. The president shall also publish the results in the official publications of the American Federation of Teachers.

Section 6. AFT policy adopted by referendum shall not be considered by the first convention following the referendum.

ARTICLE XIII
PARLIAMENTARY AUTHORITY

The rules contained in *Robert's Rules of Order Revised* shall govern this federation in all cases to which they are applicable and in which they are not inconsistent with rules regularly adopted by the federation.

BYLAWS

Note: *Underlined words indicate new language adopted at the 1992 convention.*

ARTICLE 1
SPECIAL RULES OF ORDER FOR CONVENTIONS

Section 1. The convention shall be called to order and conducted according to the printed program as prepared by the convention committee and approved by the executive council subject to such modification as the convention may make from time to time.

Section 2. The convention shall not adjourn before 3:00 p.m. on the fifth day unless all business of the convention has been finished.

Section 3. Limitations of speeches in debate shall be three minutes instead of ten minutes as provided in *Robert's Rules of Order Revised* unless time is extended by majority vote of the convention.

Section 4. A motion calling for a roll-call vote shall require a one-fourth vote for adoption. When a roll-call vote has been ordered, the presiding officer shall at once call for the next item on the agenda, action on the pending motion being automatically postponed pending the tabulation of the results of the roll-call vote. No debate, amendment or other motion affecting the question on which the roll-call vote was ordered may be made after a roll-call has been ordered. The ballots shall be distributed to the ranking delegates of each delegation under the direction of the presiding officer of the credentials committee. (These ballots shall be prepared in advance by the president.) Each delegate voting shall enter on his/her ballot the number of the roll-call, the number of his/her local, his/her full name, the number of votes he/she is casting, how he/she is voting. This record shall be included in the convention proceedings. The ranking delegation shall tabulate the votes of the delegation on a summary sheet and submit the sheet along with the ballots to the credentials committee. If a delegate's ballot is not collected promptly, he/she may deliver his/her ballot directly to the committee on credentials. No vote shall be accepted later than one hour following the ordering of a roll-call vote. The results of the roll-call vote shall be tabulated by the committee on credentials and reported to the convention immediately upon completion of the tabulation according to the following procedure:

(a) The total vote shall be read.

(b) If any delegate challenges the vote of his/her local, the roll of delegates from that local shall be read, and each delegate shall rise as his/her name is called, announce his/her vote and state the number of votes he/she is casting.

(c) The report on the roll-call vote shall then be revised to agree with the oral vote just taken.

(d) A copy of the roll-call vote shall be posted showing the vote of each delegate and shall remain posted until the end of the convention.

Section 5. Delegates shall be seated upon acceptance by the convention of the report of the credentials committee and the list of delegates shall be made available to the members of the convention. The right of any delegate to be seated as a member of the convention shall be subject to challenge within a twenty-four hour period after he/she has been declared seated by the convention. Delegates may vote unless or until successfully challenged but, in the event of a roll-call vote, a successful challenge invalidates the individual's vote.

Section 6. In the case of locals represented by fewer delegates than the number of votes to which they are entitled, the votes shall be distributed in accordance with the constitutional provision (Article VIII, Section 7), and any remaining votes shall be distributed as determined by the delegation.

Section 7. The order of business for business sessions of the convention shall be as follows:

(a) report of committee on credentials (credentials committee shall make supplemental reports at the beginning of each business session of the convention);

(b) action on minutes of the previous convention as summarized in the delegate's reports prepared by the convention reporter;

(c) reports of officers and executive employees;

(d) report of executive council;

(e) reports of convention committees;

(f) reports of special committees; and

(g) installation of officers.

Section 8. Reports of officers and executive employees given before the seating of delegates shall be referred without debate and without action of the convention to the appropriate committees.

Section 9. A quorum for the conduct of business at a convention shall be 25 percent of the delegates who have been seated.

ARTICLE II
COMMITTEE ON CREDENTIALS
Registration of delegates and visitors.

Section 1. The committee on credentials shall be appointed by the executive council and shall be notified of their appointment at least two weeks prior to the convention. The committee shall consist of at least five members and shall be responsible for registration of delegates, council members and visitors.

Section 2. Registration of delegates, members of the executive council and visitors shall begin at 1:00 p.m. on the day preceding the convention. Before the time for registration, the president shall furnish the committee on credentials with copies of the lists of delegations and the duplicates of credentials as reported to him/her by the various locals. Each delegate, member of the executive council and visitor shall be furnished with an appropriate official badge to be worn at the convention.

ARTICLE III
CONVENTION PROGRAM

Section 1. The committee on convention program shall be appointed by the executive council not later than the midyear meeting of the executive council. This committee shall prepare the tentative program of the next convention and shall submit it to the president at least six weeks before the convention. The president shall send a copy of the tentative program to each delegate as soon thereafter as possible.

Section 2. The convention program shall provide for a minimum of six (6) business sessions, including one for nominations and shall make available a minimum of three (3) hours for meetings of convention committees.

Section 3. In setting up the convention program, reports of convention committees shall be scheduled to begin not later than the afternoon session of the second day of the convention.

ARTICLE IV
GENERAL CONVENTION PROCEDURE

Section 1. The convention shall convene during the months of July and/or August at the time and place determined by the executive council.

Section 2. In any case any motion is passed that any convention address be mimeographed or printed, the maker and seconder of the motion shall constitute a committee to secure the address in printable form and to submit it to the president.

Section 3. Only credentialed delegates and members of the executive council shall be admitted to the convention floor except invited guests participating in the program of the convention. All visitors shall secure a pass from the credentials committee and shall be seated only in a special section reserved for them.

Section 4. Resolutions to the convention may be introduced by locals, state federations or the executive council of the American Federation of Teachers. No resolution shall be introduced later than six weeks prior to the opening of the convention except by two-thirds vote of the convention. All resolutions shall bear the signature of at least two elected officers of the federation introducing the resolution. The officers signing the resolution shall certify that the resolution was approved for submission to the convention by the executive board or membership of the local or by the executive board or convention of the state federation or by the executive council of the American Federation of Teachers. The resolution shall contain the title and shall be submitted to the president of the American Federation of Teachers in typewritten form, in quadruplicate. Resolutions so submitted shall be mailed from the AFT national office to locals and state federations prior to the convention.

Section 5. The president or presiding officer of the convention shall appoint an appropriate number of ushers whose duty it shall be to see that only persons entitled to admission shall be admitted to the convention hall. The ushers shall see that visitors are seated in the section assigned to them. They shall assist the presiding officer in such other ways as may be directed.

Section 6. The constitutional amendments committee shall be heard in full prior to other committee reports. The constitutional amendments committee shall report only the proposed amendments, which it recommends for adoption, with or without amendments. At the conclusion or immediately after the conclusion of the committee's full report, any delegate may move adoption of a proposed amendment not recommended by the committee. The chair shall allow one statement for the proposed amendment and one statement against the proposed amendment. The chair shall then immediately put the question of whether the convention desires to debate the proposed amendment. If this motion prevails by a one-third vote, the proposed amendment shall be before the convention.

Section 7. Each other committee shall select the three resolutions or items of business it considers most important for its initial report. When these have been acted upon or at the end of an hour, of each committee's partial report, whichever comes first, debate shall be closed and all pending questions shall be put to a vote immediately unless the time of debate is extended by majority vote of the convention. After all committees have had an opportunity to make their first reports, additional committee reports may be made in the order selected by the president.

Section 8. Resolutions upon which no action has been taken shall die when the convention adjourns.

Section 9. A copy of the rules should be provided for delegates and visitors upon convention registration and should be voted on at the opening session on the first day of the convention.

ARTICLE V
CONVENTION COMMITTEES

Section 1. Convention committees shall be appointed by the executive council. In appointing such committees, the council shall give consideration to the expressed choices of delegates as indicated on the committee choice cards, which shall be sent by the president to each delegate promptly upon receipt of credentials. However, the council shall not be bound by the choice cards but shall give equal weight and consideration to service on standing committees and to the proper balancing of committees. Members of standing committees who are delegates shall be appointed to the corresponding convention committees so far as feasible in order to coordinate the work of convention and standing committees.

Section 2. A delegate interested in a specific problem of a resolution shall have an opportunity to present his/her viewpoint to the appropriate committee at a time designated by the committee chair.

Section 3. Changes in assignments of delegates to a committee shall be made only by a committee of the executive council upon application. Such application shall include a written statement of the reason for desiring the change. No change shall be made after 5:00 p.m. on the first day of the convention.

Section 4. Reports of convention committees shall be received at the time designated in the printed program or as designated by the convention. Reports shall be made in the order assigned by the chair of the convention committee and the president who shall make such assignments upon application by the chair of committees except as the convention may desire to receive reports in a different order.

Section 5. Debate in committees may be limited by a two-thirds vote of the committee.

ARTICLE VI
NOMINATIONS AND ELECTION PROCEDURES

Section 1. All nominations of officers and delegates to the AFL-CIO convention shall be by petition signed by at least fifty delegates and presented to the secretary-treasurer no later than 8:00 a.m. on the third day of the convention. Declination of nominations shall be made prior to 8:30 a.m. on the same day. Candidates shall be introduced to the convention between 8:30 a.m. and 10:00 a.m. on the same day with the option of making a two-minute speech of acceptance. Candidates for president and secretary-treasurer shall be allotted five minutes for their acceptance speeches and remaining time allotted equally among vice-presidential candidates with the option of pooling their time. Candidates for delegate to the AFL-CIO convention shall be allotted two minutes for their speech with the option of pooling their time. No other business shall be conducted during this time.

Section 2. Balloting for election of officers shall take place from 4:30 p.m. until 7:30 p.m. of the third day of the convention under the supervision of the elections committee. No other official business of the convention shall be conducted during balloting. Only delegates who are seated by 5:00 p.m. of the second day of the convention may vote in the election.

Section 3. A majority of the ballots cast for the offices of the president and secretary-treasurer shall be required to elect the president and secretary-treasurer. In the event that no candidates for the positions of president and secretary-treasurer receive a majority, a run-off election between the two candidates receiving the highest number of votes shall be conducted by roll-call vote.

Section 4. Vice-presidential candidates receiving the highest number of votes corresponding to the number of positions to be filled shall be declared elected subject to the provision of Article V, Section 1. In the event that there is a tie for the final positions, a run-off election for that position between the tied candidates shall be conducted by roll-call vote.

ARTICLE VII
STANDING COMMITTEES

Section 1. The standing committees shall be established and appointed by the executive council not later than the midyear meeting of the council each year. The presiding officer and as many members of standing committees as possible shall be appointed at the post-convention meeting of the council.

Section 2. As a matter of policy, the executive council shall endeavor to maintain continuity of personnel of standing committees.

Section 3. Each standing committee shall make a written report for submission to the appropriate convention committee.

Section 4. In addition to the standing committees established and appointed by the executive council, there shall be a standing committee on civil and human rights. The executive council shall appoint the chair and other members of the committee, which shall perform the following functions:

(a) Recommend strategies for encouraging and coordinating local and regional conferences on civil and human rights in education, and work with locals to help establish effective local committees on civil and human rights.

(b) Identify resource materials on African-Americans and other minorities and recommend the development of such materials for use by educators.

(c) Recommend strategies for identifying, supporting, actively recruiting and retaining minority teachers and other employees.

(d) Conduct a national conference on civil and human rights.

The committee shall submit a report on its activities to the convention and a copy shall be sent to each local.

ARTICLE VIII
PER CAPITA, BUDGET, AND AUDITS REVENUES

Section 1. (a) Effective September 1, 1992, each affiliated local shall pay for each member a per-capita tax of $8.15 per month, and effective September 1, 1993, each local shall pay a per-capita tax of $8.55 per month. Effective January 1, 1975, the national office shall pay back to the office of each state federation for each member of the state a per capita of 20 cents per month.

Section 1. (b) Where a local receives fees from nonmembers for representing them under agency shop agreement, it shall pay to the national office a sum equal to the per-capita tax for all such nonmembers and shall also pay to the state federation of teachers a sum equal to the per capita of the state federation for all such nonmembers. Effective September 1, 1977, each affiliated local that has members within a unit where the bargaining rights have been won by another organization and where the other organization has obtained an agency shop or fair-share clause in the contract, the local shall pay per-capita tax at one-fourth the regular rate on those members required to pay agency or fair-share fees to another organization. Representation at the American Federation of Teachers or the state convention shall also be computed at one-fourth the constitutional formula for apportionment of delegate and voting strength. Locals whose members pay agency or fair-share fees to another organization may elect to pay full per capita for such members and receive full representation.

Section 1. (c) Any local that receives service or fair-share payments in lieu of dues from employee(s) represented by the local shall adopt procedures for such employee(s) to object during a specific time period each year to the expenditures of his/her portion of such payments for certain purposes. Such procedures shall provide that employee(s) may object to expenditure of his/her portion of such payments for activities or causes of a political nature only incidentally related to collective bargaining. Employee(s) may not object to expenditures of his/her portion of such payments used for collective bargaining including, but not limited to, negotiating, organizing, servicing, educational research and union administration. That portion of such fees spent by the union, local, state and national level for the above-described purposes will be determined in each fiscal year by the respective chief fiscal policy-making body, and rebate of a prorated portion of his/her service or fair-share fees corresponding to such proration shall be made to each individual who has filed a timely notice of objection each year.

Section 1. (d) The procedures adopted shall provide for the right to object during a specific time by registered/certified mail and for the determination of appropriate portions of money spent for purposes described in sections 1(b) and (c). The employee(s) shall have rights of appeal internally and, if not satisfied, shall have the right to appeal to an independent, outside review panel whose decision shall be final and binding.

In the event that service or fair-share fees are established through procedures of state law in such a way as to meet the above objections, then sections 1(c) and 1(d) shall not apply.

Section 2. The budget shall be prepared and adopted annually by the executive councils and shall be subject to subsequent revision when needed.

Section 3. It shall be the responsibility of the executive council to cause the auditing of the financial records of the organization annually and to submit said audits to each convention.

Section 4. Twenty-five cents of each member's per-capita tax shall be set aside each month in a building fund to finance the purchase of an AFT building. The fund shall continue until such time as the purchase has been completed and any additional financial costs of the building not covered by income from the building have been met.

Section 5. Proposed changes in per capita must be sent to the national office by March 15 and must be sent by the national to the locals by April 15.

ARTICLE IX
SUSPENSION OF RULES AND AMENDMENT OF BYLAWS

Section 1. The special rules of order contained in Article 1 of these bylaws may be suspended by a two-thirds vote in the same manner as provided by *Robert's Rules of Order Revised* for the suspension of all regular rules of order.

Section 2. The bylaws may be amended by the same procedure as in Article X, Sections 1 through 3, of the constitution. All such amendments shall require a majority vote for their adoption except those relating to bylaws, which themselves require more than a majority vote, in which case the same vote shall be required to adopt the amendment as required by the bylaws to be amended.

Interview Team Worksheet
1992

The Interview Team Worksheet serves as the questionnaire for the candidate interview. It provides order for the interview and assures that questions necessary to the endorsement process are covered.

Each team members should have a copy of the worksheet for each candidate to be interviewed. This assists team members in following the questions, provides them with a scale to rate individual responses, and space for very limited notes. Team members should not take copious notes during responses (let a tape recorder handle that).

The completed Candidate Questionnaire is the basis that guides the interview.

Reviewing the Interview Team Worksheet

1. Questions 1-4 are open-ended questions giving the candidate a chance to relax and open up. After hearing the candidate's opening statement (Question #1), you may decide to skip questions 2 and/or 3, feeling the candidate has already covered these points.

2. Question #5 seeks the extent of the candidate's commitment to increased funding for education. Many candidates may dispute the contention that the situation has grown worse. Specific information is included in this kit which explains the educational funding problem. This information can be found in the "Background on NEA Issues" document under question #1.

3. Questions #6-16 correspond to questions on the written questionnaire. They are asked in the interview because of their importance to the legislative program. Vague answers require additional probing. Try to pin the candidate down now while he/she is most acutely aware of the relationship between the issues we have identified and our political support.

If you feel that the candidate has clearly and fully answered these questions on the questionnaire, you should at least reinforce the issue. Example: "We are pleased to see that your position on (_____) is fully in support of our own program."

4. During this phase of the interview the Chair should integrate any additional questions the team has identified for candidate elaboration or on which the candidate's written response has been vague or unclear. It is recommended that these additional questions be included in the same order they appear on the written questionnaire. Note interview question #7 corresponds to questionnaire Part II, question #1.

5. Following the last question drawn from the written questionnaire, ask any other issue questions which the team may have developed. (Remember that additional questions should be asked of all candidates to maintain equity in the process.)

6. Proceed with question #17 regarding the candidate's intentions towards working with the NEA. It is important that the candidate understand that the Association, not teacher friends and colleagues, is the vehicle for communication with and about is-

sues that affect education or NEA members. Then close the first section of the interview with question #18, the closing statement.

7. Now take up the two open-ended questions relating to the candidate's campaign plans and expectations of Association help if endorsed. The team may wish to expand on these questions, particularly if there are doubts about the candidate's electability.

8. In closing be sure to let the candidate know how the endorsement process works and when he/she will be notified of the final endorsement decision.

It is extremely helpful to NEA lobbyists to know which issues were supported by the Members of Congress when they were candidates. Be sure all completed candidate questionnaires are forwarded to the appropriate NEA Government Relations field staff just in case our endorsed candidate is not elected.

| Candidate: |
| Team member: |

1992 INTERVIEW TEAM WORKSHEET

This worksheet is recommended for use by individual team members to assist them in tracking the interview and providing them with an informal means of evaluating answers and making brief notes.

INTERVIEW TEAM CHAIR Thank you for coming today. We've had the opportunity to review the responses on your written questionnaire and appreciate your taking the time to discuss your views on the issues of concern to us. We are taping (video-taping) the interview for our own reviewing purposes. Please let us know if you have any objections or would like to make some "off the record" comments.

1. Before getting into the issues would you like to make an opening statement at this time?
    Low 1 2 3 4 5 6 7 8 9 10 High

2. Tell us first of all why you believe that the NEA should support your candidacy?
    Low 1 2 3 4 5 6 7 8 9 10 High

3. What do you believe are the major problems facing education today?
    Low 1 2 3 4 5 6 7 8 9 10 High

4. What do you believe are the greatest strengths of our public education system?
    Low 1 2 3 4 5 6 7 8 9 10 High

5. The first question of Part II, NEA's Legislative Program on the written questionnaire sought your response to the critical problem of inadequate school financing and your views as to education's funding as a national priority. You may also be aware that over the last two decades nearly all candidates have said positive and supportive things about education and the need for greater financial assistance. Nevertheless the situation has grown steadily worse. Will you please elaborate on your written response and share with us what you personally would do to turn this situation around?
    Low 1 2 3 4 5 6 7 8 9 10 High

At this point in the interview, **review in order** the following questions (6-16) and those questions on the written questionnaire which:
    A. the committee has previously identified as needing the candidate's elaboration or on which the candidate's response has been vague or unclear.
    B. the candidate has indicated a desire to discuss.

6. Will you actively support through Congressional action the achievement of the six national education goals established by the nation's governors and endorsed by the President, at their election summit meeting in February 1990? (Questionnaire Part I, questions #1 & 2)

    ( ) Agrees/NEA   ( ) Disagrees/NEA   ( ) No Position

7. The current budgetary agreement between the President and the U.S. Congress creates a condition in which some federally funded programs must be funded at the expense of others. Are you willing to support substantially increasing the authorization and appropriations for elementary and secondary education under such circumstances. (Questionnaire Part II, #1)

    ( ) Agrees/NEA   ( ) Disagrees/NEA   ( ) No Position

8. Will you oppose all efforts to break down the division between church and state including the use of such devices as tuition tax credits, vouchers, or so called "choice" plans? (Questionnaire Part II, #3 & 8)

    ( ) Agrees/NEA   ( ) Disagrees/NEA   ( ) No Position

9. Will you support federal legislation guaranteeing collective bargaining rights to all public employees? (Questionnaire Part II, #13)

    ( ) Agrees/NEA   ( ) Disagrees/NEA   ( ) No Position

10. Will you support a comprehensive universal health care system provided by public and private agencies for all citizens? (Questionnaire Part II, #14)

    ( ) Agrees/NEA   ( ) Disagrees/NEA   ( ) No Position

11. Will you oppose the taxation of employee benefits, such as employer-paid health and life insurance and employer-paid education assistance? (Questionnaire Part II, #16)

    ( ) Agrees/NEA   ( ) Disagrees/NEA   ( ) No Position

12. Will you oppose mandatory coverage of public employees under Social Security or Medicare for employee groups which have declined coverage under existing federal law? (Questionnaire Part II, #19)

    ( ) Agrees/NEA   ( ) Disagrees/NEA   ( ) No Position

13. Will you support legislation to repeal the "spousal offset" which reduces Social Security benefits of certain public employees? (Questionnaire Part II, #20)

    ( ) Agrees/NEA   ( ) Disagrees/NEA   ( ) No Position

14. Will you support federal legislation to protect the civil rights of all Americans, including protection from on-the-job harassment and equitable treatment in all employment decisions including hiring, firing, and promotion? (Questionnaire Part II, #21)

    ( ) Agrees/NEA   ( ) Disagrees/NEA   ( ) No Position

15. Will you encourage and support the addition of the Equal Rights Amendment to the U.S. Constitution? (Questionnaire Part II, #23)

( ) Agrees/NEA   ( ) Disagrees/NEA   ( ) No Position

16. Will you support the right of all citizens to participate in the election process and make contributions through political action committees? (Questionnaire Part II, #25)

( ) Agrees/NEA   ( ) Disagrees/NEA   ( ) No Position

Now ask the questions not covered in this interview or on the written questionnaire which the team believes are appropriate to this campaign. Any new questions posed by the team should be asked of all candidates.

17. As a Member of Congress what kind of a working relationship would you seek to have with the NEA?

Low 1 2 3 4 5 6 7 8 9 10 High

18. As a conclusion to the issue portion of this interview, would you like to go back over any of the questions or make a closing statement?

Low 1 2 3 4 5 6 7 8 9 10 High

Now we'd like to discuss the campaign ahead. Would you please tell us something about the type of campaign you plan to run?

If the Association chooses to endorse your candidacy, in what ways could we best help your campaign?

THANK YOU FOR MEETING WITH US! We'll notify all candidates of our decision by
_____.

Response Code:

Agree/NEA—*Would vote for the NEA position*

Disagree/NEA—*Would vote against the NEA position*

No Position—*Does not have or would not give a position on the issue.*

SUMMARY OF LABOR-MANAGEMENT REPORTING AND DISCLOSURE ACT

As frequently noted, the state and local teacher unions are regulated by state, not federal statutes. Under the Labor-Management Reporting and Disclosure Act (LMRDA), unions subject to federal regulation are required to submit certain reports and union members have certain rights vis-a-vis their unions. These union obligations and member rights are summarized in Appendix E. The safeguards for union members in Appendix E were not ordinarily included in the state legislation applicable to teacher unions. The national organizations of the NEA and AFT are subject to the LMRDA but their state and local affiliates are not. The legislation providing bargaining rights for state and local public employees was initially drafted by the unions, hence it did not include member rights against the unions. Quite often, the proposed legislation was referred to state legislative committees with little or no sophistication about unions or labor relations issues. Consequently, state bargaining statutes frequently omit the safeguards for union members included in federal labor laws.

For this reason, closer scrutiny of the teacher unions is likely to reveal a great deal of negative information about them.

THE LABOR-MANAGEMENT REPORTING AND DISCLOSURE ACT

The Labor-Management Reporting and Disclosure Act of 1959, as amended (LMRDA), grants certain rights to union members and protects their interests by promoting democratic procedures within labor organizations. The Act establishes a Bill of Rights for union members; reporting requirements for labor organizations, union officers and employees, employers, labor-relations consultants, and surety companies; standards for the regular election of union officers; and safeguards for protecting labor organization funds and assets. Unions representing Federal employees are similarly covered by the implementing regulations of the standards of conduct provisions of the Civil Service Reform Act of 1978. Unions representing solely state, county, and municipal employees are not covered by either of these laws.

The Secretary of Labor enforces certain provisions of the LMRDA and has delegated that authority to the Department of Labor's Office of Labor-Management Standards (OLMS). Other provisions may only be enforced by union members through a private suit in a Federal District Court. Outlined below are the major provisions of the LMRDA.

Title I - Bill of Rights of Union Members
* Union members have equal rights to nominate candidates for union office, vote in union elections, and participate in union meetings. They may also meet with other members and express any opinions.

* Unions may impose assessments and raise dues only by democratic procedures. In addition, unions must afford members a full and fair hearing of charges against them.
* Unions must inform their members about provisions of the LMRDA.
* Members may enforce Title I rights through a private suit against the union, but may be required to exhaust internal union remedies for up to four months.
* Union members and nonunion employees have the right to receive or to inspect collective bargaining agreements. This right may be enforced by a union member or by the Secretary of Labor.

Title II - Reporting Requirements
* Unions must file information reports, constitutions and bylaws, and annual financial reports with the Office of Labor-Management Standards (OLMS).
* Officers and employees of labor unions must report any loans and benefits received from, or certain financial interests in, employers whose employees their unions represent and businesses that deal with their unions.
* Employers and labor-relations consultants who engage in certain activities to persuade employees about their union activities or to supply information to the employer must file reports.
* Surety companies which issue bonds required by the LMRDA or the Employee Retirement Income Security Act of 1974 must report data such as premiums received, total claims paid, and amounts recovered.
* The Secretary of Labor has authority to enforce the reporting requirements of the Act.
* The reports and documents filed with OLMS are public information and any person may examine them or obtain copies at OLMS offices.
* Filers must retain the records necessary to verify the reports for at least five years.
* Unions must make reports available to members and permit members to examine records for just cause.

Title III - Trusteeships
* A parent union which places a subordinate body under trusteeship must file initial, semiannual, and terminal trusteeship reports.
* A trusteeship may only be imposed for the purposes specified in the LMRDA and must be established and administered in accordance with the constitution and bylaws of the labor organization which has assumed trusteeship over the subordinate body.
* A parent union which imposes a trusteeship may not engage in specified acts involving the funds and delegate votes from a trusteed union.
* The Secretary of Labor has authority to investigate alleged violations of this Title. A union member or a subordinate labor organization may also enforce Title III provisions except for the reporting requirements.

Title IV - Elections
* Local unions must elect their officers by secret ballot; international unions and intermediate bodies must elect their officers by secret ballot vote of the members or by delegates chosen by secret ballot.
* International unions must hold elections at least every five years, intermediate bodies every four years, and local unions every three years.
* Unions must comply with a candidates's request to distribute campaign material to members at the candidate's own expense and must also refrain from discriminat-

ing against any candidate with respect to the use of membership lists. Candidates have the right to inspect a list containing the names and addresses of members subject to a union security agreement within 30 days prior to the election.

* A member in good standing has the right to nominate candidates, to be a candidate subject to reasonable qualifications uniformly imposed, to hold office, and to support and vote for the candidates of the member's choice.

* Unions must mail a notice of election to every member at their last-known home address at least 15 days prior to the election.

* A member whose dues have been withheld by an employer may not be declared ineligible to vote or to be a candidate for office by reason of alleged delay or default in the payment of dues.

* Unions must conduct regular elections of officers in accordance with their constitution and bylaws and preserve all election records for one year.

* Union and employer funds may not be used to promote the candidacy of any candidate. Union funds may be utilized for expenses necessary for the conduct of an election.

* Union members may hold a secret ballot vote to remove from office an elected local union official guilty of serious misconduct if the Secretary of Labor finds that the union constitution and bylaws do not provide adequate procedures for such a removal.

* Union members who have exhausted internal election remedies or who have invoked such remedies without obtaining a final decision within three calendar months after their invocation may file a complaint with the Secretary within one calendar month thereafter.

* The Secretary of Labor has authority to file a suit in a Federal District Court to set aside an invalid election and to request a new election under the supervision of the Secretary and in accordance with Title IV.

Title V - Safeguards for Labor Organizations

* Officers have a duty to manage the funds and property of the union solely for the benefit of the union in accordance with its constitution and bylaws.

* A union officer or employee who embezzles or otherwise misappropriates union funds or other assets commits a Federal crime punishable by a fine and/or imprisonment.

* Officials who handle union funds or property must be bonded to provide protection against losses.

* A union may not have outstanding loans to any one officer or employee convicted of any willful violation of the LMRDA.

* Persons convicted of certain crimes may not hold union office or employment for up to 13 years after conviction or after the end of imprisonment.

Title VI - Miscellaneous Provisions

* Authority is granted to the Secretary of Labor to investigate possible violations of most provisions of the LMRDA (except those specifically excluded) and to enter premises, examine records, and question persons in the course of the investigation.

* A union or any of its officials may not fine, suspend, expel, or otherwise discipline a member for exercise of rights under the LMRDA.

* No one may use or threaten to use force or violence to interfere with a union member in the exercise of LMRDA rights.

Title VII - Amendments to the Taft-Hartley Act
* Another Federal law, the Labor Management Relations Act (LMRA), is amended by the LMRDA with regard to such matters as strikes, boycotts, and picketing. The LMRA is administered by the National Labor Relations Board (NRLB), an independent Federal agency.

REFERENCES

"AEA [Alabama Education Association] employees want to know if Hubbert used members' dues." 1991. *Times Daily,* October 3, p. A8.

American Federation of Teachers (AFT). 1993. "Joining forces against school vouchers." *American Teacher,* October, Vol. 78, No. 2: 12.

——. 1993. *Labor Organization Annual Report Form LM-2.* U.S. Department of Labor, Office of Labor Management Standards. Washington: U.S. Government Printing Office.

——. 1993. *Form 990 Return of Organization Exempt From Income Tax.* Department of the Treasury, Internal Revenue Service.

——. 1993. *Voting record and legislative report of the 102nd Congress. AFT Rates Congress,* p. 1-4.

——. 1993. *AFT or NEA: What's the Difference,* January.

——. 1992. *AFT Publications Catalog,* p. 4.

——. 1992. *The 1990-92 Report of the Officers of the American Federation of Teachers,* p. 10-15.

——. 1992. *Constitution of the American Federation of Teachers, AFL-CIO.* August. American Federation of Teachers Committee on Political Education. 1993. *Federal Election Commission Selected List of Receipts and Expenditures (G) (1992).* U.S. Government Printing Office. October.

Anderson, John. 1990. "AEA gets $1 million challenge; Hubbert campaign sets funding goal." *The Huntsville Times,* April 1, p. A1.

Berube, Maurice R. 1988. *Teacher Politics: The Influence of Unions.* New York: Greenwood Press.

Blumenfeld, Samuel L. 1984. *NEA: Trojan Horse in American Education.* Phoenix: The Paradigm Company.

Bockelman, Andrew and Overton, Joseph P. 1993. *Michigan Education Special Services Association: The MEA's Money Machine.* Midland, MI: Mackinac Center for Public Policy. November.

Brimelow, Peter and Leslie Spencer. 1993. "Union knows best." *Forbes,* October 11, p. 89-90.

——. 1993. "The National Extortion Association." *Forbes,* June 7, p. 72-84.

Bureau of Census. 1987 Census of Government, Public Employment, No. 3. *Labor-Management Relations.* Washington: U.S. Government Printing Office.

California Public Employment Relations Board (PERB). 1983. *California School Employees Association and its South Lake Tahoe Chapter No. 286 v. Lake Tahoe Unified School District.* S-CE-531.

California Teachers Association (CTA). 1993. "174-Yes on TV." *No on Vouchers*, October 11, No. 13: 1.

——. 1993. "Anyone can start a school." *Election News*, October, p. 1.

——. 1993. "Tidal wave of opposition unleashed against Prop. 174." *CTA Action*, October, Vol. 32, No. 2: 3.

——. 1992. "CTA's 1992 Edition, Report Card on the California Legislature." *Making the Grade*, Vol. 9, No. 22: 4.

Cuomo, Mario M. 1984. *Diaries of Mario M. Cuomo, The Campaign for Governor*. New York: Random House.

Donley, Marshall O., Jr. 1976. *Power to the Teacher: How America's Educators Became Militant*. Bloomington: Indiana University Press.

Ehrenhalt, Alan. 1991. *The United States of Ambition, Politicians, Power, and the Pursuit of Office*. New York: Times Books.

Everhart, Robert B., ed. 1982. *The Public School Monopoly*. San Francisco: Pacific Institute for Public Policy Research.

Federal Election Commission v. National Education Association. 1978. 457 Fed. Supp. 1102 (DDC).

Freeman, Richard B. 1986. "Unionism Comes to the Public Sector." *Journal of Economic Literature*, Vol. 24, No. 1.

Garcia v. San Antonio Metropolitan Transit Authority, et.al. 1985. 105 S. CT 1005.

Geiger, Keith. 1994. "Violence, Greed, and Social Conscience." advertisement. *Washington Post*, January 16, p. C4.

——. 1993. "The 1.3 Billion Hoax." *NEA Today*, September, Vol. 12, No. 2: 2.

——. 1993. *Memorandum To Delegates to the 1993 Representative Assembly*. The history of the Special Committee and of New Business Items A and B prior to the vote in the 1993 Representative Assembly. May 26.

Gollner, Philipp M. 1993. "On the California Ballot: Should the State Help Pay for Private-School Pupils?" *New York Times*, August 4. p. B9.

Johnson, Susan Moore. 1984. *Teacher Unions in Schools*. Philadelphia: Temple University Press.

Kerchner, Charles Taylor and Douglas E. Miller. 1988. *The Changing Idea of a Teachers' Union*. London: New York: Falmer Press.

Krislov, Joseph. 1962. "The Independent Public Employee Association." *Industrial and Labor Relations Review*, Vol. 15, July.

Lester, Richard. 1958. *As Unions Mature*. Princeton, NJ: Princeton University Press.

Lieberman, Myron and Gene Geisert, 1994. *Teacher Bargaining: Practice and Policy*. Chicago: Bonus Books.

Lieberman, Myron. 1994. "The School Choice Fiasco." *The Public Interest*, Winter, No. 114: 17-34.

——. 1993. *Public Education, An Autopsy*. Cambridge, Mass.: Harvard University Press.

———. 1993. "Merger of the NEA and the AFT: Prospects and Consequences." *Government Union Review*, Summer, Vol 14, No. 3: 1-41.

———. 1980. "Professional Ethics in Education: An Autopsy." *Phi Delta Kappan*, October, p. 159-160; Karl Hostetler. 1989. "Who Says Professional Ethics is Dead? A Response to Myron Lieberman." *Phi Delta Kappan*. May, p. 723-725; and Lieberman, "A Reply to Karl Hostetler." *Phi Delta Kappan*, May, p. 726-727.

———. 1960. *The Future of Public Education*. Chicago: University of Chicago Press.

———. 1956. *Education as a Profession*. Englewood Cliffs, NJ: Prentice Hall, Inc. Although an extensive discussion of the meaning and implications of professionalism, this analysis did not recognize the basic conflict between professionalism and unionization.

Lieberman, Myron and Michael H. Moskow. 1966. *Collective Negotiations in Education*. Chicago: Rand McNally. For a detailed account of the rivalry between the NEA and AFT in the 1960s, and the transformation of the NEA into a union, see p. 21-61.

Makinson, Larry. 1990. *Open Secrets, The Cash Constituents of Congress.* Washington: Center for Responsive Politics.

McDonnell, Lorraine M. and Anthony Pascal. 1988. *Teacher Unions and Educational Reform*. Santa Monica, Calif.: Rand.

Morain, Dan. 1993. "Teacher Union Shows Clout in Fight Against Voucher Measure." *Los Angeles Times,* October 5, p. B3.

National Education Association (NEA). 1993. *NEA Handbook 1993-94.* Includes Charter, Constitution, Bylaws and Standing Rules. Washington: National Educational Association.

———. 1993. "The 1993-94 Resolutions of the National Education Association." *NEA Today.* September, Vol. 12, No. 2: 26.

———. 1993. "Public Education, The voucher battle." *NEA NOW,* August 30, p.1.

———. 1993. "NEA Standing Committee on Legislation." *Reports of Committees 1992-93,* Presented to the 72nd Representative Assembly of the National Education Association, July 2-5, p. 39-40.

———. 1993. *Financial Reports,* Presented to the Representative Assembly, San Francisco, California, July.

———. 1993. *Strategic Plan and Budget Fiscal Year 1993-94,* Presented to the Representative Assembly, San Francisco, California, July.

———. 1993. *Form 990 Return of Organization Exempt From Income Tax.* Department of the Treasury, Internal Revenue Service.

———. 1992. *Labor Organization Annual Report Form LM-2.* U.S. Department of Labor, Office of Labor Management Standards. Washington: U.S. Government Printing Office.

———. 1985. *How to Set Up and Operate a Local Association Political Action Program.* Washington: National Education Association.

National Education Association Political Action Committee. 1993. *Federal Election Commission Selected List of Receipts & Expenditures (G) (91-92).* Washington: U.S. Government Printing Office. October.

O'Neill, Colleen M. 1993. "Collective Bargaining Would Benefit From Reform." *AFL-CIO News,* October 4, p. 7.

Pipefitters Local 562 v. United States, 407 U.S. 385, 92 S.Ct. 2247, 33 L. Ed.2nd 11 (1972).

Reed, Sally D. 1984. *NEA: Propaganda Front of the Radical Left.* Falls Church, VA: Conservative Press.

Selden, David. 1985. *The Teacher Rebellion.* Washington: Howard University Press.

Shanahan-Walsh, Ann. 1993. "The Growing Presence of Absentees." *Campaign.* January/February, Vol. VII, No.1: 14.

Shanker, Albert. 1979. "A Reply to Myron Lieberman." *Phi Delta Kappan.* May, p. 652-654.

——. 1993. "A California Nightmare." *American Teacher.* October, Vol. 78, No. 2: 7.

Spero, Sterling D. 1972. *Government as Employer.* New York: Remsen Press.

Spiotto, James E. 1991. Chapter 13, "Municipal Insolvency: Bankruptcy, Receivership, Workouts and Alternative Remedies," unpublished manuscript. *Strategies for Communities in Crisis: Is There Life After a Budget Deficit?* Paper prepared for Government Financial Officers Association. June 3.

——. 1993. *Strategies for Communities in Crisis: Is There Life After a Budget Deficit?* Paper prepared for the Government Finance Officers' Association, June.

Stern, James L. 1988. "Unionism in the Public Sector," in Benjamin Aaron, J.M. Najita, and James L. Stern, *Public Sector Bargaining.* Washington: Bureau of National Affairs, 2d Edition.

Tawney, Richard H. 1920. *The Acquisitive Society.* New York: Harcourt Brace.

Toch, Thomas. 1991. *In the Name of Excellence.* New York: Oxford University Press.

Troy, Leo. 1994. *The New Unionism in the New Society: Public Sector Unionism in the Redistributive State.* Fairfax, VA: George Mason University Press.

——. 1993. The New Unionism and the New Society; Myron Lieberman discussion with Albert Shanker at the 1993 AFT convention in Washington, July 8-11, 1993; and David Selden, *The Teacher Rebellion,* 162-167. Selden emphasizes that he personally was anathema to AFL-CIO President George Meany whereas Shanker enjoyed cordial relations with Meany.

United States Department of Labor, Bureau of Labor Statistics. 1991. *Employment and Earnings,* January.

US Department of Labor, Office of Labor-Management Standards. 1990. *Labor-Management Reporting and Disclosure Act of 1959, As Amended.*

Weber, D.A. (Del). 1992. *Triumph and Uncertainty: California Issues and the NEA.* Memorandum distributed by the CTA to the 1992 NEA Representative Assembly, Washington, July.

West, Allan M. 1980. *The National Education Association.* New York: The Free Press.

Wildman, Wesley A. 1971. "Teachers and Collective Negotiation," in Albert A. Blum, *White Collar Workers*, New York: Random House.

Ziskind, David. 1949. *One Thousand Strikes of Government Employees.* New York: Columbia University Press.

INDEX

receipts of, 29
Representative Assembly (RA), 5, 13, 40, 54
representation in, 13
Republican Party, 65
Republican candidates, 59
Republican Educators Caucus (REC), 62–63, 87
Republican National Committee (RNC), 87
retirement benefits, 44
reverse checkoff, 57–58
Review Board, 13
salaries of officers, 43–44
salaries of staff, 45
school choice. *See* Vouchers
secret ballot as merger issue, 118–120
special committees, 14
Special Purpose Funds, 44–47
special services, 88
standing committees, 13, 14
state education associations, 16–19, 52, 67, 82–83, 88, 94–99, 107
strategic objectives, 14
table of organization, 15
tax exemption of, 124–125
and teacher strikes, 12, 97, 129, 130, 143, 151–152
unified membership in, 17–18
Unified Legal Service Program, 91–92
UniServ, 30–31, 43, 99
    directors, 21–22, 30–31
    funding of, 21–22, 32
    political operations, 59, 68, 83
    revenues, 30–32
United States Department of Education, 57
Urban Project, 12
National Council of Urban Education Associations (NCUEA), 20
National Foundation for the Improvement in Education (NFIE), 45–46
National Labor Relations Act, 129
National Right to Work Committee (NRTWC), 39
National Science Teachers Association (NSTA), 19, 93
National Teachers Association (NTA), 146–150
New York City, 23, 83, 138–139
New York State United Teachers (NYSUT), 18, 83–85, 116
Noncash contributions, 78–79, 87
North American Free Trade Agreement (NAFTA), 63–64, 136–137

ABOUT THE AUTHORS

Dr. Myron Lieberman

Dr. Myron Lieberman is Senior Research Scholar, Social Philosophy and Policy Center, Bowling Green State University, Bowling Green, Ohio. He is the author or coauthor of twelve books and scores of articles on educational policy and teacher bargaining; his most recent were *Public Education: An Autopsy.* (Harvard University Press, 1993) and *Teacher Bargaining: Practice and Policy.* (Bonus Books, 1994).

In addition to his publications, Dr. Lieberman has been involved in every phase of teacher union activities. He is a life member of the NEA and retiree member of the AFT and has been a frequent delegate to state and national conventions of teacher unions. From 1972 to 1975 he directed the Teacher Leadership Program, a training program for teacher union leaders on public policy issues. In addition to serving as an expert witness or consultant to the NEA and AFT, Dr. Lieberman was a candidate for national president of the AFT in 1962, receiving approximatly one third of the convention votes. Subsequently, he served as a labor negotiator for school boards in Rhode Island, Connecticut, New York, Arizona, California and New Jersey, with responsibilities for grievances and unfair labor practices as well as contract negotiations.

Charlene K. Haar

Charlene K. Haar is an educational consultant specializing in teacher/parent relations and local, state and federal educational policy. Ms. Haar was born and attended public schools in South Dakota. She graduated from the University of South Dakota with a Bachelor of Arts in French and later received a Master of Arts in Gifted Education from Augustana College, Sioux Falls, South Dakota in 1987. Following graduation, Ms. Haar taught French, English and American Government for 11 years, most recently at Madison High School, Madison, South Dakota.

In 1992, after twenty years of local and state political involvement, Ms. Haar was chosen as the Republican candidate for U.S. Senate from South Dakota. In that year, at the Republican National Convention in Houston, Texas, she made one of the seconding presentations on national television on behalf of the candidacy of Vice-President Dan Quayle.

221

In the 1980s, Ms. Haar also had extensive first hand experience with the political operations of teacher unions. In addition to being a coauthor of this book, she is the author or coauthor of articles on teacher unions in the *National Review, Government Union Review*, and other national publications. She and Robert J. Haar are parents of Elizabeth Haar, a recent graduate of the University of South Dakota.

Dr. Leo Troy

Dr. Leo Troy, Distinguished Professor of Economics at Rutgers University, received his Ph.D. degree in economics from Columbia University in 1958. He is a Fellow of the Public Service Research Council, and member of the Editorial Advisory Board of the *Journal of Labor Research*.

A frequent contributor to such professional journals as the *Harvard Journal of Law and Public Policy, University of Chicago Law Review, Government Union Review, Quarterly Journal of Economics, British Journal of Industrial Relations*, and the *Journal of Labor Research*, Dr. Troy is widely regarded as one of the nation's foremost authorities on trends in the labor movement, especially with reference to public and private sector unionization. His latest book, *The New Unionism in the New Society: Public Sector Unionism in the Redistributive State* (1993) was published by the George Mason University Press.